Inequality in Gifted and Talented Programs

Palgrave Studies in Urban Education
Series Editors: Alan R. Sadovnik and Susan F. Semel

Reforming Boston Schools, 1930–2006: Overcoming Corruption and Racial Segregation
By Joseph Marr Cronin (April 2008)

What Mothers Say about Special Education: From the 1960s to the Present
By Jan W. Valle (March 2009)

Charter Schools: From Reform Imagery to Reform Reality
By Jeanne M. Powers (June 2009)

Becoming an Engineer in Public Universities: Pathways for Women and Minorities
Edited by Kathryn M. Borman, Will Tyson, and Rhoda H. Halperin (May 2010)

The Multiracial Urban High School: Fearing Peers and Trusting Friends
Susan Rakosi Rosenbloom (October 2010)

Reforming Boston Schools, 1930 to the Present: Overcoming Corruption and Racial Segregation (updated paperback edition of *Reforming Boston Schools, 1930–2006*)
By Joseph Marr Cronin (August 2011)

The History of "Zero Tolerance" in American Public Schooling
By Judith Kafka (December 2011)

Advisory in Urban High Schools: A Study of Expanded Teacher Roles
By Kate Phillippo (August 2013)

Public Housing and School Choice in a Gentrified City: Youth Experiences of Uneven Opportunity
By Molly Vollman Makris (March 2015)

Against Race- and Class-Based Pedagogy in Early Childhood Education
By Stephanie C. Smith (October 2015)

Inequality in Gifted and Talented Programs: Parental Choices about Status, School Opportunity, and Second-Generation Segregation
By Allison Roda (October 2015)

Inequality in Gifted and Talented Programs

Parental Choices about Status, School Opportunity, and Second-Generation Segregation

Allison Roda

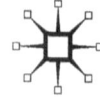

INEQUALITY IN GIFTED AND TALENTED PROGRAMS
Copyright © Allison Roda 2015
Softcover reprint of the hardcover 1st edition 2015 978-1-137-48539-7
All rights reserved. No reproduction, copy or transmission of this publication may be made without written permission. No portion of this publication may be reproduced, copied or transmitted save with written permission. In accordance with the provisions of the Copyright, Designs and Patents Act 1988, or under the terms of any licence permitting limited copying issued by the Copyright Licensing Agency, Saffron House, 6-10 Kirby Street, London EC1N 8TS.

Any person who does any unauthorized act in relation to this publication may be liable to criminal prosecution and civil claims for damages.

First published 2015 by
PALGRAVE MACMILLAN

The author has asserted their right to be identified as the author of this work in accordance with the Copyright, Designs and Patents Act 1988.

Palgrave Macmillan in the UK is an imprint of Macmillan Publishers Limited, registered in England, company number 785998, of Houndmills, Basingstoke, Hampshire, RG21 6XS.

Palgrave Macmillan in the US is a division of Nature America, Inc., One New York Plaza, Suite 4500, New York, NY 10004-1562.

Palgrave Macmillan is the global academic imprint of the above companies and has companies and representatives throughout the world.

E-PDF ISBN: 978–1–137–48540–3
ISBN 978-1-349-56344-9
DOI 10.1057/9781137485403

Library of Congress Cataloging-in-Publication Data
Roda, Allison.
   Inequality in gifted and talented programs : parental choices about status, school opportunity, and second-generation segregation / by Allison Roda.
       pages cm.—(Palgrave studies in urban education)
   Includes bibliographical references and index.

   1. Gifted children—Education (Elementary)—New York (State)—New York. 2. Special education—Social aspects—New York (State)—New York. 3. Segregation in education—New York (State)—New York. 4. School choice—New York (State)—New York. I. Title.
LC3995.N5R64 2015
371.9509747—dc23   2015016475

A catalogue record of the book is available from the British Library.

Tomy" Boys"
And the Pursuit of Equal Educational Opportunity

Contents

List of Tables		ix
Series Editors' Preface		xi
Preface and Acknowledgments		xiii
Introduction	Maintaining Their Advantage	1
One	The Case: G&T Programs within New York City Schools	27
Two	Striving to Be G&T "Because the People in It Are Just Like You"	55
Three	The Social Construction of Giftedness	75
Four	How Parents Recreate and Reproduce the Boundaries	99
Five	"The Only Thing They Got out of This Is Segregation": TCSR evisited	129
Conclusion	Putting Integration (Back?) on the Education Policy Agenda	155
Notes		167
References		177
Index		185

Tables

I.1	Positionality and category of parent	9
I.2	NYC specialized high school admissions results by race, 2012	18
1.1	NYC public school students in G&T programs by race/ethnicity before and after the 2008 centralized G&T policy change	33
1.2	Percent of the 2009–2010 New York City versus the City Limits School District student population by race/ethnicity and FRPL	34
1.3	Student's race, FRPL status, and percent of students who passed the ELA and math state tests for (1) Three "diverse" neighborhood schools (with no G&T), and (2) Comparison group of "hyper-segregated" neighborhood schools	35
1.4	Student's race, eligibility for FRPL, and percent of students who passed the ELA and math state tests for the schools with G&T programs	43
1.5	Demographic changes at The Community School, 2007–2015	46
1.6	Interview participant categories	48
1.7	Profile of the parent sample	50
5.1	Black and Latino parent sample	133
5.2	White parents who were reinterviewed in 2014	143

Series Editors' Preface

Education has remained a hotly debated topic throughout the history of the United States. Over the last 50 years, scholars, policymakers, and the general public have placed a particular focus on urban education issues. This is in part due to the struggle of urban school districts to achieve similar results as their often more affluent suburban counterparts and also due to an increasing proportion of our nation's children being educated in cities. This series provides a forum for social scientists and historians to address the myriad issues in urban education.

Urban schools mirror the social problems of the cities in which they are situated. Similar to the communities in which they are located, many urban schools are unsafe and lack the resources and human capital that are necessary to succeed. Additionally, structures in our society place added burdens on the significant number of poor and minority children in urban schools and create obstacles to their academic success.

Empirical analysis demonstrates an undeniable relationship between socioeconomic status, race, ethnicity, and educational achievement. Children from families with low socioeconomic status have lower educational attainment than their counterparts from higher socioeconomic backgrounds. Black and Hispanic students have lower academic achievement than Asian American and White students. Given the high percentage of Black and Hispanic students living in poverty who attend schools in cities, urban education systems struggle to produce similar results to suburban school districts.

Low student achievement and high dropout rates have become endemic to urban school systems. Many cities have dropout rates at or above 40 percent and mathematics and reading proficiency rates below 50 percent. Because of unconscionable statistics such as these, policymakers and scholars have engaged in an effort both to understand the roots of failure in urban schools and to develop reforms that resolve the problems.

While some scholars and policymakers attribute differences in achievement to factors within schools, others focus on factors outside of schools. On the one hand, some of the in-school factors that affect achievement include unqualified teachers, unequal funding, high turnover of teachers and principals, low expectations, and a dumbed-down curriculum. On the other hand, much of the achievement gap is due to factors outside of schools, including inadequate housing, poor healthcare, and environmental stresses. Nevertheless, despite the overwhelming number of urban schools that are struggling to educate their students, it is important to note that there are numerous examples of highly successful urban schools that beat the odds.

Currently, there is a contentious debate about how to improve urban schools. Some reformers advocate a take-no-excuses approach that focuses on issues within schools and contend that poverty is not the primary reason for low educational achievement. They support systemic reforms through the growth of charter schools and/or school voucher programs and through standards-based student and teacher accountability systems. In addition, they focus attention on ensuring that all students have quality teachers and administrators through the recruitment of high-performing candidates, new tenure laws, and the use of value-added accountability programs. Others argue that school-based reforms by themselves are limited in their ability to reduce the achievement gaps unless they also address the factors outside of schools that contribute to educational inequalities.

We are at a crucial moment in educational reform, particularly in urban districts. This is also true internationally, with countries such as the United Kingdom, Canada, Australia, Japan, and Finland grappling with these problems. There is a growing divide between those who support the no-excuses approach to education reform and those who argue that societies must concurrently address poverty and the many forms of discrimination that affect educational achievement and the life outcomes of children in urban schools.

Social science and historical research have played, and must continue to play, an important role in understanding urban educational problems and evaluating policies aimed at solving them. The goal of *Palgrave Studies in Urban Education* is to publish books that use social science and historical knowledge to analyze urban educational processes, practices, and policies from a variety of research methods and theoretical perspectives. The books in this series examine a diverse set of urban educational issues and offer compelling insights into the limits and possibilities of urban educational reforms. Moreover, the series strives to contribute to the development of best practices that improve the life chances of the increasing number of children who pass through urban schools.

ALAN R. SADOVNIK
and
SUSAN F. SEMEL

Preface and Acknowledgments

It was September 2005 and I was packing to move across the country for graduate school in New York City. This was a big move for many reasons; particularly because my family and I had been living in Montana and moving to the "Big Apple" was going to be a culture shock. Besides registering for classes and meeting my adviser, navigating a new city, finding the grocery store, and closest doctor and dentist, we also had to figure out where our seven-year-old son, Ethan, would attend first grade. Anyone who has attempted school choice research on the Internet knows that this can be a daunting task—most of all because we could not go visit the schools beforehand and had no social networks to rely on for insider information about our school options.

I quickly realized that it was impossible to register Ethan for school online and no one at the schools would answer my emails over the summer months because the school offices were closed. To make the situation even more stressful, I found out that we would have only two days after we moved into the college's family housing before the first day of school for Ethan. I would be busy doing mandatory orientation activities for college, therefore my husband was in charge of getting him into the perfect New York City school and we had only two days in which to do it.

I admit that I looked at our zoned school first, but quickly discovered that my White, middle-class son would be in the minority since it was a school that was "hyper-segregated"—meaning a school with more than 90 percent children of color, and the school had an Afrocentric curriculum. When conducting my online research I found that, of the six schools that have a sizable population of White students in them, three schools offer Gifted & Talented (G&T) self-contained programs and three schools offer more heterogeneous classroom environments, including one that is an unzoned school with a separate admission process. The G&T programs were not on my radar at the time, mostly because I did not consider my son "gifted" but also because it was too late for him to be tested. I made a list of the three schools that I considered to be "diverse"—at both the school and the classroom level, in which

Ethan would not be in the minority, and gave the list to my husband. My husband and son visited the first school on the list—giving the female secretary all of the necessary paperwork and explaining the situation, as my husband recalls, a little naively and with a little charm. He told the secretary about just moving to New York City, his wife in graduate school at Columbia, and Ethan with no school to go to. My husband said he made sure to tell the secretary what he felt our family could contribute to the school, including how Ethan had lived in different places across the country, that my husband was an artist and could volunteer his time, and my teaching background.

Ironically, this was the school that Ethan got into and it was the only school my husband and son visited that day. It was the school against which I had put two stars on my list and had been emailing for a month or two with no response. One of the reasons why it is more racially and socioeconomically diverse (meaning more White students) compared to the other schools is because it is not a neighborhood school that only draws from the catchment area. It is what the New York City Department of Education calls an "unzoned" school, in which families from across the district can fill out an application and apply. There is always a long list of families on the waiting list because of its diversity and child-centered philosophy. The reason Ethan got a spot at this highly coveted school, according to the secretary, was because they needed more boys in the first grade classroom. The other reason, I suspect, was our belief that we could just show up at the school and try to get certain opportunities for our son no matter what—what Annette Lareau calls "concerted cultivation."[1] In fact, I soon found out that the way we got accepted is not a common experience for other families at the school.

While my New York City school choice experience may sound unique, there are similarities in the ways I made sense of the different educational options compared to the parents in this book. Just like them, I grew up in a suburban town in a different state and attended a homogeneous, majority White suburban public school. I did not want my child to be in the minority in our zoned school. I also had a strong desire for Ethan's classroom to reflect the diversity of the city in which we would soon be living; yet the diverse public school options were few and far between. Therefore, I chose a school that was disproportionately White, higher-income, and had higher test score averages, because the other options I had were non-options—for example, majority Black and Latino, low-income, struggling schools.

What I did not realize at the time was that my own school choice experience would be the topic of future research with my graduate school adviser at Teachers College.[2] In particular, the comments from many of the White parents interviewed in 2006 described the struggles that they went through when choosing a school, especially when they witnessed the segregated G&T and General Education (Gen Ed) classrooms in some of the schools when they went on school tours.[3] For instance, some parents acknowledged the "problem" of segregation, but still chose the G&T program if their child passed the test and was offered a seat, and rationalized it as the best program for their child.

As a White, middle-class, former public school parent in the New York City community school district that I studied, my unique vantage point into this segregated system provided me with "insider knowledge" of the school choice options from which the advantaged parents in this book were choosing. Studying parental school choice within this large community school district several years after my own child had left the system because we moved to the suburbs, allowed me to be unknown to my respondents and yet aware of the larger context.

This book takes a closer look inside a demographically changing neighborhood school with a self-contained G&T program to examine how a racially and socioeconomically diverse group of parents in the G&T, General Education (Gen Ed), or both programs, (1) make meaning of their available school choice options and their sense of "place" within the New York City school system and larger society, (2) perceive the families who enroll their children in the different G&T and Gen Ed programs, and construct their own children's intelligence and ability, and (3) engage in "boundary work" to create, recreate, and reproduce boundaries between the G&T and Gen Ed programs within a school.

* * *

I could not have written this book (or my dissertation on which it is based), without the invaluable support and advice from graduate school faculty, mentors, colleagues, family, and friends. First and foremost, I would like to thank my dissertation sponsor, my mentor, and my friend, Amy Stuart Wells. I could not have done any of this without her enthusiasm and steady support of all my endeavors over the years. She took me under her wing and, through example, showed me the art of qualitative research. Her guidance helped shape my ideas for this research, both conceptually and theoretically.

Additionally, I have been very fortunate to have many mentors and colleagues who have given me critical feedback and support throughout the many stages of this book. I would like to especially thank Aaron Pallas, Luis Huerta, Alan Sadovnik, Erin Horvat, Linn Posey-Maddox, Carolyn

Sattin-Bajaj, Molly Vollman Makris, Laurie Hills, Paul Tractenberg, and Jeffrey Backstrand for giving me opportunities and encouragement along the way. Special thanks to my confidant and friend throughout our graduate school experience, Miya Warner, as well as Bianca Baldridge, Terrenda White, Shannon Allen, and Lauren Fox, who have become great role models and lifelong friends. During my postdoctoral fellowship at Rutgers University, I became a friend and colleague of Molly Vollman Makris. I owe her a debt of gratitude for helping me survive the ups and downs of the academic journey. A huge thank you also goes out to Kimberly Moorhead, Carolyn Sattin-Bajaj, Molly Vollman Makris, Maia Cucchiara,[4] and David Tipson for their helpful editing and insightful comments throughout the final drafts of this book. Special thanks also to Colleen McCauley for her transcription assistance, and to the editors and reviewers at Palgrave Macmillan.

I could not have done any of this without my husband, Tim Roda, and my four sons, Ethan, Rocco, Tre, and Andre, who have been not only my biggest fans but also, truly, my biggest motivation in fulfilling this and every accomplishment. I am grateful to my grandmother Eleanor Hale, who always gave the best advice and will continue to be my greatest role model even after her passing. My parents, Edward and Gail Thomson, for always believing in my wildest dreams, and closest friends, especially Ashley Zook—I thank them for knowing when to push, and when to listen and support me through the trials and tribulations of this journey. They never doubted that I could complete this book. And most importantly, I would like to thank all of the New York City parents who took the time to share their school choice experiences with me. This book would not have been as complete without their support of this project and their honest and thoughtful stories.

Introduction
Maintaining Their Advantage

Alyssa[1] is a New York City mother whose daughter is entering kindergarten. Alyssa is White. When it comes to school choice in New York City, as in many urban areas, Alyssa has options. Most children attend their zoned public school; however, there is a wide variety of school choice options, including gifted, dual language, unzoned, and charter schools. The problem is that most of these choices are racially and socioeconomically segregated. Like many other savvy parents interested in getting their children into the "best"—meaning disproportionately White—elementary schools, Alyssa attends costly school choice workshops, forms a "mommy group" that meets regularly to share insights about their public school options, and even pays for individual consultations with a school choice consultant to guide her through the admissions process.

We meet in the park for the interview. Alyssa is pushing her daughter on a swing and starts listing the schools that she is considering, which are all the non-Gifted and Talented (G&T), more diverse schools in the district because, as she adamantly explains, "we didn't want tracking." By "tracking," she is referring to the practice of separating students for the entire day to receive different instruction. She discusses how other parents will openly talk about G&T programs, but no one "acknowledges" the other side of being in the non-G&T, the "Gen Ed class." She believes that a General Education (Gen Ed) class in a school with G&T is not the same experience as a Gen Ed class in a school that does not have that option.[2] She says parents "love to say G&T, but they don't like to say tracking" or how "race and class" are intertwined with G&T and Gen Ed. While many of the parents in this book admit that the G&T and Gen Ed classes are segregated, Alyssa is the first person to use the word "tracking."

As she talks more, she explains that her "cool friends" who are into "organic food and breastfeeding" told her they are *not* "teaching to the [G&T] test." Nevertheless, she says that in every "house that she went into," these same "cool friends" who said they were not test prepping had

"Brain Quest flashcards or some kind of game that had the word 'smart' in it. That's really unfortunate." Alyssa goes on to say that "the parents that I know, for the most part, in this neighborhood they buy into the classes, the prep... And so it makes a lot of parents nervous and they need these things to get the kids out of the house." These same friends, Alyssa explains, get their child's test score back and when they find out that the child got a "99 or whatever, they're like, 'Well the test is not so bad'... and the day before the tests, they wouldn't say that. It's a magical thing. It's not a reasonable thing. Suddenly, you are what the test said you were."

Alyssa is about to answer another question when an unfamiliar White woman at the playground approaches her. The stranger explains that she is a grandmother watching her granddaughter at the park and that Alyssa is the first person in any playground she has overheard discussing tracking and G&T programs. The grandmother responds, *"Parents think their poor kids aren't going to get a job 30 years later if they don't get into the G&T."* They agree with each other and the grandmother walks away. Given Alyssa's strong attitudes against tracking and the segregation G&T causes within schools, it is surprising that she still tested her daughter for the G&T program. As Alyssa explains, she "bought into the idea that we should try everything" to give herself, and her daughter, "better" school options, even though she "felt really bad about that... I might have even cried."[3] When asked what school her daughter will be going to for kindergarten, she quickly responds that she chose a neighborhood school with no tracking, where there are exciting teachers and the parents are really involved in the school. She ends the interview by saying something that most White advantaged parents who sought to get their children into the G&T program did not say: "G&T is good for the kids that are in G&T, but I don't want her in that program, I think it's detrimental to both sides."

Alyssa's story is reflective of the themes running through this book on the relationship between G&T education, school choice, and racialized tracking within New York City elementary schools. This book breaks the silence surrounding the segregative effects of G&T education within urban elementary schools[4] as a growing number of policymakers, citizens, scholars, and even some parents like Alyssa are voicing their concern about using a single test score for G&T admission. It has been something with which White, higher-income, or advantaged New York City parents[5] have expressed discomfort, yet some choose the G&T program anyway and rationalize it as the "best" program for their child in a constrained and stratified school choice environment.[6] Despite their critique about the fairness of the G&T policy, these parents still capitalize on their advantage in order to win one of the coveted G&T spots for their children in a high-status program, thus assuring the passage of "advantage" from one generation to the next. As parents explained, the biggest advantage of securing a G&T placement is that it seems to be a "feeder for the better middle schools, which then seems to be a feeder for the better high schools." In fact, to get into the "better" middle schools and high schools, students must score well on standardized tests.

As Alyssa's story suggests, White advantaged parents in the system realize what is at stake in terms of their children's future in a highly unequal society, causing anxiety and pressure to be considered a "good parent" who gives their children educational advantages[7] in the form of high-status G&T placements and future educational opportunities. At the same time, these White advantaged parents will question the measures used to define "giftedness"—relating the gifted label more to students' advantaged backgrounds and G&T test preparation than their "true" intelligence. By exploring parental attitudes around enrolling their child(ren) in a New York City elementary school that offers self-contained G&T and Gen Ed programs, this book offers an in-depth examination of "second-generation segregation," or the within-school segregation caused by tracking based on a single score on a standardized test.[8] "First-generation segregation" refers to the segregation between schools that desegregation policies have attempted to ameliorate. The most famous example of an attempt to mitigate first-generation segregation was *Brown v. Board of Education* in 1954. "Second-generation segregation" is a phrase used to refer to within-school segregation.[9] This book focuses on second-generation segregation in the elementary schools, and it begins when students are identified for gifted or special education, and it results in racially correlated tracks. The book gives policymakers, researchers, school leaders, and parents alike a deeper understanding of the sociocultural aspects of urban school reform, including how within-school segregation operates, the social construction of giftedness, the ongoing debate about G&T tracking and best practices, and the role of social reproduction and boundaries in maintaining educational advantage.

The research findings also illustrate how education policy and the sociocultural context both facilitate and maintain racial and socioeconomic boundaries between groups.[10] By "sociocultural context," I am referring to the different ways that educators, parents, and students make sense of who belongs where in the race and class-based hierarchy within the school. Thus, when White advantaged parents enroll their children on the Gen Ed side of the boundary, contradictory attitudes emerge because there is a mismatch between the parent's sense of place in the larger society and system versus their lower-status placement in the school.[11] The book also shows the perspective of a comparison group of Black and Latino parents to see how they make sense of the programs, other parents, and students within the school.

Sociologists of education have long identified stratification within and between schools as a barrier to equal educational opportunity. What has been "often overlooked by integration advocates is the reality of 'dual school systems' operating at the curricular level, not just at the facility level."[12] US schools tend to be stratified by sector (private schools, Catholic schools), race and social class (in terms of academically oriented peers, parental involvement levels, or funding), and tracking mechanisms (exposure to a challenging curriculum).[13] Instead of schools becoming the "great equalizer" in society, through tracking and ability grouping, such as Advanced Placement, Honors, and G&T classes, elementary and secondary schools can be sites of social reproduction and can increase racial and socioeconomic status (SES) inequality in society. New York City's G&T programs, which enroll students based on a constructed definition of "giftedness" measured by a single score on a standardized test,[14] have historically started from kindergarten and tend to result in racial and SES segregation between G&T and Gen Ed tracks.[15]

School Choice, Tracking, and G&T

The literature on school choice, tracking, and G&T education is often examined in isolation. The research that most closely overlaps with this book examines these issues of parental choice and/or stratification between G&T magnet programs and the regular programs within larger high schools,[16] pullout G&T programs in suburban elementary schools,[17] and G&T programs in secondary schools.[18] Elementary schools typically use pullout models for gifted students, in which "gifted" students are given G&T curriculum outside the regular classroom for a set number of hours per week. Yet, in the context of New York City and other urban districts, full time, school-within-school G&T models are used alongside Gen Ed programs. As a result, parents are given the "choice" to request that their preschool child be tested for G&T, meaning that they fill out an online form by a certain deadline and then take their child to a designated testing location. Then, if their child scores at or above the 90th percentile on the standardized tests they can apply to district G&T programs. If they score above the 97th percentile, they become eligible for one of the citywide kindergarten G&T programs.[19] This book crosses the boundaries of the three bodies of research on school choice, tracking, and G&T, and situates itself in a local school district context where parents are given the "choice" between two hierarchical, academic tracks within one elementary school.

Conceptually, tracking in elementary schools is defined as the practice of separating students for the entire day to receive different instruction.[20] Researchers who examine school choice and tracking policies within schools include self-contained G&T programs on their list of programs that track students.[21] While most of the tracking literature has been conducted at the secondary school level where students and teachers have the most power in choosing track placements, this book explores how the G&T policy and parents' decisions to have their child tested (or not) act as gatekeepers in determining G&T/Gen Ed track placement at the elementary school level.[22] Because these parents are making these choices as their children are entering kindergarten, teachers and students are not part of the decision-making process.

Elementary school tracking provides a better context (than secondary school) in which to explore issues of boundary maintenance because the parents' social construction of their child's ability as it interacts with several material circumstances, including district policies and G&T test scores, is one of the central factors in the decision-making process. What's more is that G&T policies based upon measures of student "ability" are often seen as merit-based, but in fact have many cultural biases that relate to privilege in terms of race and class.[23] Therefore, this book explores how the social construction of students and their ability is related to broader social structures and the ways in which those structures are embodied in the parents.

In this way, tracking and G&T programs come to symbolize how parents socially construct where students belong within academically tracked schools, based solely on a standardized test score and their cultural capital exchange. Roslyn Mickelson and colleagues explain, "Choice options designated for gifted students, particularly schools that require certain test scores to enter, will by design resegregate students by achievement. And because achievement is correlated with race and SES, [G&T] students tend to be disproportionately White, Asian, and middle-class."[24]

In New York and other urban school districts across the country, G&T programs are strategically placed within historically Black and Latino, lower-income schools in an attempt to attract higher-income White students and improve student achievement levels.[25] As Lauren, a kindergarten Gen Ed parent, explained, "But you know why they have the G&T? I mean, you know, it's so middle-class families will stay in the schools. Supposedly it wasn't—it was supposed to get bright kids from not-so-good school districts to be able to come [to the G&T], but I was told that was all smoke and mirrors and that it's to make sure that middle-class families stay in the schools and don't all go to private." Consequently, while this practice can desegregate schools at the building level, students are resegregated by race and SES at the classroom level. This racialized tracking has been called, "desegregation without integration"[26] and therefore "subverts" any potential benefits of desegregation school wide.[27] Since standardized tests have been found to be racially and culturally biased[28] and many Black and Latino, low-income parents do not get their children tested for G&T, second-generation segregation is prevalent in New York City schools with self-contained G&T and Gen Ed programs.[29]

This book adds to the small body of literature that explores how school structures and practices create, maintain, and legitimize segregated gifted tracks.[30] Mara Sapon-Shevin, an advocate for inclusive education, argues for more research on the interplay between diverse parent constituencies in schools and the policies and school practices that help to legitimate and perpetuate resegregation of students in separate and unequal classrooms within these same schools:

> For parents to become a positive force in building successful integrated schools that do not reproduce social inequities and social stratification, understanding of the interplay among diverse groups of parents and schools must increase. In particular, a more comprehensive understanding of inequalities in social and cultural capital among parents and the role of schools in the reproduction of advantage is needed.[31]

This book fills this gap in the literature. It allows readers to understand how within-school segregation operates by showing how parents on both sides of the G&T/Gen Ed boundary line make sense of their school choice options and their child's placement in a G&T or Gen Ed program (or both) amid these racial distinctions across programs and schools. The within-school segregation caused by G&T programs is partly due to the fact that the central goal of the school choice program is to maximize parental choice, not to racially or socioeconomically diversify the schools. In this way, the kindergarten school choice program is "color-blind," letting school diversity chips fall where they may. The political argument that we now live in a "color-blind" society and do not need to consider race when developing educational policies, particularly school choice policies that can exacerbate segregation, does not hold in this context.

The research clearly demonstrates that parents' school choices are anything but color-blind and, absent policies designed to support school-level diversity, parents' decisions of what a quality education looks like leads to greater racial and SES segregation between and within schools.[32] Like Makris (2015) posits in her book on school choice and gentrification in Hoboken, New Jersey, deregulated school choice policies are designed to give the appearance of color-blindness, yet allow parents to opt out of public neighborhood schools where they could actually help desegregate schools.[33]

The Local Context Where Race and Class Intertwine

Gentrifying cities such as New York[34] are potential sites for a growing number of racially and socioeconomically diverse public schools, as higher-income, White parents are utilizing the public system. This is due to the fact that many White advantaged parents are choosing public over private schools because of the housing market collapse, the move toward urban living, and the economic recession of 2008—causing overcrowding in the most popular, disproportionately White schools and G&T programs within schools.[35] While most of the 32 New York City community school districts (CSDs) have predominantly Black and Latino student populations, the significance of studying the "City Limits" CSD, is due to the racially and socioeconomically diverse student body overall. In the context of one of the most racially and ethnically segregated public school systems in the country, the *City Limits* student population stands out with roughly 30 percent each of White, Black, and Latino students. Yet, the options that *City Limits* parents have to choose among do not reflect the diverse student population within its borders. These mostly segregated options include: (1) private schools (if they have the money for tuition or are awarded a scholarship, and get accepted), (2) zoned schools that are typically hyper-segregated,[36] (3) G&T or dual language self-contained programs that oftentimes attract White parents into separate programs within otherwise diverse public schools,[37] (4) unzoned K-8 school or charter schools[38] with their own district wide lottery applications. A fifth option of last resort cited by parents is moving out to the suburbs.[39]

Out of the three G&T programs in the highly diverse *City Limits* School District, the elementary school that is the subject of this book, "The Community School" (TCS), was chosen because the total student enrollment consists of a more even mix of different race/ethnicities and social class backgrounds in the school overall, compared to the other schools with G&T programs that are popular with White parents. This is the case because TCS's catchment area includes public housing in the northern section, as well as high-priced apartment buildings and brownstones that constitute the majority of homes in the area.

Since the G&T program began in 1997 with its separate admissions criteria, both White and some Asian families from across the district have been drawn to TCS's highly reputed G&T program.[40] The Gen Ed program, on the other hand, has historically enrolled a majority of Black and Latino students from the catchment area, who live in public subsidized housing and rent stabilized apartments, or from lower-income districts outside of the *City Limits* School District that were bused in to fill the Gen Ed seats.[41] In recent years, a growing number of White advantaged TCS parents living in the catchment or who have older children in the G&T program are starting to consider a fourth option for their children's education. This option is the historically Black and Latino Gen Ed programs within schools that also offer highly popular G&T programs.

This influx of White families to the Gen Ed program in the younger grades has caused the segregation in the Gen Ed classrooms to break down slowly over time. Since 2008, the school's White student enrollment has increased. The Black and Latino student population in the school, however, has steadily decreased. Why? As more and more seats in the Gen Ed program are being filled by White advantaged students from the neighborhood, fewer seats are available for Black and Latino students who live outside of TCS's attendance zone. The neighborhood itself is not really changing residentially, except for rising housing prices; it's the White neighborhood families choosing their zoned school instead of private schools or other public neighborhood schools/programs that are popular with White families. Jessica, a first grade Gen Ed parent, made clear that the "Gen Ed program itself" is not becoming more "acceptable" to White families in the catchment area. The "demographics are becoming more acceptable. I really think that's what it was." This points to the relationship between race and class and perceptions of public school quality when choosing schools and programs within them.

Parents who "know their place" in the educational system are simply following what seems natural to them when raising their child(ren). Determining educational placements serves to rank them in the stratification system because they are rewarded, or not, in their struggle for resources and "status." This stratified system ultimately gives advantages and entitlements to the parents who have their children in the G&T program and creates tension for the White advantaged parents who strive for G&T but whose children do not get a high enough score to get a seat or their seat is taken by a sibling who gets priority.

This book explores how 51 parents of different racial/ethnic and socioeconomic backgrounds, who are either in the process of choosing schools for their children or have elementary school children already enrolled in TCS's G&T, Gen Ed, or both programs make meaning of their available school choice options and their sense of "place" within the New York City school system and larger society. The parent interviews were conducted in two waves of data collection. In 2011, initial interviews were conducted with 41 White advantaged parents, including 16 G&T parents only, 16 Gen Ed parents only and nine parents with children in both programs. In 2014, follow-up interviews were conducted with eight of the White parents who had their children enrolled in the kindergarten or first grade Gen Ed program in 2011, along with nine Black and Latino parents, and one new White Gen Ed parent.

This book focuses on TCS, an urban elementary school that is starting to enroll White advantaged families into two stratified G&T and Gen Ed academic programs within the same school. The phenomenon has led to a change in the school's culture and reconceptualization of what it means to be a "G&T" and/or "Gen Ed" parent in the school—particularly for parents with children in both programs who straddle the boundaries, and advantaged, White Gen Ed parents who have to negotiate their lower-status position in the school. It shows how the White advantaged parents differed in important ways regarding how they constructed their sense of "place" within the structures, depending on whether or how many of their children were in the high-status G&T program. As the initial interviews were conducted in 2011, four distinct groups of White advantaged parents, each with different ways of making sense of the boundaries and categories that their children are given within the school, were identified (see Table I.1).

Table I.1 Positionality and category of parent

	G&T Defenders $n=9$	*Savvy Negotiators* $n=16$	*Conflicted Followers* $n=11$	*GenEd Reconcilers* $n=5$
G&T Only	Kate Cecelia Claire Courtney Rachel Jennifer Anne Kathy Melody	Rosie Dana Carrie Chrissy Caitlyn Lillian		
Gen Ed Only		Jane Maya	Alyssa Kelly Trudie Lauren Denise Domenica Beatrice Colleen Jessica	Tara Lisa Tanya Elaine Trista
Both programs		Alice Amy/Joe Margaret Lindsay Melissa Violet Betsy	Veronica Tessa	

1. **G&T Defenders (n=9)**: This category of parents include the G&T parents who actually believe their children are truly gifted since their child scored high enough on the standardized test to be offered a G&T seat. This group of parents tends to be the G&T parents in the younger grades that do not live within the school's catchment area, and have little experience with the Gen Ed parents, children or classrooms. They often feel that their child is not being challenged enough because the G&T and Gen Ed curriculum is the same.
2. **Savvy Negotiators (n=16)**: Most frequently, these are G&T parents in the older grades, some of whom have younger children in the Gen Ed program. The parents who have children in both programs and have experienced the school the longest are most adept at negotiating the boundaries between the two different programs by developing strategies to downplay the differences. They are simultaneously bothered by the divisions that this system creates between parents and children in the school, yet continue to retest for G&T. They retest, even if they do not "buy into" the labels, because they experience the stigma associated with the Gen Ed label the most—particularly from the G&T parents in their older child's class.
3. **Conflicted Followers (n=11)**: This group of Gen Ed parents in the younger grades agrees with the Savvy Negotiators in terms of not believing in the gifted label and supporting the G&T program phase out. Yet, just like the parents with children in both programs, they continue to prep, test, and retest their children for the G&T program because of the G&T status and the negative stigma associated with the Gen Ed label. They seem to be more "disgruntled" and unhappy because their child is not in G&T and feel they are not getting as good of an education in Gen Ed, mostly because of the high levels of parent involvement in G&T.
4. **Gen Ed Reconcilers (n=5)**: This group of Gen Ed parents originally tested their child for G&T in kindergarten, but has subsequently stopped testing them either because their child is not eligible to test anymore after third grade or because they do not want to put their child through the testing process again. In other words, they make the best of the situation and resign themselves to their child's Gen Ed placement. They believe the diversity in the Gen Ed program in the younger grades, meaning more White students, is a great thing for the school because the segregation is diminishing. They hope it is a sign that the school will phase out the G&T program.

The in-depth interviews with parents suggest that when the advantaged, White parents are given the choice between mostly segregated schools and programs and the ability to use their uneven cultural capital exchange, they all strive to be in the Whiter, and higher-status programs and schools with other parents like them. White advantaged parents do this because they believe G&T programs are the better educational option in terms of peer effects and peer environment, even if they also value diversity for their children's education in mixed ability classrooms. They also strive for G&T programs because it matches their privileged position in the larger society and prevailing messages about worth, value, and opportunities in an environment in which parental anxiety runs high regarding their children's future in a competitive society.[42] At the same time, what many G&T and Gen Ed White parents desire are more undivided and diverse school options to choose from, as evidenced by their contradictory attitudes about whether the G&T program should be phased out or not. Amid this proliferation of G&T services as the answer to keeping White families in the public school system, as shown in the Conclusion chapter, there is evidence beyond this research that more New Yorkers are questioning the validity of these separate classrooms because of the use of a single standardized test when children are so young.

The main argument portrayed in this book is that the New York City G&T policy context within which parents are operating creates the status distinctions between schools and programs. This is the case because parents are allowed to use their cultural capital to "play the game" of school choice and get their children into high-status G&T programs by prepping and tutoring for the G&T test and using social networks for information about the G&T process. The structures in the system set parents up to make these difficult decisions that by necessity result in "winners" and losers. Parents essentially win the "game" if they can pass along their advantages to their children through G&T placements. In other words, this book not only illuminates the educational decision making of New York City parents, but also how their decisions are grounded in a larger stratified social context that encourages and rewards more advantaged parents in particular (i.e., by exclusionary access to private preschools, test prepping, insider information about the school choice process from their social networks and consulting services, etc.) and allows them to convert "social hierarchies into academic hierarchies."[43] It shows how race and class structure school opportunity through G&T placements, and provides recommendations for stopping the cycle of social reproduction in schools.

Leaders in diverse schools have the agency to promote a culture of inclusion rather than exclusion that celebrates and encourages all families to bring their unique contributions to their learning environment. *Inequality in Gifted and Talented Programs* serves to inform stakeholders in New York City and other metros as they consider how this story relates to their own community and schools.

The Role of Cultural Capital and Boundaries in Maintaining Educational Advantage

This book is framed by Pierre Bourdieu's social reproduction theory and Michele Lamont's work on boundaries. In general, Bourdieu's theory[44] explains how members of the upper classes in France sustain privilege by passing along their cultural dispositions, attitudes, and behaviors to their children (e.g., cultural capital) in a stratified, unequal social system, while legitimizing their privilege and their children's accomplishments in the educational system. Bourdieu believed that the educational system, through the "transmission of cultural capital, pedagogy, and academic selection processes," was the main institution to reproduce social class stratification and inequality in society.[45]

In France, cultural capital is more visible and can be applied more neatly, simply because French culture is steeped in a hierarchy of cultural distinctions from birth, based on an individual's social class position.[46] Even though there are not as rigid social class boundaries in the United States, there are cultural distinctions that signify an individual's social class standing or status. For instance, one of the ways that cultural capital is related to the US's stratified system is through the use of culturally biased standardized test scores for G&T admission.[47] In this way, through the use of standardized tests, and knowing which students get rewarded for their "high-class" culture, White advantaged parents' sense making about their place[ment] *within* TCS leads them to either internalize (to varying degrees) or resist the categories or labels that their children are given based on their score on a standardized test.[48]

Bourdieu also argued that individuals possess differently valued forms of cultural capital that correlate with social class in a stratified society.[49] In the US context, and in TCS in particular, this is highly intertwined with race as well, since the two programs are sharply divided by race and class, and parents classify themselves and others into categories that relate to their race and class backgrounds, as well as what they perceive to be cultural values and attitudes about education.[50] Bourdieu defined the distinctions between these different forms of cultural capital as cultural signals used for social and cultural exclusion. These "cultural signals" that individuals use to determine their place in the stratified social system are related to the theories on boundaries and boundary work in education. Boundaries is a key theoretical concept but also one based very much in reality as school district and attendance boundaries help structure patterns of school and residential segregation across urban and suburban spaces—in the New York metro and elsewhere. Many social scientists define boundaries as the point where group similarities end and differences begin.[51] "In this sense, a boundary can be seen as a juxtaposition of what 'we are' and what 'we aren ot.'"[52]

Michele Lamont's work goes a step further and distinguishes between social and symbolic boundaries that separate individuals and groups on different social, cultural, and moral levels.[53] Symbolic boundaries are the "conceptual distinctions" that individuals use to categorize people into groups based on group similarities, and social boundaries are the patterns of "social exclusion and race and class segregation" that result from symbolic boundaries and unequal access to resources and opportunities.[54] This book captures how parents make sense of and interact with both the social and symbolic boundaries that separate the G&T and Gen Ed program and guides parents into the places where they said they belong. This interaction not only assists parents in distinguishing where their children belong in this stratified school context, but later helps them make sense of where their children are placed in the gifted–Gen Ed hierarchy.

In TCS, the social boundaries include the physical, academic, and social segregation of students in separate classrooms, which, particularly for the G&T program, correlates to the race, class, and academic backgrounds of the students. The symbolic boundaries, meanwhile, include perceptions of student's classroom behavior in either program, the degree to which parents are involved in their children's education, whether parents get their children tested for G&T or not, and so on. White advantaged parents determine where they belong in this stratified system by using social and symbolic boundaries to define "us" (e.g., White parents) and "them" (lower-income parents of color who choose the Gen Ed program)—even if they were technically in the Gen Ed program themselves. The majority White G&T program became a status symbol of where the better behaved students, more involved parents, and higher achieving students were located, which strengthens the symbolic boundaries between groups.

Symbolic boundaries only become real to the people involved when they are "widely agreed upon" and develop into social boundaries.[55] But, as shown in chapter two, there are moments when symbolic boundaries do not always translate into social boundaries in this context. White advantaged parents are enrolling their children in the Gen Ed program now and the G&T and Gen Ed distinctions cannot always be determined "based on skin color alone." The findings reveal how parents rationalize, negotiate, and reconcile their child's placement in the G&T/Gen Ed hierarchy and the ambivalence that some White advantaged parents feel about being part of these privileging processes and programs.

By studying how White advantaged parents make sense of their children's placements in a segregated school context, this book captures how they either navigate the status associated with giftedness or the stigma of the Gen Ed label by rationalizing and reconciling where they belong. White G&T parents reconcile their contradictory attitudes by rationalizing that their children are being exposed to school-level diversity, and Gen Ed parents are getting *diversity by default*. In fact, the desires of White advantaged parents to have their children educated in a "diverse" setting, conceptualized at the school or classroom level and meaning different things to different parents, gets reconstructed depending on their child(ren)'s placement(s) in the school. For parents, "diversity" is used to refer to different things at different times, from a mix of students from different race/ethnicities and SES backgrounds in the K–2 Gen Ed classrooms (e.g., integration) or in the school overall (e.g., desegregation), to mostly low-income students of color in the 3–5 Gen Ed classrooms (e.g., segregation).[56] On the other side, Gen Ed parents of color believe G&T is a tool for segregation, status, and power within the school. Studying how parents make sense of the boundaries between G&T and Gen Ed programs is key to illuminating the effects of school structures on parent's school choice practices and children's opportunities to learn.

The G&T Debate

New York City Department of Education (NYCDOE) officials addressed the long-standing criticism from some parents and the popular press that G&T programs were "gifted in name only," and that the admissions process was not transparent, by changing the decentralized admissions process in 2008.[57] Leading up to the New York City district wide G&T policy change, the New York City School's chancellor described the G&T classrooms "as a hodgepodge of offerings with varying and often opaque admissions criteria that tend to favor children with well-connected parents."[58] In fact, one of the DOE's stated goals with the policy change was to increase the enrollment of Black and Latino students into G&T programs by making the G&T testing free and expanding the number of programs.

Prior to 2008, the G&T admissions process relied on multiple criteria for G&T admission, such as teacher recommendations, interviews, and observations, which allowed community school districts to tailor their G&T admissions criteria to their community and enroll a more diverse G&T program. The new centralized policy, however, was changed to use a single test score as the sole criterion. Despite warnings from experts that using standardized scores alone would lead to fewer Black and Latino students in G&T classrooms because the tests have been found to be racially and culturally biased, policy officials pushed forward with the new G&T admissions policy anyway.[59]

The problem remained and merely offering more G&T programs across the city, testing more children (because the testing is free now), setting a unified cutoff score to the 90th percentile, and having a standardized application process citywide did not equate to more diverse enrollments as the NYCDOE had hoped. Actually, just the opposite occurred. More White students and half as many Black and Latino students were admitted to G&T programs after the centralized admissions policy was implemented, primarily because the criteria for admitting students to these programs actually narrowed to place more emphasis on the one measure that had a clear correlation to both race and class: standardized tests.[60] Diane Ravitch, a historian of the New York City school system, writes about how the NYCDOE's centralized G&T admissions "halved the proportion" of Black and Latino students in G&T programs: "Any education researcher could have predicted this result, because children from advantaged homes are far likelier to know the vocabulary on a standardized test than children who lack the same advantages."[61]

This is evidenced by the fact that in the New York City school system, where Black and Latino students make up the majority of the total student population, in the year 2013, White students were three times more likely to be enrolled in G&T programs compared to Black students, and seven times more likely than Latino students.[62] This trend of within-school segregation caused by G&T programming is not limited to New York. It has been reported that the Charleston, Memphis, and Atlanta school districts classify six times more White students as G&T than Black students, and in Philadelphia and Los Angeles White students are three times more likely to be labeled G&T as Black students.[63]

Critics of G&T tracking generally point to the research evidence that reveals the educational and social harms of segregation for students, including achievement disparities and negative stereotypes.[64] They argue against using a single test score for G&T admission when children are in preschool because it further advantages students from higher-income families and acts as "pipelines" to higher-quality middle school and high school placements. Additionally, "because they are often embedded within larger schools, the programs bolster a false vision of diversity."[65] Advocates of tracking and ability grouping, on the other hand, believe that grouping students according to ability allows teachers to target instruction to student's needs and that G&T programs are needed to cultivate America's talent.[66] These same advocates tend to blame lower-income families and neighborhoods through a cultural deficit framework for G&T inequality, instead of placing the blame on the G&T programs or admissions policies themselves.

Jeannie Oakes, an expert on tracking, conducted a study of 25 racially and socioeconomically diverse secondary schools. She deconstructs the supposed "merit-based" system used to legitimize racialized tracking by calling into question how the tracking system continues to award more advantaged parents and their children with better educational opportunities through higher track placements, and why we continue to blame lower-income families for "their own lack of ability and effort or on their failure to take advantage of schooling" opportunities.[67] Researchers have consistently found that White, higher-income students are more likely to be placed in higher-tracked classrooms (Advanced Placement, G&T, College Prep) whereas Black/Latino and lower-income students are disproportionately placed in lower-tracked classrooms. There are little to no educational or social benefits for either track.[68]

According to the US Education Department, during the 2011-2012 school year, 26 percent of Black and Latino students were enrolled in G&T programs compared to 70 percent of White and Asian students nationwide.[69] With regards to G&T placements, research has shown that Black, Latino and Native American students have been perniciously underrepresented in gifted classrooms by as much as 70 percent since G&T programs started operating in the early nineteenth century.[70] As Ford and Grantham (2008) write, "This historical problem is rooted in the deficit views of culturally diverse groups, as well as in the overreliance on intelligence tests as the single or primary means of selection." Indeed, as a response to the influx of immigrant children into the public school system in the early 1900s, intelligence testing and tracking systems in the schools (including G&T programs) were implemented to sort students based on perceived ability into different "tracks." These rigid tracking structures sorted students into academic, general, or vocational tracks for their secondary school careers. In fact, G&T programs remained even after tracking policies started to lose popularity based on an extant body of research proving that they were "ineffective."[71]

This debate has played out in the courts, as well, with legal challenges to racialized tracking practices in various school districts across the country. One such case, called *Hobson v. Hansen* in Washington, DC, found that both poor students and students of color were disproportionately placed in low-track classes. The court found that this practice violated the equal protection clause of the Fourteenth Amendment because the district was using culturally biased tests for admission, "reduced curricula" in the lower track, rigid track placements, and, for the students placed in the lowest track there was an academic and social stigma.[72] A similar case in the 1990s, *People Who Care v. Rockford Board of Education* stemmed from the resegregation of students within schools after court-mandated desegregation. The federal court found that the district's strategy of creating separate, majority White G&T programs within majority Black and Latino schools was unconstitutional. These separate programs not only provided students with different curricula, but students were being placed in programs that used unfair student assignment policies. Although some have understood the US Supreme Court's 1954 *Brown v. Board of Education* decision to contemplate *integrated classrooms* as well as desegregated schools and to apply nationally not just in the South, that may be an idealized view. In any event, the reality is that in much of the country White students and students of color remain segregated not only between schools and school districts, but also within schools. According to Karolyn Tyson (2011), racialized tracking still exists, despite the legal challenges to tracking, because of the stubborn achievement gaps between White students and students of color that districts use to "justify the segregation."[73]

The G&T debate is particularly timely given the recent attention to the racial disparities associated with the NYC Specialized High Schools (SHS) admissions policy that, like G&T, also relies on a single test score for admission. For example, the NAACP Legal Defence Fund (LDF) reports that in 2014, "out of the 952 eighth grade students who received offers to matriculate into Stuyvesant High School this year, 7 are Black and 21 are Hispanic. Of the 968 eighth graders who have been admitted to Bronx High School of Science, 18 are Black and 50 are Hispanic."[74] Of the nearly 30,000 students that took the exam in 2012, only 5 percent of Black test takers were offered a spot in one of the specialized high schools compared to 31 percent of White students who took the exam (see Table I.2).

The LDF, along with other law, education, and social justice organizations filed an Office for Civil Rights (OCR) federal complaint against

Table I.2 NYC specialized high school admissions results by race, 2012

	Students who took the exam	Students who received an offer of admission to an SHS	% of test takers who received an offer of admission to any of the SHS
Black	6382	319	5
Latino	6143	414	7
Asian	7119	2490	35
White	4101	1253	31

Source: All 2012 statistics were taken from the NAACP/LDF website: http://www.naacpldf.org/case-issue/new-york-city-specialized-high-school-complaint.

the SHS in NYC that, since 1971 have relied upon the SHS Admission Test (SHSAT). Like the G&T admissions exam, this practice of using a single test for high school admissions is aligned with the broader policy focus on narrow measures of accountability and testing in public school systems across the country. The test, however, is considered bad practice because it results in racial and SES inequality. Additionally, the group that filed the complaint argue that the NYCDOE has never proven that the test itself predicts future success in the SHS. Reportedly, NYC is the only city in the country that uses this type of high school admissions policy.[75]

As a result of the complaint and in advance of the OCR decision, New York State has proposed legislation to use multiple factors for admission into SHS that would expand access and opportunity for students of color, eliminate the use of costly (and unfair) test prep services for the SHSAT test, and ensure diversity in all New York City public schools. Sean Corcoran and Christine Baker-Smith from The Research Alliance for New York City Public Schools conducted a simulation of SHS admissions using multiple measures (i.e., state test scores, attendance, and grades). The researchers found that while the share of Latino, White, and female students would increase, it would not "appreciably increase" the share of Black students admitted to SHS.[76] Therefore, future work is needed to develop strategies to expand access and diversify the SHS. New York City is not the only district that has come under fire and been investigated by the OCR regarding racial disparities in advanced course taking patterns, and other specialized programs and specialty schools. In recent years, the federal government has been more focused on eliminating the opportunity gap and has "branded tracking" as a "modern day form of segregation." *The Atlantic* magazine recently reported that there are 40 open civil rights cases currently under investigation regarding racial inequities deriving from tracking policies.[77] Districts typically have to identify the problem, come up with a plan to remedy it within one year, and obtain OCR's approval.

The core problem of offering G&T programs at the elementary school level is that by using a single test score for admission and by assuming that all parents will apply for testing and use school choice to gain access to G&T programs, the NYCDOE is not necessarily identifying "gifted and talented" students. They are merely identifying advantaged students in the system. In this way, deregulated, color-blind school choice can undermine the importance of school integration.[78] This realization can assist New York and similar districts interested in closing the opportunity gap in education—or the "accumulated differences in access to key educational resources" between White students and students of color and poor and nonpoor students, and develop strategies to ensure equality of educational opportunity. Institutional racism in the form of unequal access to high quality G&T programs, coupled with deregulated, "color-blind" school choice policies that favor advantaged families and consistently lead to second-generation segregation widens the opportunity gap and can "cast a long shadow" in terms of a student's future schooling opportunities and academic success.[79]

The Benefits of Diversity

Reams of social science evidence show that attending racially and socioeconomically diverse schools, including de-tracked classrooms, benefits all students especially lower-income students. These diverse schools have higher academic achievement and attainment, and they foster other short- and long-term social benefits for students, such as higher self-esteem and more diverse social networks.[80] Within this G&T policy context, many parents say they would prefer to enroll their children in diverse schools that have strong educational programs. Due to the fact that such options are not available, they continue to make choices that privilege their children and perpetuate the status quo.[81]

A prominent theme in the school choice literature is that many parents are aware of the benefits of diverse schools and say they believe in integrated schooling in the abstract, but when they actually choose a school their actions do not match their stated beliefs.[82] In the current post–civil rights era when racial tensions have seemingly improved, parents in this book seemed to struggle with their decision to choose the segregated G&T program at TCS, but ultimately chose it anyway for the status and opportunities that the G&T label afforded them and their children. Thus, the contradictions between what parents say they want and what they think they need given the existing choices and their place within the structures is brought to the foreground. Parents say they value integrated school environments but only when it does not pose a threat to their end goal, which is to obtain advantaged school spaces for their own children. Furthermore, these parents support integrated academic environments but want to maintain boundaries between low-income children of color and their own children.[83]

A similar theme emerges from Wells, Holme, Revilla, and Atanda's qualitative research on White graduates of desegregated schools from the 1970 and 1980s.[84] The authors found that these graduates harbor extremely fond memories of their own experiences in racially diverse schools. Yet in this new era of high-stakes assessments, a highly competitive college admissions process, and growing income inequality, many of them are drawn to the public and private schools that they see as the most selective and highest status for their own children. And, at a time when fewer public policies support the creation or maintenance of racially diverse schools, these high-status schools are more often than not predominantly White and affluent. Therefore, Wells et al. saw this tension within White parents in a very blatant form. Graduates of desegregated schools, who experienced the benefits of racially diverse schools first hand, understood what their own children were missing when they chose to put them in more segregated schools but did so in spite of this.

White advantaged parents in this book also embodied contradictory attitudes in regard to exposing their children to racial/ethnic and socioeconomic "diversity," as long as their children were not in the minority, and provided their children with what they consider to be the "best" education alongside students and families like their own. Parents said they would prefer to enroll their children in "diverse," meaning desegregated, schools that have strong educational programs. They specifically point to the "diversity" in the Gen Ed classrooms in the younger grades (K-2)—meaning more White students—as a "positive thing" for the school since the segregation between programs is breaking down slowly over time. Yet, instead of choosing what has been coined "diversity by choice,"[85] the White advantaged parents in this context who enroll their children in the more diverse Gen Ed programs for kindergarten are receiving *diversity by default*. This is the case because they are not intentionally choosing the Gen Ed program because of its diversity. Rather, the Gen Ed program is considered the next best option if parents do not initially get their children in the high status G&T program that they prefer.

This phenomenon occurs when parents have older children enrolled in G&T, but their younger child does not make the G&T cutoff score and they want both of their children in the same school, or they live in the school's catchment but are placed in a different school with a G&T program that is less desirable because of location. Parents explained that the other two G&T programs that the district offers are not as popular to White families because the Gen Ed portion in those schools is majority Black and Latino. Lauren, who has both of her sons in the G&T program, said in some schools with G&T programs "that pull from the projects, it is not an option for everybody because some people are like, 'Oh great, they're giving me a G&T spot in a school where my kid's going to be a huge minority.'"

What is unique about this demographically changing school site is that White advantaged parents are starting to choose the lower status Gen Ed program for kindergarten. Parents explained that the G&T program benefits the whole school because it "brings up the academics" and reputation, "so people start being more willing to go to the Gen Ed program" if they live in the neighborhood. According to TCS parent estimates, enrollment in the three kindergarten Gen Ed classrooms was roughly 30 percent White, or about 8 to 9 White students per class, and growing as more and more White "neighborhood" parents made the choice to enroll their children in their neighborhood public school even if their child did not get into the G&T program.[86] As parents explained, the sharp racial distinctions between the G&T and Gen Ed programs for students in grades 3 to 5 remained since White families would prep and retest their Gen Ed children because of the negative stigma, peer environment, and perceived advantages of the G&T label until most of them eventually switched to the G&T program or left the school for better options.

For most of these White advantaged parents, having their children enrolled in a program with other students "like them" in terms of their social status and privilege and thus being associated with other parents "like them" was the most important factor, superseding all other desires.[87] And, as Alyssa confirmed at the beginning of the chapter, once parents get their children into what they believe is the best program for someone like them, they are more likely to "buy into" the labels or categories that their children are given within the school because of their child's G&T test score, even if "they try not to."

One of the primary reasons parents cited for retesting their children for the G&T program was because of the negative stigma associated with the Gen Ed label. This academic and social stigma is felt by parents in terms of parent involvement and for students in terms of academic ability. This is contrary to the tracking/de-tracking literature that found that academic achievement and teacher quality were driving the support of tracking.[88] Instead, in this book, White parents downplayed the curriculum and teaching differences between programs and spoke about the G&T program in code language in order to be "sensitive" to advantaged Gen Ed parents and relieve the tension between the two sets of parents. Since there is no "advanced specialty curriculum" in the G&T program, some G&T parents thought that their child could be challenged more, but there was no way to do that with the standardized NYCDOE curriculum. Even with the same curriculum, parents still felt that a G&T placement guarantees entry into the "best" middle schools because students have higher academic self-esteem. G&T students are also being pushed by their stronger academic peers and the teachers are better for preparing students to take the fourth grade tests that are used for middle school applications.

In fact, many of the White parents were aware that their actions and choices privileged their own children and perpetuated the status quo. Yet, they still strove to be in the majority White G&T program because their choices are nested within the broader context of our stratified society, especially in cities like New York City with high degrees of income inequality, patterns of gentrification, and residential and school segregation. To be fair, though, these parents do not have many other high-quality public school options to choose from. Ultimately, the larger structures of inequality and privilege that these parents are operating within shape their school choices and opportunities.

Overview of Chapters

This book, situated within a social and political New York City community school district of residential and school segregation, SES bifurcation, and a test-driven G&T admissions system, is a key site to study the issues of social reproduction and boundary maintenance with White advantaged parents whose children get placed into two different hierarchical academic tracks. Chapter One describes the local school and neighborhood context in more depth, including the different school choice programs that have been adopted in the *City Limits* district, and the history of the NYCDOE using G&T programs to attract White parents into public schools in New York City. It provides a picture of the community school district, schools, and neighborhoods where the parents in this book choose to live and send their children to school.

Chapters Two to Four are based on the in-depth interviews with the 41 advantaged White parents in the sample. Chapter Two illustrates the multiple ways that parents use social and symbolic boundaries to distinguish the G&T and Gen Ed categories and labels in their school. It shows how White parents go through all necessary steps to get their children placed in the G&T program, which better matches their advantaged position as signified by plenty of people "like them," despite the seemingly paradoxical attitudes they have about "diversity" and segregation. The distinctions that parents make between "us" (White parents) and "them" (lower-income parents of color in the Gen Ed program) reinforced the feeling that advantaged parents belong on the G&T side of the boundary line and contributed to the contradictions that developed inside them if they were not where they said they believed they belong (e.g., their "place"). Parents use boundaries to imagine who they are by imagining who they are not, whether it's comparing TCS to a school that recently phased out their G&T program or comparing themselves to a Gen Ed parent who is perceived to not value education because they did not get their child tested for G&T.

Chapter Three shows how even White advantaged parents—particularly those with at least one child in the Gen Ed program, who have resources to help get their children into G&T programs and G&T parents in the older grades who have experienced the school culture longer—struggle with the meaning of the measures used to define "giftedness" in this context, namely a single score on a standardized test. The Savvy Negotiators and Conflicted Followers, in particular, best articulate their belief that the "gifted" label is socially constructed, meaning that "giftedness" in this context is related more to students' advantaged backgrounds and G&T test preparation than their "true" intelligence. Their definition of giftedness is different than the DOE's arbitrary 90th percentile cutoff score and who can do really well on the G&T test by being prepped. The chapter concludes by describing why some G&T parents, particularly the "G&T Defenders" in the younger grades, who have the least experience with the school or with the Gen Ed program, tend to embody or internalize the G&T label more than others because of their child's high score on the G&T test.

Chapter Four demonstrates how the findings discussed in the prior two chapters shift and become redefined as a growing number of White advantaged parents are choosing the Gen Ed program. Readers will learn how the White parents make sense of and adapt to the changing social and symbolic boundaries within the school by choosing the Gen Ed program when that was their only option in TCS and then redefine what the symbolic boundary of the two programs meant. In this moment of recreating the boundaries, parents on both sides of the boundary line considered the "diversity" in the Gen Ed classrooms as "positive" and a sign that the school could (and should) phase out the G&T program. But, regardless of what they said about the positive benefits of diversity in the younger grades, the boundary between G&T and Gen Ed in the upper grades gets reproduced because the White Gen Ed parents retest their children for G&T, and most of these White students then move over to the G&T program. In this way, these same advantaged parents who would support the G&T program being phased out, also argue that the G&T program is still "needed" at their school to attract the right kind of parents to the school and create distance from the "other." In the current, post–civil rights era, where White racial attitudes seemingly have improved, parents' simultaneous desires to phase out the G&T program and hold onto it highlight their contradictory attitudes in this segregated two-track school.

In chapter five, data and analysis from follow-up interviews with eight White parents who had their children in the K-1 Gen Ed program in 2011, including one new Gen Ed parent, are highlighted to see whether their child eventually switched to the G&T, left the school, or chose to stay in the Gen Ed program. The findings show that White advantaged parents are continuing to use their cultural capital to test prep and secure a G&T seat because of the perceived advantages and the stigma of the Gen Ed label, with six out of the eight parents switching their child to G&T or leaving the school. There is also less critique of phasing the G&T program out now that there is more competition to get a G&T seat. Additionally, a comparison group of nine Black and Latino mothers who enroll their children in the Gen Ed program at TCS were interviewed regarding their perspective of the two different programs, parents and children in the school. The Gen Ed parents of color believe that G&T is used as a tool for segregation, status, and power within the school. They question the definition of giftedness in this context because parents are tutoring for the G&T test, and, compared to White parents, have limited information about school choice from their social networks or preschools.

And finally, the Conclusion summarizes the main points and arguments of the book, mainly that the New York City G&T policy context that parents are operating within creates the status distinctions between schools and programs in the first place and results in the social reproduction of the system. The argument is made for de-tracking the segregated G&T programs within otherwise diverse neighborhood schools, and using school choice as a policy tool to achieve diversity since right now integration is not the goal. This concluding chapter explores other policies that could be implemented to combat the segregation that this system maintains, discusses the theoretical and empirical contributions of the book, and proposes ideas for future research on this important topic. The chapter ends by questioning how school districts can redefine what is considered to be the "best" school—from schools with a critical mass of White, higher-income students to schools with racial and social class integration that promote cross-cultural understandings and prepare students for our increasingly diverse twenty-first-century society.

CHAPTER ONE

THE CASE: G&T PROGRAMS WITHIN
NEW YORK CITY SCHOOLS

The year is 1996 and the *City Limits* superintendent of schools has proposed moving a district-run G&T program from one highly regarded elementary school, called "Riverside Elementary" into another less reputable school, "The Community School" (TCS).[1] A *New York Times* education article dramatically reports about the parents' "agony" over the movement of the gifted program to a different school site located a mere five blocks away. The author questions how extreme parents will be in their efforts to stop the G&T move by participating in "candlelight vigils, crowded sidewalk protests, placard-waving pupils, furious letter-writing campaigns—all for the plight of the gifted and talented?"[2] As reported, the highly involved Riverside parents quickly gather to protest the plan, but to no avail as the local school board votes to move the G&T program to TCS anyway the following school year. The rationale behind the move is that TCS is handicapped accessible and Riverside is not.

The article explains that parents are in an uproar because prior to the G&T program being implemented, Riverside Elementary was considered failing and was losing students. Because of the efforts and presence of the highly involved G&T parents in the school, Riverside was "credited with keeping the middle class" from leaving the public school system. "Enraged" parents accused the superintendent of moving the G&T program from Riverside to improve TCS, a historically Black and Latino school, which had experienced declining test scores in recent years. Riverside parents believed that moving the G&T program from their school would be like "ripping the heart out" of it—meaning losing the advantaged families who provide valued resources to the school. In other words, this was *not* a fight over keeping G&T opportunities for district students since they would still be offered in a different school location. It was a fight to keep advantaged parents in a particular school to make it better. The threat of losing the G&T program and parents to another school threatened Riverside's reputation and ability to attract other highly involved parents to the school. This rationale to keep G&T in certain schools is reflective of how the parents in this book imagine who they are—a school community that "needs" G&T because it has lower-income students and wants to attract the right "kind" of parent (chapter two). Ironically, this is the same reasoning that the advantaged parents use in this book about whether the G&T program at TCS should be phased out or not (chapter four).

The backstory of the G&T program at TCS and Riverside have a great deal in common. Both schools target and implement G&T programs in historically segregated, Black and Latino low-income schools. These two programs were established in hopes that White, higher-income parents will be attracted to the school, bring their valued resources, and improve student achievement levels. Once that process is accomplished and more White families from the catchment start enrolling their children in the Gen Ed program, which is starting to happen at TCS, then they can phase the program out and implement G&T at a new school. Courtney, an incoming G&T parent, explained why she thought they were phasing out a G&T program at one disproportionately White school and starting a new program at a segregated Black and Latino, neighborhood school: "I mean they said ['GT2' in Table 1.4] was phasing their G&T program out because they had more regular [Gen Ed] applicants, and they ran out of actual physical space, which may be true. But I also feel like it's a good way to get [the new G&T program] to work better. So they're spreading the wealth a little."

Additionally, Kathy who is an upper-class fourth grade G&T Defender responded, "I believe that G&T programs can elevate a school and then they can be phased out and the school will stay a great school, you know?" Parents in this book believe that the G&T program "pulls the school up" because they attract the right type of "G&T" parent—one who has money to donate and gets involved in the PTA, which in this case are the majority White, higher-income parents. Then, the theory goes, once the school gets a better reputation because of who is enrolling their children there and what they are doing for the school, then parents from the neighborhood will want to go to the school regardless if there is a G&T program or not. Kelly, who is an incoming G&T parent asked "How long do you keep [the G&T at TCS] before you move it some place else and improve those schools, too?"

TCS has maintained a segregated G&T program for nearly 20 years. As policymakers in New York City and elsewhere contemplate the most effective urban school reform strategies, the question remains whether the practice of using G&T programs to attract White, middle-class parents into the public system is the best policy when the result is second-generation segregation within schools? Are there more equitable strategies that can be implemented to attract New York City parents who want diversity *and* high-quality school options without resulting in "dual segregation"?[3] Linn Posey-Maddox, in her study of middle-class parents' motivations for choosing a Title I urban public school in Northern California, argues that "relying upon middle-class parents as major drivers of school reform is bad practice, as their volunteerism and fundraising efforts may marginalize low-income and working-class families in a school community."[4] In this context in which G&T programs are seen as the answer to the problem of how to keep the middle class invested in New York City public schools, low-income families of color get marginalized and undervalued in terms of parent involvement efforts for school improvement. For instance, Mercedes, who is a Latina mother in the Gen Ed program, explained that every year the PTA asks for $2,500 from each family to pay for teaching assistants in the classroom. She replied: "It's public school. Why do you want $2,500 from me? Why? I'm not paying you $2,500. If the teacher needs me, I'm there. If they need snacks, I'll provide whatever you need from me. I'm there. But don't ask me for $2,500. That, I don't see." Because the White advantaged families are paying for the teaching assistant salaries, and not the lower-income parents, Mercedes said, "they walk around like they are better than you."

Prior to 1997 when TCS implemented its G&T program, it was a typical neighborhood school and served mostly Black and Latino children from the catchment area[5] and, by some reports, was considered to be a low-performing school. Since the G&T program began with its separate admissions criteria, though, White (and some Asian) families from across the district have been drawn to its highly reputed G&T program. The Gen Ed program, on the other hand, enrolls the Black and Latino students from the catchment area who live in public housing or rent-stabilized apartments. The program also enrolls from lower-income districts outside of the *City Limits* School District who, until recently, were bused in to fill the Gen Ed seats. Tanya, a first grade Gen Ed parent who lives in TCS's attendance boundaries, explained that older women from her neighborhood had told her that TCS was not a place where you would have sent your [White] children to back in the 80s and 90s because it was majority students of color.

Since 2008 when the G&T admissions policy changed and the economic recession hit, the Gen Ed program has slowly started to enroll White neighborhood children or younger siblings of older G&T students who do not initially make the G&T cutoff score—breaking down the racial and social class boundaries in the younger grades but not in the older grades because, by then, most of the White students retest and switch to G&T.

The advantaged parents in this urban school choice context are an interesting and unique group to study on many levels, especially within a demographically changing school where White families are located on both sides of the G&T/Gen Ed divide. Moving the G&T program into TCS in 1997 sets the stage for this research and is symbolic of the larger social, political, and economic context that the parents in this book are operating within. This local context is also important theoretically and conceptually because the New York City school system is an ideal place to learn about the multiple ways that social reproduction and racial and SES segregation *within* schools is maintained and perpetuated at a more micro level by both the NYCDOE's G&T policy and parent's elementary school choices. This book furthers our understanding of how race and class are tightly intertwined regarding parents' (1) perceptions of school and program quality, (2) symbolic boundary work (rules, codes and expectations), and (3) interactions with other parents, teachers, and administrators, which serve to influence and structure student's opportunities to learn.

Although New York City schools are often seen as unique cases, the consequential boundaries that are created and maintained between the G&T and Gen Ed programs *within* New York City elementary schools are more layered and complex. The two programs are in closer proximity to one another, as opposed to choosing a school or school district that is in a different neighborhood and thus further removed from sight and mind. In New York City, racial and SES distinctions are more blatant because the "gifted" and "Gen Ed" students are placed in self-contained classrooms in the same schools, literally across the hallway from each other. In the current post–civil rights era, the racial/ethnic demographic contrast between the two programs become a more visceral experience for the parents, students, and school community, especially when parents are determining where their children belong in this two-track segregated system. This chapter describes the social context of the book in more detail to provide a picture of the New York City school choice policy landscape that parents are operating within.

School Choice in NYC

By far the largest school district in the country, the New York City School System educates roughly one million students in 1,600 schools across the five boroughs of Manhattan, Brooklyn, Queens, the Bronx, and Staten

Island.[6] While New York City is hailed as one of the most racial/ethnic and socioeconomically diverse school districts in the United States with an overall student population of 15 percent White, 15 percent Asian, 40 percent Latino, 30 percent Black and 71 percent qualifying for FRPL,[7] it is also notoriously one of the most segregated.[8] Within urban areas such as Chicago, Dallas, and New York City, school segregation is linked to gentrification, isolated poverty, and residential segregation—meaning that roughly 80 percent of Black and White students in these urban centers would have to move to a different school for racial integration to be achieved.[9] This racial disparity occurs between and within the 32 Community School Districts (CSDs) across New York City, reflecting the segregated neighborhoods surrounding each school's catchment area and parents' school choices.

Race and class are highly intertwined in New York City. US census data confirms that in Manhattan, for example, the median household income for Whites is $100,128 compared to a mere $33,110 for Blacks and $31,779 for Latino households.[10] The majority of New York City Black and Latino students are concentrated in schools that enroll a majority of low-income students of color, while White, higher-income students are "overexposed" to other White students.[11] Gary Orfield has called this phenomenon "double segregation"[12] by race and class in schools, which serves to disadvantage lower-income students of color even more because segregated schools, as compared to integrated schools, tend to be less well-resourced, hire less experienced teachers, and have higher rates of behavior problems and student mobility—all resulting in lower achievement, reputations, and rankings.[13] The Civil Rights Project reports that many of the CSDs such as *City Limits* have "One or two well-resourced schools filled with predominately White and Asian, middle-class students in contrast to the other and under-resourced schools, serving lower-income and majority minority students."[14]

Neighborhood and school segregation is compounded when you add in deregulated, color-blind school choice policies that many CSDs implement. Advantaged parents in the system are more likely to use market-based school choice plans to flee their zoned, neighborhood schools for Whiter and higher-income schools and programs, thus exacerbating the segregation in the system. Moving away from the desegregation era of using school choice as a policy tool to reduce racial isolation, current school choice policy is typically enacted to maximize parental choice and create greater competition for students across schools and programs—leading to more and not less segregation between schools.[15] This choice-based segregation, between and within schools, occurs even as more White parents are saying they want more racially diverse schools to choose from.[16]

At the time of this study, *City Limits* offered several school choice avenues for parents who were unhappy with their assigned zoned school: (1) a district-wide deregulated school choice system for general education programs (public and charter) in which parents fill out individual school applications and then school administrators choose students if space is available (2) a NYCDOE gifted and talented (a.k.a. G&T) admissions process, involving a separate online application decided by sibling priority, students' scores on the G&T test, and space/capacity issues in each school's program, and (3) an unzoned, "magnet" school option with a separate application and lottery process.

Because of the deregulated and color-blind school choice policy, racial segregation at the school and classroom level is rampant across *City Limits* schools, as well as the New York City School System as a whole. *City Limits* district does not report the demographic breakdown or standardized test score differences for G&T programs versus Gen Ed. Site visits to many of these schools, as well as newspaper and advocacy reports and interview data, however, demonstrate that G&T programs in *City Limits* schools are almost entirely White. In contrast, Gen Ed classes in the same schools are comprised almost entirely of students of color. In TCS, the Gen Ed program is demographically changing as more and more White families from the neighborhood or younger siblings of G&T students are enrolling in Gen Ed in the younger grades. Parents report that, academically, G&T students tend to score higher on the state standardized tests as evidenced by their higher rates of admission into the selective middle schools.

In an effort to diversify G&T programs citywide by switching to a more transparent, centralized admissions policy, the racial disparities between the two separate programs have gotten worse. This is evidenced by the fact that in the New York City School System, which is only 15 percent White and 15 percent Asian overall, G&T enrollments for the 2010–2011 school year were 73 percent White and Asian students, up from 68 percent the year before. Meanwhile, although Black and Latino students make up about 70 percent of the total student population, they constitute only 11 and 12 percent respectively of the students in G&T programs across the City(see Table1 .1).

Ultimately, the disparities that exist between and within schools across the city are perpetuated by school policies that are implemented in ways that advantage the most privileged New York City families even more, and disadvantage the families and students who need access to high-quality schools the most. For instance, parents first need to be aware of the G&T testing process. If parents want to be able to apply to G&T schools, they must fill out an online request to get their children tested and then take

Table 1.1 NYC public school students in G&T programs by race/ethnicity before and after the 2008 centralized G&T policy change

	Latino (%)	Black (%)	White (%)	Asian (%)
NYC Incoming K G&T Population—before 2007	15	31	33	20
NYC Incoming K G&T Population—2008–2009	9	13	48	28

Source: Gootman & Gebeloff, 2008.

them to the designated testing place. It is important to highlight how the policy context itself shapes the distribution of opportunities for the parents in the first place by creating the status distinctions between schools, programs, parents, and, most importantly, students.

Site Selection: "*City Limits* School District" and "The Community School"

The public school enrollment in *City Limits* is incredibly diverse with more Black (33%) a growing number of White students (27%, up from 23% in 2006) and fewer Latino (34%) and Asian (5%) students than the citywide school system.[17] See Table 1.2 for a comparison of the racial/ethnic breakdowns between the *City Limits* School District and the larger New York City school system.

In theory, *City Limits* has the ability to create integrated schools. Because of racially segregated housing patterns, the fact that many parents choose their neighborhood schools, and the G&T policy that uses standardized tests for admission into kindergarten, most schools are racially and socioeconomically segregated both between and within schools. Many of the elementary schools that offer G&T programs may appear racially diverse. Students are separated into different homogeneous tracks, however, from kindergarten through fifth grade. G&T parents will rationalize that their children are being exposed to school-level diversity, even though there is little interaction between the G&T and Gen Ed parents and students inside the school.[18] In fact, parents explained that the only opportunity for students to socialize with the other track is during recess, lunchtime (where they sit with their own class), field trips (if Gen Ed is included), and afterschool activities and sports (if they participate, and which also tend to be segregated). As described in chapter two, this separation contributes to the feeling that the G&T is "getting something better" or special, even

Table 1.2 Percent of the 2009–2010 New York City versus the City Limits School District student population by race/ethnicity and FRPL

	Latino (%)	Black (%)	White (%)	Asian (%)	FRPL (%)
NYC Schools	40	30	15	15	71
City Limits	34	33	27	5	54

Source: All 2009–2010 statistics are taken from the New York City Department of Education website, http://schools.nyc.gov.

Note: FRPL = free or reduced price lunch.

though technically the G&T and Gen Ed students are receiving the same standardized NYCDOE curriculum and have access to the same resources, pushing parents to retest for G&T every year until most eventually get in or leave the school.

The end result of White advantaged parents sorting their children based on where they determine they belong in this stratified and segregated system is that most *City Limits* schools are racially and socioeconomically segregated with 13 out of the 19 elementary schools comprised mostly of low-income children of color and the remaining six schools disproportionately enrolling the White, higher-income student population.[19] For example, of the six schools that have a sizable population of White students in them, three schools offer G&T programs (including The Community School) and three schools offer more heterogeneous classroom environments (see Table 1.3 for a comparison sample of "diverse" schools and "hyper-segregated" schools with more than 90% children of color).

Like Alyssa described in the Introduction, many of the advantaged White parents in this book voiced their frustration with the fact that there are only three *City Limits* schools that they consider to be "diverse" at the school and classroom level, which are virtually impossible to get into because they are oversubscribed (see Table 1.3). These "diverse" schools not only enroll a majority of White, higher-income students as compared to the hyper-segregated schools, they also enroll more students (because they are popular and oversubscribed), and are higher performing, based on test scores. Currently, some of the students zoned for these schools are being placed on waiting lists due to the lack of available seats. The DOE responded to the overcrowding by opening a new elementary school for the overflow, and a charter school that attracts White, higher-income families. In contrast, the hyper-segregated neighborhood schools in the district are undersubscribed, high poverty, and low-performing schools. As a result, more parents who live in one of these areas prep and test their children for G&T programs to escape their "failing" zoned school.

This constrained school choice environment that consists of choosing between majority White and higher income schools and G&T programs within schools, versus majority Black and Latino and lower-income schools pushes parents to apply for every "acceptable" option—like Alyssa explained in the Introduction. For most advantaged parents, this includes getting their children tested for G&T and choosing the program if they score high enough, even if they were initially hesitant to choose that option because of the segregation.

Not only do some advantaged parents feel discomfort about choosing segregated G&T programs, if they have the choice between one of the three majority White neighborhood schools and a G&T program, there are strong opinions about which one is the "better" choice in terms of segregation, test scores, and future school opportunities. This debate played out in a 2011 "UrbanBaby" blog exchange below, in which a *City Limits* parent was trying to decide between G&T at TCS or Gen Ed at school A (see Table1.3).

Table 1.3 Student's race, FRPL status, and percent of students who passed the ELA and math state tests for (1) Three "diverse" neighborhood schools (with no G&T), and (2) Comparison group of "hyper-segregated" neighborhood schools

Public School	Total Students	% Black	% Latino	% White	% Asian	% FRPL	% ELA Score	% Math Score
1. "Diverse" Neighborhood Schools (with no G&T)								
A	962	10	17	68	7	10	84	85
B	774	5	12	68	11	9	88	91
C*	705	18	24	57	7	21	68	70
2. "Hyper-segregated" Neighborhood Schools								
D	404	81	18	1	0	86	25	47
E	395	75	21	1	1	78	25	30
F	155	70	26	2	3	88	21	34

Source: All 2009–2010 statistics are taken from the New York City Department of Education website, http://schools.nyc.gov.

Note: All schools were renamed using alphabetical order to protect confidentiality and are kindergarten to grade 5 schools unless otherwise noted. G&T = gifted and talented program; FRPL = free or reduced price lunch; %ELA score = percentage of students who passed the yearly English Language Arts standardized test; %Math score = percentage of students who passed the yearly Mathematics standardized test.

* School C is a K–8 school and has its own district-wide lottery application for admission.

- "look at the [district] results [school A] blows [TCS] out of the water and it does not have a segregated program."
- "[School A] is the Whitest school in [the district]. 71 percent White, 13 percent Asian, 11 percent Hispanic, 5 percent Black. And only 7 percent free lunch. (In a district that is 31% Black, 32% Hispanic, and 45% free lunch.) [School A's] demographics aren't particularly anyone's "fault," but I would counsel anyone at [school A] to be circumspect about labeling other schools as "segregated.""
- "At least you don't have Black in one class and White in another, and you cannot compete on scores, which is the main thing for middle school."
- "Basically at [TCS] g&t you have the White kids, then the gen ed has some White kids but half kids of color. So, if you like that segregation, go for it!"
- "Or you could go to [school B] and just be with White kids? How is this an improvement?"[20]

These posts reflect the fact that parents are keenly aware of the segregation between and within schools, and also what is at stake regarding standardized test scores and middle school placement. This blog exchange between parents goes back and forth, with different parents giving their take on the situation and commenting on the "big divide" that exists between "good" schools that have parents who "value education" versus "bad zoned schools" with "lots of poor people of color." One parent writes, "My zoned public is absolutely terrible on all fronts and there is no way I'd send my dc ['darling child'] there." But then, the conversation turns to what factors go into making a school "good"—like great teachers, an effective leader, and parental involvement. Another parent writes that in her zoned school, which just added a G&T program in kindergarten, "there is a small core group of parents who are really involved and we really just need more." She asks "parents" to "not shy away" from her school—implying White, higher-income parents who are most likely contributing to and reading UrbanBaby blogs should come to her school to help turn it around. In this constrained and segregated school choice environment, it is perhaps not surprising that parents are conflicted between diversity, segregation, and providing their child with, as one TCS advantaged parent said, the "best education that you can...within your means."

In recent years, a growing number of advantaged parents in the *City Limits* School District are starting to consider a fourth option for their children's education. This option is Gen Ed programs within schools that also offer highly popular G&T programs, like TCS, which is located in a mixed income neighborhood. Therefore, what is happening is if their kindergarten child does not originally get a high enough score on the G&T test to get offered a G&T seat in TCS, they choose the Gen Ed program within that same school for kindergarten (either because they are zoned for that school or their older sibling is in the G&T program and the administration allows them to enroll their younger child even though they live outside the catchment). Then, these same families retest their children for G&T until most eventually get in.

The G&T Admissions Policy

The NYCDOE decided to address the long-standing criticism from some parents, DOE officials, and the popular press that G&T programs across the city were "gifted in name only" and the admissions process was not transparent by centralizing the process in 2008.[21] Leading up to the New York City district-wide G&T policy change, the New York City School's chancellor described the G&T classrooms as "a hodgepodge of offerings with varying, and often opaque, admissions criteria that tend to favor children with well-connected parents."[22] In fact, one of the DOE's stated goals with the policy change was to increase the enrollment of Black and Latino students into G&T programs. But, like Lauren's quote suggests, that could have been just "smoke and mirrors," the real reason being to attract middle-class parents into public schools to make them better.

Prior to 2008, the G&T admissions process relied on multiple criteria for admission, such as teacher recommendations, interviews, and observations. This process allowed CSDs to tailor their G&T admissions criteria to their community and enroll a more diverse G&T program. The new centralized policy, however, was changed to use a single test score as the sole criterion. The former chancellor pushed forward with his new G&T admissions policy despite warnings from experts that using standardized test scores alone, which were found to be racially biased, would lead to fewer Black and Latino students in G&T classrooms.[23]

This relatively new G&T admissions policy is based on a single score on a standardized test that children take in preschool. Thus, parents can choose to have their children tested to become eligible for two types of G&T programs. The first G&T option is a community school district program for students who score above the 90th percentile. These G&T programs are located within certain neighborhood schools that also house Gen Ed programs for students living in the neighborhood, like TCS. The other G&T option is for children who score above the 97th percentile on the G&T tests. These students become eligible for the five citywide G&T schools, which are open to students from all five boroughs if space is available.[24] This new G&T admissions process favors parents who send their children to private preschools and have more time, knowledge, and resources, not only to navigate the system but also to prepare their children to take the test and get the highest score possible. Melissa, an upper-class White parent with experience in both programs pointed out, "I never went into the G&T program thinking that my kids were gifted, you know, they were in the G&T program because I was able to send them to a good preschool. I knew they needed to take the test, I knew the whole deal."

At the time of this study, the two standardized tests that preschool children took included the Otis-Lennon School Ability Test (OLSAT) and the Bracken School Readiness Assessment (BSRA). According to the NYCDOE's website, the OLSAT G&T test measures "verbal comprehension, verbal reasoning, pictorial reasoning and figural reasoning," and the BSRA asks questions about colors, letters, shapes, sizes, numbers/counting, and comparisons in a multiple-choice format. Parents in this book described the BSRA as a basic kindergarten readiness test that children can easily pass if they attend preschool and learn their colors and shapes. The OLSAT test, on the other hand, was described as being a little more "tricky" and was the test that parents were prepping their children to take because they said it was more about test taking skills than actual "academic prowess." As Elaine, a third grade Gen Ed parent explained, "The questions are just confusing [on the OLSAT]. And you have to really be a good test taker, which I don't think everybody is. And you have to really be able to decipher what they're actually asking. The questions are all very tricky. A lot of logic and almost puzzle-y kind of questions."

The majority of parents in this book did some kind of test prep activities with their children either at home, at preschool, and/or with a private tutor. Many parents said they used the DOE's website, which provides a practice OLSAT test that parents can print out. Parents also bought practice tests and workbooks online and even hired professional tutors (usually privately at their home). In chapter three, parents' justifications for prepping their children for the G&T tests are explained as a way to give their children "every advantage" in the system even when they say it is not who they are, they do not believe their child is truly "gifted" and "talented," and/or they admit that tutoring for the G&T test is cheating. The growing test-prepping industry contributes to the uneven cultural capital exchange among parents, which serves to strengthen the boundary line between G&T and Gen Ed programs and children, and leads to the reproduction of this stratified system.[25]

The G&T test process varies for various age groups, which can also help or hinder test performance. Since the children are only four years old when they first take the tests, professional proctors (who are usually school teachers) read the questions and fill in the test form bubbles for the children. Older children are pulled out of their classroom in small groups and fill in the bubbles themselves. Kelly, an Incoming parent to the school, thought that it was more about "listening skills than test taking skills at this age." Other parents in the book said that some children who are shy and are not "comfortable going off with strangers" have more difficulty performing well on these tests because of their "personality." Children who are more outgoing and comfortable talking to adults, according to parents, are more likely to get higher G&T scores. Students who do not pass the G&T test for kindergarten can take subsequent G&T tests each year up until third grade.

Before parents can rank the G&T schools on the application form, they are required to fill out an online "Request for G&T Testing" form, take their children to get tested at their assigned place and time, and receive their children's scores. The NYCDOE combines the student's two test scores to come up with a percentile rank by weighting the OLSAT 75 percent and the BSRA 25 percent. The percentile rank score shows a student's score relative to other children in that age group who also took the test. If the student scores above the 90th percentile, then she/he gets placed in schools according to sibling priority, percentile rank, ranked school preferences, and available seats in G&T programs. Parents receive one offer, and if they decline their seat they do not get put on a waiting list or receive another placement offer.

Since TCS's G&T program is popular, parents said that students had to get a top score of a 98 or 99 to get a seat at TCS (except for younger siblings who are guaranteed a seat if they scored above 90). They also explained that there are so many younger siblings that there are hardly any available seats for first-time incoming students. As Rachel, a first grade G&T parent explained:

> I don't know of anybody that scored under a 98 in the G&T from last year [in kindergarten] or for the first grade. So if you scored a 90, you could get in because you were a sibling. And I think it's pretty easy to get a 90 in the way that—I don't know if you've seen the stats, but somebody from the G&T, they sent me a spreadsheet that had all the boroughs and all the stats on how many kids scored in each—in which bracket, and [City Limits School District], you know, blown out of the water. And half the kids score above 90. And a really high percentage scored above 97. So to even get considered for citywide, I mean you had to have a 99, and then it was the luck of the draw whether you got picked or not.

In other words, if a student gets between 90 and 99 on the G&T test, they are still considered "gifted" according to the DOE's standards because they made the cutoff score, but unless they are the younger sibling of an older G&T student, they are offered a G&T seat in a less desirable school. This caused many parents who lived within TCS's catchment or had older children in the G&T program already, to choose TCS's Gen Ed program for their children's education, instead of choosing a less desirable G&T program or having their children enrolled in two different schools. Then, parents would continue to retest their child until they eventually got into the G&T at TCS. This entire process clearly favors parents who know the "rules of the game," as Bourdieu would say, and activate their cultural capital exchange[26] in order to maintain or improve their position in the school choice field, and, as will be described in chapter two, avoid the negative stigma of the Gen Ed label.

This book stems from an earlier study on parent's satisfaction of a 2006 school choice lottery system, which is now defunct.[27] The comments from many of the White parents who were interviewed described the struggles that they went through when choosing a school, especially after witnessing the segregated G&T and Gen Ed classrooms during school tours.[28] For example, some parents were very bothered by the segregation between the two programs when they toured the schools, and ultimately chose a different school, either a private school or one of a few non-G&T neighborhood schools with a majority of White students—meaning more than 50 percent. But others, acknowledged the "problem" of segregation, yet still chose the G&T program and rationalized it as the best program for their child. This book takes a closer look inside a neighborhood school with a G&T program to see how a diverse group of parents in the G&T, Gen Ed, or both programs make sense of their different placements within a segregated two-track school.

Schools with G&T programs, however, continue to be popular choices because, as Alyssa pointed out in the Introduction, they are perceived to be "better" than the Gen Ed classrooms within the same schools, even when they are highly stratified racially and socioeconomically. In fact, the NYCDOE recently reported that the district-wide number of kindergarteners enrolled in G&T programs almost doubled from 874 students in 2008 to 1,554 students in 2009, which they attributed to more four-year-olds who took the standardized tests and passed the 90th percentile cutoff.[29]

It is also important to note that there were a few parents who were considered to be outliers because they either did not attempt to switch their child from the Gen Ed to G&T in first grade for academic reasons (n=1), got accepted into a different G&T program but chose the Gen Ed program at TCS because of location or reputation (n=2), or technically made the 90th percentile score for G&T placement but did not get a G&T seat for first grade because of sibling priority (n=2). The presence of parent outliers illustrates that there are factors beyond test scores that contribute to the competition for a G&T seat.

Therefore, the problem remains that merely offering more G&T programs across the city, testing more children (because the testing is free now), setting a unified cutoff score to the 90th percentile, and having a more standardized application process citywide did not equate to more diverse enrollments as the DOE had hoped. The opposite occurred. More White students, from 33 percent to 48 percent, and half as many Black and Latino students were admitted to G&T programs after the centralized application policy was implemented. See Table 1.1 for a comparison of New York City public school students in G&T Programs by race/ethnicity before and after the 2008 centralized G&T policy change.

By 2008–2009 the entering G&T kindergarten population was Whiter and came from higher-income families than in prior years. A third of the new class of gifted kindergartners came from New York City's wealthiest and Whitest community school districts. On the other hand, students of color made up 70 percent of the public school population overall, but only 22 percent of students in the new gifted classrooms, down from 36 percent before the policy change.[30] In addition, out of 32 total CSDs in New York City, nine districts that enroll a majority of low-income Black and Latino students overall currently do not have enough students who passed the test to offer *any* G&T programs.[31]

While no systematic study of the new 2008 G&T admissions process has been done, the demographic shifts that occurred are obvious. The criteria for admitting students to the 2,700 available G&T seats across the city actually narrowed to place more emphasis on the single measure that has a clear correlation to both race and class: standardized tests.[32] It also points to the NYCDOE's assumption that because the G&T tests are free, more Black and Latino parents will get their children tested, which does not seem to be the case. What did change about the process, however, was that individual schools no longer had the ability to choose a more diverse group of students for their G&T programs and the NYCDOE implemented a 90th percentile cutoff score for the G&T tests.

The Community School—the School, the Neighborhood and the Parents

Generally, when asked to describe TCS to someone who is not familiar with the schools or programs in the *City Limits* School District, the vast majority of interviewed parents described it as a "great school" with "excellent teachers" and "very involved parents." In terms of the curriculum and pedagogy, parents said they liked that the school was very "traditional" and "structured," as compared to other schools such as the unzoned, magnet school that was considered to be more child-centered and progressive. They explained that because the G&T program does not have a separate G&T curriculum, the teachers are expected "to go faster and go a little deeper, but they're not working a grade or two ahead" like they do in the citywide G&T schools. The citywide G&T schools do enrich the curriculum and reportedly are working a grade ahead in specific subjects, such as Math.[33] What also stood out to parents was the overall diversity at TCS, which they cited as one of the key reasons they chose this particular school. Diversity is seen as a "positive thing," especially now that there are more White families choosing the Gen Ed.[34] Yet, even though the Gen Ed program is becoming more White in the younger grades, when describing the two academic programs within the school, parents would say that the segregation is still "visible," particularly in the upper grades, because the G&T program remains majority White and advantaged parents who have a child in the Gen Ed program retest their children for G&T. As Lisa, a kindergarten Gen Ed parent described:

> When I toured it, you go into the G&T classrooms and its White and Asian predominantly, maybe a couple Indian children. You go into the Gen Ed, and it's just across the board—completely diverse, and you have children with special needs. And then you go into first or second grade classrooms, and it's predominantly African American and Hispanic. It's very—the school is very split like that. I guess because in the past, they didn't have a lot of interest from people in the neighborhood so they were busing in kids from other zones to fill in.

In fact, based on its overall demographics in 2011—roughly 10 percent Black, 24 percent Latino, 56 percent White, and 10 percent Asian with 36 percent eligible for free and reduced-price lunch—this school has the potential to be a truly integrated school, breaking down racial and social class boundaries. But on the inside, its students are racially segregated into separate and unequal "gifted" and "non-gifted" or Gen Ed classrooms.[35]

Out of the three G&T schools in the *City Limits* School District, TCS was chosen to be the focus of this book because it does not have a dual language program (which might confound the results), is the only school housed in the building (e.g., the school building is not shared by multiple schools), has two G&T classrooms and two Gen Ed classrooms for each grade from kindergarten through fifth grade,[36] and has a more even mix of different race/ethnicities and social class backgrounds in terms of the overall school enrollment compared to the other two G&T programs that are popular with White parents (see Table 1.4; Schools "GT2," "GT3," and "The Community School").

Table 1.4 Student's race, eligibility for FRPL, and percent of students who passed the ELA and math state tests for the schools with G&T programs

Public School	Total Students	%Black	%Latino	%White	%Asian	%FRPL	%ELA Score	% Math Score
Schools with G&T programs								
TCS	610	12	24	54	8	31	62	73
GT2	561	10	21	60	8	19	83	93
GT3	612	25	40	28	6	48	60	70

Source: All 2009–2010 statistics are taken from the New York City Department of Education website, http://schools.nyc.gov.
Note: All schools were given pseudonyms to protect confidentiality and are kindergarten to grade 5 schools. G&T = gifted and talented program; FRPL = free or reduced price lunch; %ELA score = percentage of students who passed the yearly English Language Arts standardized test; %Math score = percentage of students who passed the yearly Mathematics standardized test.

GT2, the most popular G&T program, decided to phase out their G&T program because there were too many neighborhood students filling the Gen Ed seats. Therefore, school officials said they did not have space for the G&T program anymore. At the same time when GT2 was phasing their program out, the district decided to open a new G&T program in a low-income Black and Latino school across town, as Courtney said, "spreading the wealth a little." GT3 is considered the least popular of the three G&T schools because as parents explained, there are "projects" right beside the school. Overall, it is a majority Black and Latino, low-income, and lower-performing school. According to the parents who were reinterviewed in 2014, TCS became the most popular G&T option because GT2 decided to phase out their program. It became even more competitive for parents to get their children into the program and the pressure increased to achieve the highest possible score on the G&T test (see chapter five).

The decision to study TCS within the *City Limits* School District was strategic and paramount to uncovering what role *cultural capital and boundaries* play in parents' decisions to live in the *City Limits* district and yet enroll their children into public elementary schools. Segregative aspects between and within schools are maintained and perpetuated by neighborhood segregation, the G&T policy, and parents' school choice decisions.

The TCS Neighborhood

Within the highly diverse catchment area of TCS, which encompasses four city blocks north to south (about a quarter of a mile in length) and five long blocks east to west (about ¾ of a mile), there is public housing a couple of blocks away from TCS in the northern section. The catchment area of TCS also includes rent-stabilized apartments and high-priced apartment buildings and brownstones that constitute the majority of homes in the attendance area. These higher-priced housing units are, according to parents, home to much more affluent families; the average rent for a two-bedroom apartment in one of the luxury apartment buildings in this neighborhood is in the $4,000–$5,000 per month range. The sale price of a two-bedroom apartment in this neighborhood averages between $1 million to $2.5 million. Furthermore, the sales price for a brownstone ranges from $3.3 million to almost $20 million.[37] According to parents, the affluent families living in the catchment could certainly afford private school (and some do decide to choose that option), but others decide to enroll their children at TCS instead.

A New York City real estate website that describes The Community School's neighborhood to prospective renters and buyers, states: "Some parts of the neighborhood are extremely wealthy, most of it is upper-middle class, but there are a few blocks in the northern section of the neighborhood that are visibly poor."[38] According to the New York City Housing Authority's 2000 census data on families with children in public housing, of the 7,518 families in public housing in the *City Limits* School District, 47 percent were Black and 47 percent were Latino compared to a mere 4 percent White.[39] Many of these lower-income families live in the catchment areas of *City Limits* schools with G&T programs but enroll their children in the Gen Ed programs in those schools. Approximately 35 percent of families with children in TCS are receiving public assistance and are eligible for the federal Free or Reduced Price Lunch program.[40] Chapter Two describes how advantaged parents characterize "those" parents who live in the "project housing" within TCS's catchment as the "other" in the Gen Ed classrooms. Because of this, advantaged parents with children in the Gen Ed program, retest their children for G&T to create distance from the parents and students who are not "like them" in terms of race and class, which gets conflated with parent involvement levels, student behavior, and so on. According to parents, the catchment area is also home to working-class parents of color who reside in rent-stabilized apartments and/or live with other family members.

Perhaps surprisingly, the vast majority of parents in this book did not move to the *City Limits* district because of the schools. At the time of their move, the schools were not on their "radar at the time" because it was before they had children. Instead, they explained that the reason they moved there after college was due to the location, parks, and amenities of the area. Then, once they had children, they never left. The parents living within the boundaries of TCS's catchment could "choose" between the G&T or Gen Ed program at TCS. The parents living outside of TCS's catchment, though, only had the G&T program as an option out of their zoned school. For instance, Cecelia, a kindergarten G&T parent, when asked what her school choice options were for her daughter, explained, "Well, first of all, she got a 99 on the test, so that opens up all the citywides [G&T schools] to you, and plus the district...G&T's are all good, so you rank them all, you get one, you know? There's like no ifs, ands or buts." She went on to explain that if she did not get her daughter into a G&T program, she would have moved out to the suburbs because, like many other parents said, private school was not, financially, an option for her family and she lived in a "failing" school catchment area.

For parents like Cecelia who lived outside TCS's catchment and did not have the Gen Ed program as a "fallback," getting into a G&T program was sometimes perceived to be the only option out of their "failing" majority Black and Latino zoned school. This situation created stress and anxiety for parents to have their children score high enough on the G&T test to be "in their right place" with other families like their own. TCS, nested within a segregated public education system with rigid student assignment policies, is the site where advantaged parents' contradictory attitudes emerge between finding their right "place," wanting "diversity," and providing their children with the "best" education.

The Changing Demographics of The Community School
In recent years, the Gen Ed program within TCS has been demographically changing over time as more and more White "neighborhood" families and younger siblings of G&T students have enrolled their kindergarten children there. In fact, since 2008 the school's White student enrollment has increased from 46 percent of the total in 2008, to 56 percent in 2012, and up to 59 percent in 2015.[41] Meanwhile, the Black and Latino student population has decreased steadily in the school, going from 48 percent in 2008 to 25 percent in 2015 as more and more seats in the Gen Ed program were being filled by White advantaged students from the neighborhood, leaving few seats for Black and Latino students who lived outside of TCS's attendance zone to choose to come. Parents explained that instead of Black and Latino students being bused in to fill the Gen Ed seats, over time an increasing amount of White and Asian students are being bused in to fill the highly sought-after G&T program. Table 1.5 displays the demographic changes from 2007 to 2015.

The parents attribute these demographic shifts in the Gen Ed program to the fact that the program is becoming more popular to White

Table 1.5 Demographic changes at The Community School, 2007–2015

	2007–2008	2011–2012	2014–2015
White	46%	56%	59%
Black	19%	10%	7%
Latino	29%	24%	18%
Asian	7%	10%	11%
FRPL	37%	31%	28%
ELL	11%	5%	6%
Total Enrollment	574	610	624

Source: All 2007–2015 statistics are taken from the New York City Department of Education website, http://schools.nyc.gov.

Note: FRPL = free or reduced price lunch; ELL = English Language Learners.

neighborhood families. They are getting shut out of other options because of the overcrowding issues in the most popular, disproportionately White schools (especially schools A and B in Table 1.3, which are in close proximity to The Community School). Jessica, who is a first grade Gen Ed parent, made it clear that the "Gen Ed program itself" is not becoming more "acceptable" to White families in the catchment area. The "demographics are becoming more acceptable." Rachel, a G&T parent who lives outside the catchment, spoke about a friend who did not want to send her daughter to the Gen Ed program, even though she lived in TCS's catchment "because the local kids still hadn't started going there yet, so she didn't want to put her daughter in a general education class. So that was—that's kind of then. Now you know, everybody, you know, they're happy with it." This provides additional evidence that when parents are choosing schools and programs it is more about the people enrolled there than any other school-related factors.

As this shift was happening, TCS even had to stop offering their pre-k program and use that space instead for a third Gen Ed kindergarten classroom to accommodate the increasing number of catchment students. Thus, the demographic shift in the early grades (K–2) is creating a more White Gen Ed program, which is attributed to a number of reasons, including the recession, the change in the G&T admissions policy, and the subsequent overcrowding issue in the most popular and disproportionately White schools.

Starting around 2008, the economic recession hit New York City. According to parents and the popular press, this economic instability caused many *City Limits* parents to choose public over private schools.[42] This was the case not only for kindergarten admission, but according to parents, some private school parents started to enroll their youngest children into public schools because they could no longer afford private school tuition for all of their children. In this way, TCS has become a "good" option that is starting to be "recommended" by other similarly advantaged parents in their social networks, especially since there is also a G&T program that parents know will have "engaged parents and students" like them. Lauren, a kindergarten Gen Ed parent, said that advantaged parents are more likely "to try out" The Community School now:

> Especially with the G&T program there, people are more into it. The word has gotten out... so I think people definitely are more apt to try out that school. It wasn't actually—when we did our admissions interview at [our preschool], it wasn't one of the schools they recommended as a good New York City public school. They recommended [school A and B] and obviously Anderson [a citywide G&T school], but it wasn't a school they recommended—I think now they're a little more open to it. They were suggesting trying it, especially the G&T program.

At the same time that the economic crisis was affecting the school choice decisions of families in New York City, the DOE changed the G&T admissions process to be a single score on a standardized test. This policy change led to the G&T programs becoming less racially diverse over time (see Table 1.1). Therefore, getting into the most popular G&T programs such as the one at TCS, became more and more competitive because students had to get a top score (e.g., a 98 or 99) for a chance to attend. This also caused many White families in TCS's catchment area who did not initially get into the G&T program to choose the Gen Ed program for kindergarten. In addition, families who already had older children enrolled in TCS's G&T program, but whose younger children did not make the 90th percentile G&T score for siblings, began to choose the Gen Ed program in order for all of their children to attend the same school. For example, nine parents in this book had older children in the G&T program and younger children in the Gen Ed program.

And finally, there was severe overcrowding in the most popular non-G&T schools, school A, B, and C (see Table 1.3) because there was an influx of White, higher-income, *City Limits* School District parents into the public school system. Demand for the G&T programs increased substantially, therefore more parents were getting shut out of these highly sought-after options. This caused some parents who were zoned for the schools with G&T programs, including GT2 and The Community School, to choose the Gen Ed program for kindergarten if they did not initially test into the G&T program.

All of these factors combined to change the racial composition of TCS's Gen Ed program in the younger grades (K–2), which made it a more acceptable option for some White families who lived in the catchment because there were more parents/students like them in those classrooms. Before this demographic shift occurred, though, the racial segregation was very stark between programs and still remains so in grades 3–5 because parents retest their children for the G&T program until most eventually get in or leave the school.

TCSP arents

In order to understand parents' sense making of where their children belong versus where they are placed in a school that offers two hierarchical academic programs, 41 advantaged parents whose child(ren) were enrolled in the G&T, Gen Ed, or both programs participated in in-depth interviews (see chapters two to four). Parents were asked questions about their school choice process, beliefs about giftedness and the G&T policy, and their experiences with the G&T and Gen Ed programs. Of the original group of 41 advantaged parents, eight parents who had their children enrolled in the k/1 Gen Ed program in 2011 were reinterviewed three years later, including one new Gen Ed parent, to see how the school had changed and whether their children switched to G&T, left the school, or stayed in Gen Ed. In addition, nine parents who identify as Black or Latino and had enrolled their child(ren) in the Gen Ed program were interviewed in 2014 (see chapter five).

During the initial interviews in 2011, the 41 advantaged parents were purposefully chosen because they had been actively involved in the school choice process, had their children tested for G&T in preschool, and were mostly middle- to upper-middle class, college-educated White mothers. Five different entry points into the school were employed to obtain a well-rounded sample of advantaged parents from different social networks, programs, classrooms, and grade levels (see Table 1.6).

During the interviews, several White parents referred to themselves, and other parents like them, as "middle- to upper-middle class" or "wealthy." A *New York Times* 2013 article titled "What is Middle Class in Manhattan?" reported that the median income for New York

Table 1.6 Interview participant categories

Participant categories	N
White G&T Only Parents, 2011	16
White Gen Ed Only Parents, 2011	16
White Parents in Both Programs, 2011	9
Black and Latino Gen Ed Parents, 2014	9
White Gen Ed Only Parent, 2014	1
School Choice Consultant	1
Total	52

City residents when adjusted for cost of living is between $80,000 and $235,000 per year.[43] Given that definition of "middle-class" status, there are some families in this book that are classified as upper class, since they live in multimillion dollar brownstones and condos in TCS's catchment, and their husbands work on Wall Street. The upper-class families could afford to have one parent (usually the mother) stay home to be a full time caregiver, and some had older children in private school.[44] The 41 White parents in this book are classified as "advantaged" since they all were either employed in a professional or managerial position (or their partner was) and/or were highly educated with advanced degrees.[45] They also possess valuable cultural and economic capital in the system, as evidenced by the ability to afford private preschools (and private schools for older children), live in TCS's catchment area or higher-income neighborhoods within the *City Limits* district, and pay for private tutoring, and so on.

The comparison group of Black and Latino parents come from lower-middle-class or working-class backgrounds.[46] Seven of the nine parents of color lived within TCS's boundaries in rent-stabilized apartments or with extended family members. They worked part-time or full-time in white-collar jobs. One African American mother was a single parent and full-time student who lived in public housing. The two African families in the sample moved to New York City for college. Both families lived outside of the catchment area in more affordable housing. They used the G&T program for their oldest child to gain entry into TCS. Then, their younger child(ren) were permitted to enroll in the Gen Ed program because they did not make the 90th percentile on the G&T test. See Table 1.7 for a profile of the parent sample.

In order to compare different perspectives, parents were chosen because they were relatively new to the school (Incoming parents to second grade) or had experienced the school's culture longer (grades 3–5), as well as parents who had children in both programs across different grade levels. As the interviews were conducted, four distinct groups of advantaged, White parents, each with different ways of making sense of the boundaries and categories that their children are given within the school, were identified. These four categories include: (1) *G&T Defenders* (n=9), who tend to be the G&T parents in the younger grades, have the least experience in the school and believe in their child's G&T label the most, (2) *Savvy Negotiators* (n=16), who are the G&T parents in the older grades, some of whom have younger children in the Gen Ed program, have experienced the school the longest, are bothered by the segregation between programs, but still prep and retest their younger child in the Gen Ed because of the negative stigma of the label for themselves and their children, (3) *Conflicted Followers* (n=11), who

Table 1.7 Profile of the parent sample

Name	Race/Ethnicity	SES	No. of Children	School Program	Referral	Zoned School
I. G&T Only						
Jane	White (Jewish)	Stay at home mom; College-educated	1	PreK	Rachael (Classroom Network)	Out of Zone
Jennifer	White	PT professional job; College-educated	2	G&T	Rosie's e-mail to whole class	Out of Zone
Anne	White	Stay at home mom; College-educated	2	G&T	School's Website	Out of Zone
II. Gen Ed Only						
Alyssa	White	Stay at home mom; College-educated	1	Pre-K	School Choice Consultant (e-mail to her listserve)	Zoned School
Lauren	White (Jewish)	Stay at home mom; College-educated	2	Gen Ed	Margaret (Classroom Network)	Zoned School
Domenica	White (Italian American)	FT professional job; College-educated	1	Gen Ed	Jessica (Classroom Network)	Zoned School
Elaine	White	PT professional job; College-educated	2	Gen Ed	Chrissy (Classroom Network)	Zoned School

III. Both Programs

Amy and Joe (married couple interviewed together)	White (Amy is Portuguese American)	Amy= FT graduate student Joe=PT professional job; College-educated	2	G&T and Gen Ed	Elaine (e-mail to whole class)	Out of Zone
Margaret	White	PT professional job; College-educated	2	G&T and Gen Ed	Preschool Network	Out of Zone
Melissa	White	Stay at home mom; College-educated	2	G&T and Gen Ed	School's Website	Out of Zone

IV. Gen Ed Parents of Color

Mercedes	Latina/ Domenican	PT; College Educated	2	Gen Ed	Jessica (Classroom Network)	Zoned School
Althea	African American	FT Student	1	Gen Ed	Margaret (Classroom Network)	Zoned School
Amara	Black/ African	PT; College Educated	1	Gen Ed	Jessica (e-mail sent to the whole class)	Zoned School

are the Gen Ed parents in the younger grades, have no direct experience with the G&T program and are most critical of the labels and categories that children are given based on their score on a standardized test, but still prep and retest for G&T anyway because of the negative stigma of the label, and 4. *Gen Ed Reconcilers* (n=5), who are Gen Ed parents in the older grades, have subsequently stopped testing their child for Gen Ed, and have resigned themselves to the lower-status Gen Ed label.

What was most interesting before the interviews began were the parents who had children in both programs since they had to negotiate between the status of the G&T program and the negative stigma of the Gen Ed label. Although there were rumors that the Gen Ed program was starting to enroll more White advantaged families, it was unexpected that some of these families already had older children enrolled in the G&T program. As described in more detail in chapter two, parents with children in both programs, the Savvy Negotiators, were especially critical of what they viewed as an arbitrary distinction between the G&T and Gen Ed program, which results in very different learning opportunities (academically and socially) for their two children that they view as similar. The Negotiators are simultaneously "concerned" about the segregation that exists within the school and advocate for the G&T program to be phased out, yet they also "defend" the system and retest their younger Gen Ed children until they eventually get into G&T (see chapter four).

The White advantaged parents also varied in terms of parent involvement, with some parents being highly involved in the school by being a member of the Parent Teacher Association (PTA) or School Leadership Team (SLT), and others being less involved in the day-to-day activities of the school, but still knowledgeable about what was going on by talking to other parents at drop off or at the playground, and so on. The "highly involved" parents in the school were described as being nonworking mothers whose spouse made enough money to support the family financially. Parents were purposefully sampled in each category and across all grade levels—G&T only, Gen Ed only, G&T and Gen Ed (both), and incoming parents—until data saturation was reached.

In order to triangulate the data and situate the findings, a professional school choice consultant was interviewed. Observations were conducted at TCS's G&T school tour, a PTA meeting, and a public school choice workshop for incoming parents that were led by the school choice consultant. The school choice consultant was interviewed because many parents utilized her services, and one parent even referred to her as the "G&T guru." In fact, many of the G&T parents said that they utilized her private consulting services and/or attended one of her school choice workshops when they were going through the school choice process. She was an extremely valuable resource since she worked as an educational consultant for 14 years, had children that went through the public school system (in the *City Limits* district), stayed abreast of all the school choice policy changes, and had insider knowledge about all of New York City's schools and programs (including private schools). She also hears what parents are saying about each school and what the enrollment trends and demographic changes have been over time.

During the observations in the school and at the school choice workshop, close attention was paid to which parents attended in terms of race/ethnicity, gender, G&T vs. Gen Ed parent, how parents interacted with each other and the school's administration, and what kinds of questions were asked and topics covered. For example, most of the parents giving the school tour were White and on the PTA, and the incoming G&T parents attending the G&T school tour were also majority White women. The parents attending the school tour asked questions about the difference between the G&T and Gen Ed programs, if the students know about the two programs within the school, and if the G&T program was going to be phased out eventually. And finally, documents were reviewed such as newspapers, NYCDOE website information, census data, and other admission material in order to learn about changes to the G&T admissions policy, the district-wide school choice policy for Gen Ed and other specialized dual language or magnet programs, and recent demographic changes to the schools and neighborhoods in this district.

This book, situated within a social and political New York City community school district context of residential and school segregation, SES bifurcation, and a test-driven G&T admissions system, is a key site to study the issues of social reproduction and boundary maintenance with parents whose children get placed into two different hierarchical academic tracks. A case study research design is a holistic way to examine deeper meanings behind advantaged parents' sense making of where their children belong versus where they are placed within two separate and stratified programs in a single elementary school.[47]

Given this context of the parents studied, this research ultimately helps us understand the ways in which parents use their different forms of capital and boundary work to gain advantages for their children in the school system. This book helps to answer the broader question of how individual parents—connected through social networks, local context, and a set of available possibilities—interact with and help perpetuate social reproduction, social stratification and school segregation within and between schools. It questions the use of school-within-school G&T programs as a policy tool to attract White, middle-class families into the public system and improve schools.

Chapter Two illustrates the multiple ways that White advantaged parents use social and symbolic boundaries to distinguish between the G&T and Gen Ed categories and labels in their school. It shows how advantaged parents go through all the necessary steps to get their children placed in the G&T program, which better matches their advantaged position as signified by plenty of people "like them," despite the seemingly paradoxical value they also place on "diversity."

CHAPTER TWO
STRIVING TO BE G&T "BECAUSE THE
PEOPLE IN IT ARE JUST LIKE YOU"

Amy and Joe, a young White, middle-class couple from Louisiana,[1] just moved to New York City because Amy got accepted into college. They remember being "apprehensive about moving" because they have two young children and "heard all the rumors of the nightmares of elementary education in the city." After experiencing a brand new school in Louisiana with "fields of green grass," they enroll their second grade son in their zoned public school. They are stunned to see how culturally and socioeconomically different it is in comparison. Joe explains that when he drops his son off the first day: "It was a shock. I mean, I took my son to school and I signed him up and I left with tears streaming down my face, literally. I was, like, I turned around. We're not going to school here. I don't feel good about this. I mean, it looked like a prison, it felt like a prison. Ya know, he didn't, just culturally it's so far from where we're from. I know some people would say that would make me racist. But it's not, it's a culture and a class thing." Joe responds that above everything else, he wants his son to "get the best education," but his zoned school is a "non-option" because it has what he calls a "resigned failure vibe." He is not willing to send his son there just so he can be a "martyr for Civil Rights." As Joe explains, his son would "culturally not fit in" because it is a majority Black school.

After their first glimpse of what a New York City public school looks like, Amy spends a couple of days searching for a "better" school in the *City Limits* district and takes "a bunch of notes" on available choices, looking at test scores and parent's comments online—"this schools ranked really high but it's a little far...these parents complain about this...in this school the parents seem very competitive." They end up with a list of three schools, one of which is TCS because of its emphasis on the arts. By now it's already the second week of school, but luckily TCS has a spot in the second grade Gen Ed program for their oldest child. Amy and Joe reiterate that it's not a race and class issue—"it's just got to be a good school." However, what they did not realize before enrolling him in Gen Ed was the level of within-school segregation between the Gen Ed and G&T tracks. Because G&T programs are often "embedded within larger schools, the programs bolster a false vision of diversity."[2]

When asked if they heard about the G&T program at TCS before enrolling their son there, Joe explains that, "being fresh off the boat" other TCS parents would say, "Hey, you need to get your kids tested for G&T." In their minds, though, G&T was a label for children who were "geniuses" and "little Einstein kids with Bunsen burners and stuff,"—not their own kids who they thought were "pretty normal IQ." Joe says that parents continually pulled him aside, telling him that he really needs to get them tested—they "were looking out for me." He recalled that "It took me a little while to read between the lines. What they were saying was that 'we,' the middle, upper middle class, well more or less, are over here. We don't want to be over there. They were trying to give me a code, ya know. So it took me a little while to figure that out. Of course when you go to the school, it's quite obvious, the G&T classes are White." Joe explained that it was not like gifted and talented, it was like "are you with us or not?"

Yet, even though Amy and Joe say they are happy with their son's Gen Ed teacher and with the school overall, their daughter will be entering kindergarten the following year so they decide to get both kids tested for G&T "entirely for the cultural experience...and because everybody else was doing it." They also decide to "quiz" their second grade son and incoming kindergarten daughter on the practice G&T test packet that the district provides so they can learn test-taking skills. They soon find out that their daughter passes the 90th percentile cutoff score. Their son, however, gets an 89—one point shy from being labeled "gifted and talented." After that, Joe wonders why parents are allowed to "somehow game the system to separate people, but they've done it and part of it is parental involvement" in the form of G&T test prepping. The other reason for the G&T being predominantly White, according to Amy, is "cultural" since "immigrant" families might be less involved in the "day to day" of their child's education and sometimes have to work all the time. She relates it to her own background growing up in a Portuguese family. Her parents did not help her with homework or get involved in her education—at least to the extent that schools expect parents to be involved now.

Again, Joe explains that he is fine with his son being in the Gen Ed class for third grade because his teacher is good, even though the reaction from other parents about being there reflects the negative stigma associated with the Gen Ed label: "It was very interesting when parents would say, 'So did your son pass the G&T?' And I was like: 'no, he missed it.'

And they're like, 'Oh.' They just seemed ya know, really sucks to be you. You're kids going to be in there with all of those other kids... they feel pity for you, like we're not going to be friends anymore. There's this weird vibe about it." Amy and Joe both go back to the same point throughout the interview, though, that they are not "mad" about the G&T test or that their son missed the cutoff score by one point; they are "happy" with his Gen Ed placement because he has an "incredible teacher" and "he's getting a wonderful education with her." They admit, though, that they would be "upset" if their son was not given a good teacher, and would "try something else" to get him into the G&T.

Joe believes, like many other parents in this book, that the G&T test is "not a measure of gifted and talented, it's something else." The "something else" is like that "magical thing" that Alyssa explained in the Introduction when parents get their child's test scores back. It is characterized by spending time and money to teach your child how to take the test, which makes other parents think of you as a parent who prioritizes education and that puts you in the "group of parents that care" category. In Joe's view, the schools and G&T classrooms that have "a bunch of upper middle class" White "yuppie" parents who are "involved" in the school makes them "better." He concludes that "it's quite remarkable to come to New York City. It's supposed to be this great melting pot, and then you have all this coded sort of class/race stuff you have to wade through and find out the system is set up to split people into groups, White, Black, or Brown. It was like: What, really?"

Amy and Joe's story is reflective of the findings in this chapter about the struggles and contradictions that emerge when advantaged parents interact with a policy context that gives them the choice between mostly segregated schools and G&T programs. As Joe explains, the system "is set up" to divide students racially and socioeconomically because of their advantaged backgrounds and boundary work. The "advantaged" White parents in this book compete for high-status positions in the status hierarchy across schools, programs, and classrooms in their district. If they live outside TCS's catchment, parents use the G&T policy to escape their "failing" zoned school because they do not have TCS's Gen Ed program as a "fallback."[3] Meanwhile, they embody contradictions between their sense of the place where their children belong versus their placement within TCS, their desire for their children to be exposed to "diversity"—at least in the abstract and if their children are not in the minority, their discomfort with the segregation between programs, and their drive to provide their children with what's considered to be the "best" education alongside "good kids" and involved parents like them.

The parents in this hierarchical school context distinguish where they and their children belong (their "place") in this segregated school system and school setting by drawing social and symbolic boundaries[4] around what constitutes "us" (schools and programs with advantaged White parents) versus "them" (schools and programs with lower-income parents of color), *even when their own children start out in the "other" Gen Ed category*. These boundaries, like Amy and Joe describe, are composed of the rules, codes, and expectations that parents use to distinguish where their children belong within the structures. For instance, parents know that they belong in the G&T program with the other middle- to upper-middle class White parents who are perceived to "care" about education because they got their children tested for G&T—all definitions and classifications that distinguish themselves by "marking differences" that set them apart from others. Additionally, they describe the negative reaction from other advantaged parents if their child does not initially pass the G&T cutoff score—pushing them to prep and test for G&T because everyone else is doing it, even if they are happy with the education in the Gen Ed program or do not necessarily believe their children are gifted and talented (chapter three).

This chapter captures how parents make sense of their place[ment] within TCS by navigating the status associated with the G&T label and/or the stigma of the Gen Ed label amidst their stated desire for "diversity" and their discomfort with the segregation that G&T causes within the school. Parents' struggles or contradictions represent the sense of division that they embody between who they are, where they believe they belong, and where their children are placed within the social hierarchy, even if they also appreciate the diversity in the school overall (for G&T parents) or in their own children's classrooms, for example *diversity by default* (for parents with children in the Gen Ed program).

Out of 41 total parents in the White parent sample, 33—or 80 percent—said that the reason that they chose public over private school for their children's education was because of their own public school experience (n=37) and the "diversity" of the New York City public schools. These parents explained that their own experience made them public school "advocates." They also said that one of the main reasons that they chose public school, as opposed to private school or moving out to the suburbs where it is more homogeneous, was mainly because they wanted their children to be exposed to racial and socioeconomic diversity—with the cost of private school being a secondary reason.

An important and helpful truth when examining the role of boundaries in maintaining advantage is that White parents within the sample, depending on whether or not they have one or more children in the high-status G&T program, differ in terms of how and when they either internalize or resist the categories or labels that their children are given based on a single score on a standardized test. The analysis goes one step further by also showing how parents reconcile their seemingly contradictory attitudes andb eliefs.

Setting up the Boundaries between "Us" and "Them"

The interview data strongly suggest that the boundaries between G&T and Gen Ed tracks become signifiers of race and class in the school choice field. These cultural signals get complicated when White advantaged parents initially enroll their child in the historically Black and Latino Gen Ed program. Parent choices are initially based on race, class, their perceptions of their children's academic ability, which preschool they send their children to, and where they live, and so on. Once their children are enrolled in the G&T and/or Gen Ed program, the boundaries become more about the symbolic meanings of race and class in this context, which are related to children's scores on standardized tests, perceptions of student behavior in the different programs, and parent involvement in the classrooms. As Bourdieu explains, "each field prescribes its particular values and possesses its own regulative principles. These principles delimit a socially structured space in which agents struggle, depending on the position they occupy in that space, either to change or to preserve its boundaries and form."[5]

A main reason that parents are all striving to be in disproportionate White neighborhood schools and majority White G&T programs is because in this school choice context their only other option really is to choose a majority Black and Latino low-income school. Like Joe describes above, they do not want to be the "minority" in their neighborhood school. They also do not want to be the "minority" for too long in TCS's Gen Ed program since it is comprised of mostly Black and Latino students—particularly in the upper grades. As Dana, a first grade G&T Savvy Negotiator, explained she would *not* have initially chosen the Gen Ed program at TCS for her son since "You can tell when you were walking into the classes. It was not diverse, it was like the White class and Brown class, and not that I don't want Brown kids (laughs) in my kid's class, I do. I don't know that I want my kid to be the only White kid in the class." And, even if parents value diversity, the "diverse" school options with a mix of race and SES students are extremely limited to a few choice schools that are oversubscribed and hard to get into.

Caitlyn, who is a fourth grade G&T Savvy Negotiator, explained, "I do get the sense that the average person is just looking for—they don't necessarily want a G&T program, they just want a good basic education for their kids. And I think in New York there are such extremes. I feel like it's hard just to find a middle of the road." Domenica, a first grade Conflicted Follower in the Gen Ed program, whose daughter technically passed the G&T cutoff score but did not get a seat at TCS because her score was not high enough, explained that "you'll want your kid to be in the G&T program, because the people in it are just like you." Domenica describes herself as being "privileged, because I'm totally, completely [financially] independent" (as a single mother) and involved in the school. These two points make her feel as though she belongs in the G&T program with other "privileged" and highly involved parents like her. She believes the "real problem is the lack of diversity" in the G&T and Gen Ed programs at TCS, which, for the Gen Ed advantaged parents, contributes to the overall sense of *not* being in the place where they feel they belong in the school.

Betsy, an upper-class Savvy Negotiator and G&T parent whose son started in the Gen Ed program, explained the difference between the two sets of parents in the school: the G&T parents "are totally committed and into it [meaning involved in the school] and have actually chosen to send their kids to school here over other schools." The Gen Ed parents, according to Betsy, are characterized as being mostly lower-income, Black and Latino parents, "[for] who[m] it's just their zoned school and...they're not involved because they're working parents or they're parents who are under a lot of maybe financial hardship because we have in our district, we have several housing projects too." This perception is present even if their children are in the Gen Ed program. Lillian, who is an upper-class fourth grade G&T Savvy Negotiator, when asked to describe the parents who are most involved in the school, said, "They are the G&T parents. They're professionals, they're educated. They're hard working. They have passions for things. They're passionate about their kids and their kids' education and the public school. They spend a lot of time."

Betsy and Lillian are using symbolic boundaries or "conceptual distinctions" to categorize people into groups based on similarities when determining where they and others belong in the social hierarchy.[6] Parents in this context imagine who they are (privileged and involved in the school) by imagining who they are not (uninvolved parents who live in the projects), which is related to their race and class backgrounds, as well as what they perceive to be cultural values and attitudes about education. These "cultural signals" that parents use to determine group membership can cause anxiety and pressure to do what other similarly advantaged parents are doing to get into the G&T program. For instance, Tara, who is a third grade Gen Ed Reconciler, explained that she retested her daughter for G&T every year because she felt pressure to do so because the G&T students are perceived to be getting a better education. The children are smarter and better behaved, and so on. When asked, "What do you believe are the biggest distinctions between programs?"—the majority of parents, like Kelly, an Incoming Gen Ed parent to the school, explained: "Honestly, I think what's really driving the differences [between schools and programs] are the peer group and parent involvement."

Good School/Program = "Good Kids"

A strong theme that emerges from the interviews and observations is that who you "brush shoulders" with in school is more important than other school-related factors like the school's philosophy, school leadership, teacher quality, or even whether it is a G&T or Gen Ed program. Trudie, an incoming parent and Conflicted Follower, explained that she wanted to get her children into TCS's G&T program because *who* she was exposing her children to mattered the most: "I'm not lying, if I would have gotten [into G&T] I would have sent my kid regardless of who the principal was because I also recognize being surrounded by good kids as more important than the other things." This is the case because they do not want to be the minority in their "failing" majority Black and Latino neighborhood school (if they live outside TCS's catchment), and they want to be surrounded by what they consider to be other similarly advantaged and involved parents like them. They use the G&T policy to escape "failing" zoned schools because they do not have TCS's Gen Ed program as a "fallback." When asked about her zoned neighborhood school with a majority of students of color, Trudie replied: "I'm zoned for a failing school... I live on [a particular street] so *I'm zoned for a school that no one you or I know would ever send their kids to*" (emphasis added). She went on to explain what she felt was the most important factor in her school choice decision:

> Getting Accepted (laughter)... G&T, I mean, all of this is coming from a parent that was zoned for a failing school. I think that makes a huge difference in my whole mentality because all of my friends who aren't, were like "Oh, well I can always go to [TCS]." They had a fallback; I absolutely did not have a fallback. G&T was more like—okay, this is our way to get out of the dilemma of not having a fallback, but not necessarily because I felt so strongly that they had to be in a G&T. It was more like I need them to be in a good school—just another option.

Parents use test scores to justify their decision to avoid "failing" *City Limits* schools, yet continue to choose TCS even though it does not always receive the highest standardized test scores (see Table 1.4). TCS even received a "D" school rating one year. Melody, who is a G&T Defender with two children at the school explained that for TCS "you can't just rely on the stupid scores, you know what I mean? It's ridiculous. People don't realize what goes into those scores—and they're like, 'Ooo, I couldn't go [to TCS], they're failing.' And I'm like, 'No, they're not. You should go inside the door.' It's a perception.... I mean a nice score is really nice, but you can't just look at a number." In fact, parents in this book were not always aware of specific test scores or would disregard them when they made their choices.[7] In addition, they often failed to look at other school-level comparisons, like extracurricular offerings, curriculum, or quality of instruction.[8] As Trudie explained, what mattered the most in her school choice decision was getting her children into a "good school," which meant being surrounded by "good kids" and "like-minded families."

Trudie said that she grew up in a "nice suburb of DC" and her high school did not have a "huge demographic swing." She wanted some "diversity," but she replied:

> I didn't want my kids to be the only kids who have an apartment that's bigger than we needed. *So I think partially I just want them to be surrounded by kids that are somewhat like them, or at least half of the kids.* I think living in New York gives them a good view on what the world is like and different types of people and they see all kinds. But I didn't want them being at school with people that weren't coming from like-minded families. I hope it doesn't sound racist, but I think your friends are a big influence on how hard you study and how motivated you are. So it was important to me that they were somewhat surrounded by kids like that (emphasis added).

To a certain extent, parents in this book intuitively know that school diversity is beneficial for their children because they live in New York City and they "expect that in the public schools," but what was most important to Trudie and other parents like her was that there would be "like-minded families" from similar race and SES backgrounds in the school—just like they had in their own more suburban and homogeneous public school experience.[9] Parents of color at TCS, however, explained that what they were looking for is a "multicultural" school with a mix of racial and SES backgrounds. Althea, who is an African American Gen Ed parent, said she decided which school to send her son to "by what kind of kids were there. Was it multi-cultural?... How many different kinds of kids? With these kids—no. Too many of those kids—no. Too many of these kids—no."

Jane, a White, upper-class Savvy Negotiator who is also zoned for a "failing" school, described her school choice process: "It was kind of a shock dealing with—realizing that our catchment school, everybody said, 'you cannot go to that school. It's a terrible school. You cannot send your kid there. Forget it. Don't even look at it.' Which of course I did look at it because I thought how bad could it be? (laughs)." After touring the school, Jane realized that it wasn't "appropriate" for her son "since there's projects right around there and it kind of seems like, you know, it's not the people living west of [a certain street], it's the people living east of [a certain street], you know?"

Advantaged White parents strive for G&T programs even if they are bothered by how segregated they are. Jane ended up choosing the G&T program for her son's education, even though she initially said she was "hesitant" to choose that option. In fact, she said she would have preferred a school where there "wasn't like such a big shocking difference between what's the classroom like and what the rest of the school is like, it seemed much more rough around the edges in terms of who was going there and what was going on." When Jane refers to schools with G&T programs being "rough around the edges," the underlying message is that exposing her son to low-income students of color will negatively affect his educational experience,[10] even if he is somewhat sheltered in the separate, majority White G&T classroom,[11] the curriculum is the same between programs, and so on. In many qualitative school choice studies, researchers documented that parents rationalize their decisions for choosing non-diverse schools in nonracialized terms, and since the "best" schools tend to be in the Whiter, higher-income areas, the school choice system rewards children from families with highly valued cultural capital.[12]

Jane told a story about taking her son to visit his new G&T classroom the spring before school started. She recalled that her son "liked" the G&T classroom all right, but then he got scared to go into the bathroom with the other "Gen Ed" children:

> He had to go to the bathroom and I was like, you know, "There's the bathroom," you know, the boys were in there, and like I looked in and there were some of the kids from Gen Ed that were horsing around and being kind of rowdy and it was like he didn't even want to go in the bathroom. So it was like, come with me into the lady's room, it was just like, all right (laughs). Like I know people that grew up in the city that said to me that they went to public school and they were afraid to go into bathrooms and they held it all day and they got urinary tract infections because they were scared, because some rough stuff used to happen—they were unsupervised. It makes me nervous as a parent. You don't want your kid so uncomfortable that they don't want to leave the classroom alone or they don't feel safe going to the bathroom.

Contradictory attitudes emerge when parents are simultaneously bothered by the segregation between G&T and Gen Ed programs within diverse schools, yet choose G&T programs anyway where there is a concentration of other families like their own. Jane rationalized her choice of a majority White G&T program by saying that "none of these options are perfect."

Parents use social and symbolic boundaries to distinguish where they belong, based on where other advantaged parents from their private preschools are going, what type of housing people live in (e.g., projects), and which neighborhood a school is servicing (e.g., living west and east of a certain boundary line). This boundary work illustrates just how tightly race and SES are intertwined in this context. Parents are given the "choice" between low income, majority Black and Latino schools on one side and disproportionately White and higher-income schools/programs on the other side. As Caitlyn explained, in New York there are such "extremes." It is "hard" to find a school that is in the middle ground.

Good School/Program = Parent Involvement

What was abundantly clear from the parent interview data was that race and class became signifiers of better parenting, more parent involvement, and better schools and programs with better-behaved children. These understandings directly related the school or program's "assumed" quality to the status of the parents and students within them, not on any actual objective measures.[13] In other words, parents spoke less about the actual academic differences in either program because the curriculum is the same, and more about the people on either side of the boundary line. Jessica, who is a first grade Conflicted Follower in the Gen Ed program said she worried about the difference in parenting between advantaged White parents and the lower-income parents of color in the Gen Ed classrooms. When her children got older she would have less control over their choices. Therefore, she wanted to be with other parents like her who were raising their children in similar ways and, as she stated, "that there was some [parent] oversight and involvement and—you know what I mean? That was really what mattered to me more than anything." This speaks to the stigma of the Gen Ed label that advantaged parents are trying to avoid by retesting their children for G&T.

Jessica went on to explain why the G&T parents label the Gen Ed parents as being less involved in the school:

> I can understand to some degree why like a G&T parent labels the Gen Ed parents because I do think that the G&T parents are more responsive to things like a class parent sending out an email, you know, I think they

get more participation. I found out two years in a row being a class parent of Gen Ed, it can be very frustrating because people just—they seem like they don't care or they don't have the time. Maybe it's because maybe both parents work, maybe there's just a single parent, I don't really know.

As Jessica's comments indicate, White advantaged Gen Ed parents struggle with their place[ment] the most and strive to be in the G&T program to be around other similarly advantaged parents like them. These White Gen Ed parents felt like they were in a "second tier" program because of the high levels of parent involvement in the G&T classrooms. This abundance of parent involvement in the G&T classrooms gives them the appearance of being "better" because of how much G&T parents donate to the school or how many parent volunteers they have to "lead the class auction project" or chaperone field trips. Anne, who is an upper-class G&T Defender with two children in the G&T program said she would organize "class events" after school hours for G&T families to get to know each other better, such as a "parent cocktail party" at someone's house for the second grade G&T class or a "play date at the park" with pizza where families could drop by and "say hi." Anne explained that there was always good "responsiveness" for the get-togethers, and that they helped "people feel like they have a school community."

The Gen Ed program, however, does not have this same level of parent involvement. Tanya, who is a first grade Gen Ed parent explained that she "tried not to judge" but a lot of other parents in her son's classroom would not respond to "emails about very simple things." She explained that "the class project was really hard to get people to participate. No one helped at all. It was just two of us doing all of it. Even though we sent out countless emails for resources for the class, [requesting] everyone to bring a dollar for the magazine. It was really, really hard to get people to donate, or you know, actively participate and come into the school." Jessica, as well as other advantaged Gen Ed parents, explained that in her Gen Ed classroom there were only a few White parents who got involved and the rest of the parents were never around. Jessica said, "It was like pulling teeth" to get them to donate money or their time, while the "G&T parents are there all of the time." Another parent said "G&T runs the school."

Similarly, Elaine, a third grade Gen Ed Reconciler, attributed the differences between the two sets of parents as being a "culture thing"

> because a lot of these [Gen Ed] families are low-income families... [and] a lot of that culture, that economic level or person or however you want to put it doesn't really participate in the school as much. So it becomes a more frustrating experience for parents like me, where every year I end up being the parent that does everything.... And the other class is the G&T classes,

parents are much more involved. They're much more interested in building the school and working towards raising money for things at the school. Gen Ed just never really seems to have interest in that.

Similarly, Margaret, who is an upper-class Savvy Negotiator with experience in both programs said that the G&T parents tend to be "much more vocal and whiny about what they wanted and what teacher they wanted for their children." She claims that G&T parents are also more "present in the PTA" and that the difference in parent involvement in the classroom was pretty noticeable. For instance, in her daughter's kindergarten Gen Ed class she was the only parent who volunteered to be "Class Rep" compared to her son's fourth grade G&T class where there were eight parent Class Reps. Margaret explained: "I think [Gen Ed parents] come in and they're not sure what the expectation is or what they're supposed to do...I mean, it's not a free ride really. I mean, there's a lot of expectation for people to donate all over the place...I don't know, it seems like in [my daughter's Gen Ed] class, people don't really quite understand that that's kind of an obligation."

In this way, when parents labeled someone in the school as a Gen Ed parent, they were also criticizing them for not showing "interest" in getting involved or donating time or money to improve the school. At the same time, they were making their own approach to their children's education (e.g., how much they were involved in the school) the one that should be emulated and the one that the system rewards because they got their children into the high-status G&T program.

Amara, an African mother who has experienced both programs told a story about a time that she was volunteering at the school. She said it was "like a tele-thon" in which parents called up other parents to ask them to donate money for the school, "and we were sitting and they were telling us what to do and we have to call everybody, and they said 'now, you're not going to call anybody from the General Ed,' and I was like 'why'? They said, 'Even if we call them they won't give much, so why even bother' and I was pretty upset, I thought let's say this at home...oh my gosh, but that's what they did and of course nobody can afford to pay more." Amara explained that the PTA parents had already asked everyone to donate "$2,500 a year and for some people $2,500 is nothing...for me it's a lot of money and why are we giving this money? Really, why are we giving this money, really, because your kids can go on more field trips, they got more assistant teachers, more than what we get? Why are they doing it?" Again, we see how relying on G&T programs to attract White, higher-income families into the public schools can marginalize lower-income families of color in the Gen Ed programs.[14]

Ultimately, besides the visual differences, the biggest distinction that parents make between the two different sets of parents was how much value they place on their children's education, which is determined by how much money people donate and how much they are involved in the school. The more advantaged Gen Ed parents in the school did not want to be placed in the same category as the other typical "Gen Ed parents" who, they all assumed, were "low-income," using cultural deficit perspectives[15] and implying that those parents do not care enough to volunteer and do not have extra money to help improve the school.

Thus, it should come as no surprise that White advantaged families are activating their uneven cultural capital exchange[16] to sort their children into what's considered to be the "best" and high-status educational option that matches their position in the larger system and society. This option is disproportionately White, higher-income, and segregated from the rest of the school. In this way, G&T becomes the best option when it is the *only* option within a sea of majority Black and Latino, low-income schools where White advantaged parents would be in the minority.

Navigating the Status of G&T and Stigma of Gen Ed with a Desire for Diversity

Although there was no direct question during the interview about how important school-level diversity was when they were choosing schools/school programs for their children, more than half of parents said that diversity was a major factor in their decision to send their children to public school, and specifically TCS, which nearly all parents described as being racially and socioeconomically diverse overall. Although diversity was a "positive thing" in the school as a whole and in the Gen Ed program more specifically (at least in the younger grades), in these parents' eyes, school-level diversity is a whole different thing than classroom-level diversity.

To illustrate, Anne, a G&T Defender with two children in the G&T classrooms, when asked what was the most important factor in her school choice decision, explained: "I think we felt comfortable that, because there was a test that narrowed—that was a bar to entry that the kids would be of similar enough abilities...so I think a part of it was just that we knew that because there was a test that people had to take, that it would be an engaged class and parent body. I think that probably was what drew us." Therefore, Anne knew that the parents who went through the "hassle" of getting their child tested for G&T (e.g., symbolic boundaries) would be more involved or "engaged" in the school (e.g., social boundaries).

The G&T test acted as a gatekeeper or "bar to entry" that sifted out the "engaged" students and more involved parents who could navigate the system—which also happens to be correlated to their race and class backgrounds—from the rest. Although Anne said that a reason for choosing TCS was because she and her husband "liked the idea of a bigger range, socioeconomically than we had growing up.... we sort of liked the idea of diversity of the public school *and it felt like the only way to get that—get both sort of things was through the G&T*." In this way, Anne was getting the best of both worlds by choosing separate, White G&T classrooms for her children's education within a diverse school setting.[17]

Navigating the Status of G&T with a Desire for Diversity

Another example of this boundary work was an upper-class Savvy Negotiator named Alice, whose son started in the kindergarten Gen Ed program before he switched over to G&T in first grade. Alice explained that she likes "the idea of diversity" in the public schools, as opposed to a private school with "no diversity," but, in the same sentence, thought it was "too bad" that the two academic programs within the school were segregated. She said:

> I just like the fact that my kids [are going to] a public school and it meant a city public school. That said, the G&T classes honestly are not that diverse. They're diverse in kids from all over the world. They're diverse in, you know, there is an international diversity, it's a somewhat Asian diversity. It's not minority diversity, you know, Hispanic, Black. We have a couple but not, you know, and it's too bad.

While Alice appreciated the *diversity by default* her son was experiencing in the Gen Ed classroom before he switched over to G&T and said she would have been "fine" if he stayed in the Gen Ed, she was apparently more concerned about the status and opportunities that being on the G&T side of the boundary line would afford him.

Alice explained that she knew the G&T program was the place where her son belonged because the other parents in her neighborhood and preschool who got into the G&T program "were really smart." Alice added that one of the students she knew from her son's preschool, who attended TCS's G&T program, got into a high-status G&T middle school, "so clearly she got a good education." She explained that there's a certain "status to being chosen" for the G&T program and that students in the G&T program are perceived to be smarter. This perception "connotes a certain level of achievement that I'll buy into and make him look more attractive to other parents... so why wouldn't I want my child to have that, for people to judge him as well as possible?"

The majority of advantaged Gen Ed parents will continue to retest their children for G&T to transmit "every advantage" to their children in the form of high-status G&T placements, as well as avoid being the minority in the older grades. For example, Lauren is a Conflicted Follower whose son was in the kindergarten Gen Ed classroom. When Lauren was asked to identify the biggest difference between the programs, she quickly replied the "diversity in the Gen Ed classrooms." She explained that she "likes" the Gen Ed program because "my child goes to school with some non-White children, you know? I like that. In the other [G&T] classes, you don't get that." But, she still retested her son for G&T because she wanted to give him "every advantage," even though she would lose the *diversity by default* that she liked so much in the Gen Ed program.

Lauren went on to say that in the older grades, there is more "diversity" in the Gen Ed classrooms, meaning more Black and Latino students, because they used to bus in students of color from outside the neighborhood. She told a story about her children playing basketball in the park the other day: "And, like this older Black kid I'd never seen before, he goes, 'Hey dudes, how you doing?' and he came and high-fived them. And I was like, I love that! I love that they have these acquaintances with these older kids that aren't exactly like them and that are kind of cool and fun, and not just boring, same as them, you know, middle-class, you know, I kind of like that."

Lauren clearly felt that racial and socioeconomic "diversity" was a good thing both in her son's class and in the school as a whole. While Lauren, and many other Gen Ed parents, praised the Gen Ed program for the diversity, she still retested her children for G&T for first grade primarily because she heard from a teacher that the behavior problems in the Gen Ed classrooms become an issue in the older grades. In fact, out of the 35 parents who said that the racial differences were the biggest distinction between programs, 21—or 65 percent—also pointed out that there are more severe behavior problems in the Gen Ed classrooms, especially in the older grades when the children's behavior "manifest themselves" more. Melissa, an upper-class parent with children in both programs, described TCS overall as being, "a great cross-section of the New York City population." When Melissa was asked specifically to describe the two different programs within the school, however, she said that she noticed a difference in the behavior of the Gen Ed students "because of the family background that a lot of the Gen Ed kids are coming from. There's just—there's not as much support, there's probably not as much time and attention with their parents, and I think it shows." The behavior problems in the Gen Ed classrooms were attributed to less parental involvement or support in their children's education because of cultural or economic reasons—pushing advantaged White parents to retest their children for G&T.

When asked if most people in her kindergarten Gen Ed class were retesting their children, Lauren answered: "Yes, I think everyone feels like, well, we owe it to our kids, we might as well, is it better? I don't know. So I mean, you feel like you want to give your kid every advantage, right? I mean, if you lived in the city, you would probably have your kids tested for G&T, right? Because that's what you do. I don't think you're going to say, 'No, I'm going to hold my kids back.'"

Lauren retested her son for G&T because "that's what you do" to give your child "every advantage." This connects to the literature on the increased pressure parents face to push their children to succeed in a system where student success is defined by a narrow focus on student's scores on standardized tests.[18] Lareau (2003) would argue that the advantaged parents in this school context are better equipped to activate their capital by making sure that their children have certain opportunities no matter what—what she calls "concerted cultivation." Again, these within-school distinctions between programs, parents, and students would be less pronounced if the G&T admissions policy did not create the distinctions in the first place.

Advantaged parents such as Alice and Lauren, whose children do not initially make the G&T cutoff score, attempt to reconcile their place[ment] within the school by switching over to the G&T program. This decision goes against their stated beliefs in diversity but otherwise matches what other people in their social networks are doing. These codes, behaviors, and expectations (e.g., symbolic boundaries) can cause anxiety and pressure to be in the place where other families like them are located. This confirms one of the strongest themes to emerge from the existing school choice literature: parents are influenced by other people in their social networks when they are choosing where to live and where they send their children to school. For instance, Holme (2002) reported that the parents in her study used "status ideologies," or the commonly held beliefs that linked a student's motivation, behavior, and academic outcomes to their race and class background. Ultimately, the G&T label is a status symbol that matters to many parents, particularly "wealthy" parents, even though, as one G&T Defender, Cecelia, replied, "it shouldn't matter."

Stigma of Gen Ed

On the contrary, Gen Ed parents of color were seen as being less involved in the school. These parents were perceived as being not as invested or supportive of their children's education. For example, incoming parents to the school voiced concern about the stigma involved with being in the Gen

Ed portion of the school. Kelly, an Incoming "Conflicted Follower" to the Gen Ed program made a comment about not wanting to be "pegged as a Gen Ed parent and not one of the G&T parents" in the school, meaning one that is not involved in their children's education.

Jessica, a "Conflicted Follower" with a son in the first grade Gen Ed program, explained that both parents and teachers have this perception that the G&T parents are better. She recalled a time when she was helping a teacher at a school fundraiser—who apparently did not know she was a Gen Ed parent—who said to her, "Well, you know those Gen Ed parents, you know, they don't do what they're supposed to do" in terms of being involved in their child's education. Jessica said that comment kind of "cut me like a knife. I was really annoyed because I thought, oh my God, if the teachers in kindergarten have that perception, I don't like that at all. But it definitely speaks to a problem that exists." She went on to say that everyone has a perception about the two programs, even the parents, since at the very same fundraiser she heard a parent say, "Those Gen Ed parents do nothing!" Jessica said she was "shocked that that's the mentality" but admitted that there is some "truth to it" because of the lack of parent participation in the Gen Ed classes. She said you could see the difference in parent involvement if you look at how many parents volunteer to be the class parents. For instance, in most G&T classrooms there are up to eight parents who volunteer to be class parents, compared to Gen Ed when there are times when nobody volunteers.

Jessica's experience was not unique. There were similar stories from several advantaged Gen Ed parents, particularly PTA parents, who got "shocked" expressions when G&T parents found out that they were *not* "G&T parents" like them. Melissa, a Savvy Negotiator with a daughter in the kindergarten Gen Ed and an older son in the G&T program, explained: "There's an attitude that G&T parents are better [than Gen Ed parents] because I know parents, they'll meet me and they know I've been in the school for a long time and they see me around all the time and they're just kinda shocked, like, Oh wow, what teacher does your daughter have?" This also happens in the reverse when parents of color are in the G&T program. Amara, an African mother who had an older daughter go through the G&T program in which she was the only Black student in the G&T class, said "everybody of course doesn't think I'm in the G&T because... even if I say I am, they're like Ohhhh, you are? Who's your daughter? And I'm like, 'it's OK, I understand.'"

This speaks to the social and symbolic boundaries that parents use to signal group membership, in terms of race and class, and the stigma that is associated with the Gen Ed label. It is also a unique example of when symbolic boundaries do not translate into social boundaries particularly since highly involved White parents can be on either side of the boundary line now—leading to fewer stereotypes and a broadening definition of the Gen Ed parent label.

The "Oh" Response. For all of these reasons, advantaged Gen Ed parents felt like they were in a "second tier" program because of the status and stigma of the labels, not only for parents but for their children as well. Lisa, who has a child in the kindergarten Gen Ed program, felt that G&T parents acted "superior" because their children scored high enough to get into the program. She explained that the G&T program "just creates too much animosity between two groups, a feeling of being better because one is in the program. It creates a lot of tension." She explained that there is "no relationship between the G&T and non-G&T.... The two G&T classrooms had their own special thing and the Gen Ed had their own thing. I think we kind of felt like second best."

Later in the interview, Lisa told a story about having friends from preschool who have their children in the G&T program now that "always used to talk to her before," but ever since her son was placed in the Gen Ed program, they "don't even acknowledge" her when she walks by. She said, "If I feel it, I'm sure other parents do. It creates a distinction, especially in this day and age. It's ridiculous. Again, it's weird." Gen Ed parents of color also recalled similar stories about White parents who start in the Gen Ed program being their friend, but after they switch over to G&T they stop talking to them (chapter five).

In other words, some parents felt a judgment or stigma about their child's intelligence based on their child's placement in the Gen Ed classroom. For instance, Denise, a first grade Gen Ed mother said, "Moms would be like, 'What class are you in?' and it's like 'Oh, she's in the Gen Ed class.' 'Oh.' And you kinda get that 'Oh' thing." Similarly, Margaret, a Savvy Negotiator with children in both programs, said that she struggled with her daughter's placement in the Gen Ed classroom because of the judgment from other G&T parents: "People will say out loud in front of [my daughter], 'Is she in the Gifted and Talented program?' and I'll say, 'She's in K101 with [teacher's name].' *'Oh.'* I mean she hears that. It's so obnoxious... I look at my children and there's no difference between them... [my son] is not more gifted than [my daughter], absolutely not." The social and academic stigma of the Gen Ed label was a main reason that parents cited for getting their children retested for G&T because they did not want it to affect their child's academic self-concept (see chapter five).

Tanya, a Gen Ed Reconciler with a son in the first grade Gen Ed program, reported that about half of her son's kindergarten class retested for G&T and "a lot of the parents were really prepping them, and getting worried about the testing... it's like a big stigma, everybody's asking you on the playground, 'did you get G&T?'" Tanya got her son tested for G&T both years, even though academically he was not, as she put it "G&T material." She said that if her son had gotten into the G&T program she would have been "okay with that." What really bothered Tanya about being in the Gen Ed program, however, was the segregation between programs, the problem of children realizing what program they are in when they get older, and the "pressure on him to perform on the G&T test." Tanya ended up homeschooling her son and said she would not recommend the school because the "G&T and Gen Ed program are so different."

The more advantaged Gen Ed parents in the school did not want to be placed in the same category as the other typical "Gen Ed parents" because of the negative stigma of the Gen Ed label for both parent and child. The advantaged Gen Ed parents sense that many G&T parents "buy into" or internalize the labels and categories in the school, like the status and exclusivity of the program, and act like their children are special or better than other children because of their score on a standardized test.

This preference to be with "like-minded" families[19] in the high-status G&T program overshadowed their desire to expose their children to classroom-level diversity if they were initially enrolled in the Gen Ed program (*diversity by default*). According to parents, having a diverse student body in the school overall was a "positive thing," but it was also "disturbing" since the two programs remained highly segregated across race and class lines, especially in the older grades. The majority of advantaged parents (eventually) navigate to the G&T program or leave the school because of the status or stigma that the G&T / Gen Ed labels connote. The symbolic boundaries that divide G&T and Gen Ed parents and students by race and class also reflected the larger structures of inequality that the school embodied—particularly a set of educational policies that draw sharp distinctions between those who are "gifted" and those who are not and then give parents only one choice—between separate and unequal classrooms.

Chapter Three expands upon these contradictory attitudes by showing how even advantaged parents—particularly those with at least one child in the Gen Ed program who have resources to get their children into G&T programs, struggle with the true meaning of the measures used to define giftedness in this context (e.g., a single score on a standardized test administered to students when they are in preschool). This theme illuminates how "giftedness" is a socially constructed term that some parents believe in or "buy into" more than others. This chapter also provides more detail about the differences between the different sets of parents regarding how they made sense of the labels and categories within the school, and how that relates to the contradictions between who they are, where they belong, and, most importantly, where they are placed in the social hierarchy.

CHAPTER THREE

THE SOCIAL CONSTRUCTION OF
GIFTEDNESS

Lillian is an upper-class White mother with four children. She quit her career as a lawyer[1] to stay at home and take care of her children nearly 20 years ago. She has lived in TCS's catchment since her oldest child was born. She moved into the city because her husband grew up in the suburbs, but "despised them." He preferred the city lifestyle of diverse restaurants and walkability. Her older two children went to private schools in the city. Lillian's oldest child now attends college and her second oldest is currently enrolled at a private New York City high school. Meanwhile, her two younger children both attend public schools. The middle child is enrolled in a highly selective and diverse public middle school and is a graduate of TCS's G&T program. Lillian's youngest child is currently enrolled in the fourth grade G&T program at TCS.

Lillian and her family have lived in TCS's zone for nearly 20 years, but when she toured the school for her oldest daughter, the G&T program was in its infant stage. The school seemed "disorganized and they didn't know who the teachers were going to be." Lillian knew that if she sent her oldest child to private school, she would be "getting a good education and she will not fall through the cracks. I'm not going to be up at night worrying, I'm not going to spend every day at the school wondering what's going on. We slept easier. But then the bills came in and we weren't sleeping so easily. [Laughter]."

When her third child was ready for school, Lillian got her daughter accepted at the same private school that her two older children were attending. Yet, they quickly realized that "it was too much [money] to have three kids going to private school. So it was a very difficult decision. I felt incredibly guilty about it." She went through public education herself and "socially" felt that "it was the right way to go, I like that we had a nice mix of kids there, socioeconomically and ethnically—I felt the diversity was really good." For logistical reasons over everything else, Lillian decided to take another look at the G&T program at TCS because she "knew parents that liked the school," and it was her catchment school so it would be easier for her to drop off and pick up her children at two different schools. She explained that she did not choose TCS because it had a G&T program. It was apparent, though, that the majority Black and Latino Gen Ed program was a non-option for her because of the student population. When asked to describe TCS to someone who is not familiar with the schools or programs in the *City Limits* district, Lillian, who has witnessed the demographic changes at the school, says that the school attracts "a fairly odd mixture of [*City Limits*] families and then maybe families that are—I don't know— where their kids are bussed in or come in from less-privileged areas. And the school is fairly segregated…but in my opinion the G&T program just exacerbates that problem."

Although Lillian attended a G&T program within a public school in North Carolina while growing up, she feels "all schools would be better off without any G&T programs" because "it sort of indiscriminately separates kids for sort of no reason—based on a test they take that I think has very little prognosticating value." She relates the process of getting into the G&T program as "sort of the luck of the draw, the parenting, the tutoring, whatever they do to get their kids in, and then they sort of have the upper hand for the rest of the time that they're in school. I don't think that's really fair. That being said, my kids are in that."

When asked if she prepared her two youngest children to take the G&T test in preschool, Lillian explained that she does not "really believe" in tutoring or prepping for the G&T test. She does not even believe that four-year-olds should be taking a test at all: "It's so bolloxed up I think because if everybody's doing it, then your kid is sort of behind the eight ball if they don't. But I feel like if you have to prep your kids for the test then they probably should not be going into that program." Lillian thinks it is all a big "charade that we're playing" to get children into the G&T program. She also believes that it is "premature" to have them tested so young: "It is sort of imposed on us, the system that we have in New York. I guess people feel like they want the best for their child, so they should prep them. I never did it. We sort of slipped in under the wires without having done that. But I don't know, now for the SATs everybody preps."

Lillian tells a story of a friend who spent $300 per hour for an "intensive tutor," which resulted in the student's SAT scores going up by 200 points after the tutoring sessions. Lillian explains that the difference between getting tutored for the SATs and G&T tests, though, is that "these are young adults and they're doing it for themselves, but with a four-year-old they have no idea what they're doing." There's no "motivation" for preschool children to perform well on the test, and it is, in Lillian's opinion, "unnecessary torture for them to have to go in and learn how to do it." She relates a funny story about a friend who is prepping her child for the G&T test by asking the question, "If Henry and his two friends buy a pizza, and there's eight slices of pizza, and his friends each eat two slices, how many slices are left for Henry?" "And the kid goes, 'Uh, who's Henry?' [Laughter]. That was the perfect response, because what do they care? They're four."

When asked whether her children know about the G&T and Gen Ed labels and different classrooms inside the school, Lillian replied, "Sometimes they'll say—my son said to me this year—I don't remember how it came up, it was a show or something—I said 'what did this class do?' and he said 'Oh, the dark-skinned kids?' I was like 'What?' He goes 'You know, the class with the dark-skinned kids.' I mean, he just observed that in his class, there's one or two maybe." She adamantly explains, though, that she never says "gifted"[2] because she does not "think they're gifted or talented. I think it's just a joke that they took the test and they're in there. So we don't really talk about that, but they know that—it's so stupid because they can see that they're a different sort of demographic than the other class.... And that it was based on testing and stuff." Because of the G&T test prepping and all of the parents who get their children tested in the first place, Lillian says, "you have this artificially created hierarchy of kids...[that] fall along socioeconomic lines. Minorities tend to wind up in the Gen Ed and I think that's a disadvantage, to divide them up in that way. These kids shouldn't be exposed to that sort of division that young in life." Lillian thinks that the students eventually "figure it out" that the White students are in one program and the "other kids" are in another "so they feel somehow superior to those kids. I think that's all wrong, to start that at such a young age." She thinks students should be mixed up by academic ability so the higher-ability students can help the lower-ability students learn. Lillian describes her daughter's "fantastic" public middle school that is "mixed" with students from all over the city and all different backgrounds.[3] She believes that a school with *no G&T* is "preferable." Even though she has children in the G&T program herself, she makes a point to say that "I don't really think there should be a G&T program, in case you haven't guessed yet."

This chapter shows how advantaged parents struggle with the meaning of the measures used to define "giftedness" in this context, namely a single, arbitrary 90th percentile score set by the NYCDOE. These parents have at least one child in the Gen Ed program, have resources to help get their children into G&T programs, and include G&T parents in the older grades, like Lillian, who have experienced the school's culture the longest. The "Savvy Negotiators" and "Conflicted Followers," in particular, best articulated their belief that the "gifted" label is socially constructed; meaning that "giftedness" in this context is related more to students advantaged backgrounds and G&T test preparation than their "true" intelligence. In fact, as described in chapter two, parents with children in both programs often noted that they do not believe one of their children is more "gifted" than the other.

In this context where White students are being placed into two hierarchical academic programs, parents explained that "G&T" is a socially constructed term that some parents, namely the G&T Defenders in the younger grades, "buy into" more than others. They "play the game" (e.g., test prepping) that other similarly advantaged parents are playing to get their children into the G&T program. It also describes parents' sense of how their children perceive the structures within the school and the negative stigma of the Gen Ed label in terms of student's intelligence and academic self-concept.

Advantaged parent's efforts to have their children "properly" sorted into the G&T program is being fueled by practices that have been in place for many years. For some parents, they have (or had) older children in the G&T program already. Parents get their children tested and retested for G&T to be with other students who are "like them" in terms of race and class within a system that is highly stratified by both factors. These parents who live in New York City in 2011, however, do not feel comfortable saying that their strong drive to get their children into the G&T program is about segregating them by race and class. As seen in chapter two, the advantaged parents virtually all said that they would prefer their children to be in more diverse classrooms—so as a result, they use different language to discuss where they want their children placed and why.

The chapter concludes by describing why some G&T parents, particularly the "G&T Defenders" in the younger grades, who have the least experience with the school or with the Gen Ed program, tend to embody or internalize the G&T label more than others because of their child's 98 or 99th percentile score on the G&T test. In other words, their sense of place in the larger system and society matches their high-status G&T placement in the school, thus making it more likely to "buy into" the structures. For all parents, contradictory attitudes emerge as they embody, resist, and reproduce the structures, all at the same time.

The Social Construction of the "Gifted" Label—"I Never Went into the G&T Program Thinking My Kids Were Gifted"

According to the interview data, the vast majority—a full 84 percent of advantaged parents (or 34 out of 41), did not believe the G&T tests adequately measured "giftedness," as the DOE defines the term. This was the case because, they felt, most children were being prepared for the tests (either at home with workbooks or with a private tutor). Yet, despite how advantaged parents with children in the Gen Ed program question the legitimacy of the G&T label, they still resist their placement and "play the game" by prepping and retesting their children every year to get into the G&T program to reconcile their sense of place. White advantaged parents retest for G&T to succumb to the anxiety and pressure that other White parents, and some teachers, place on them to be in the G&T program, where they belong.

For example, when asked to describe the differences between the G&T and Gen Ed programs, Jessica, a "Conflicted Follower" who has children in both programs, illustrates the ways that parents simultaneously embody, resist, and reproduce the structures all at the same time:

> You know, it's really interesting. I don't like it [the G&T program]. I think it's too bad. But you just are either in Gen Ed or you're in G&T and it's a marker, and it stays with you. I find it really interesting, especially—so I was telling my husband about this too, and I said, "You know, what are your feelings about it?" And he said, "Well"—this is so funny, I mean he means it comically, but he said, "*Well, if our daughters get into G&T, I love it. And if they don't, I think it's a terrible program.*" And I think that really is—I think a lot of people in their heart of hearts really feel that way (emphasis added).

Melissa, who is an upper class Savvy Negotiator with children in both programs described how parents socially construct the labels and categories in the school when she admitted, "I never went into the G&T program thinking that my kids were gifted. They were in the G&T program because I was able to send them to a good preschool. I knew they needed to take the test, I knew the whole deal. So I don't really think there's a whole lot of difference between the G&T and the Gen Ed, certainly in the early grades."

Questioning the "Measures" Used to Define "Giftedness"

Melissa and the other parents with children in both programs were, understandably, the most critical of having both programs within the school. They did not believe one of their children was more "gifted" than the other and thus questioned the meaning of the distinction between the two, but still retested for G&T because that's where they felt they belonged. Parents like Melissa simultaneously embody the broader social structures because of their child's G&T placement, but also resist them when their other child(ren) is placed in the Gen Ed program with the students and parents who are not like them in terms of race, class, and academic ability. Thus, *who* is enrolled in the G&T program is apparently more important to these parents than their beliefs about whether or not their children are "gifted."

Another Savvy Negotiator with children in both programs, Joe, was skeptical of the reasons for having a G&T program at TCS and the validity of the G&T tests since he considered both of his children to be "really intelligent." Meanwhile, like was described in the previous chapter, his son missed the cutoff score on the G&T test by one point, thus he was labeled "not-gifted" and assigned to a Gen Ed classroom while his daughter got a very high score and was placed in the G&T classroom. He questioned whether it is a "real" G&T program in this context, because it's about:

> Sifting kids from like smart, and less smart… And it [the test scores] doesn't tell me anything about the kid's intelligence, really. The [G&T] test is very one-dimensional. And like I said, both my kids took the test. They're both very intelligent kids, but they're intelligent in different ways. And so, at first, when my son didn't pass I said, what's his score? And they said 89. So he was off by like one point. You know. So you know, because of that point, now he's not gifted and talented? What is this? Really, what is this? I just thought that was lame.

Joe's quote relates to the social construction of the G&T label and the arbitrary test score cutoff that the DOE has implemented (90th percentile) to label the students whose parents get them tested in the first place.

An incoming Gen Ed parent and Conflicted Follower, Kelly, also questioned what "gifted" means in this context. Her son technically passed the 90th percentile cutoff score for the district's G&T requirement since he received a 94. But, he did not get placed in the G&T classroom within TCS because other first time incoming children were getting 98s or 99s on the G&T test. Kelly was offered a G&T seat in a less desirable neighborhood school, so she decided to choose the Gen Ed program in TCS instead. When asked if the G&T tests adequately measure giftedness, she said,

> Not at this age, no. Absolutely not. First of all, a G&T test is an ability test, not an IQ test, so the OLSAT is a ridiculous measure of that in my opinion because it's really—what can they do in a certain amount of time, how long can they sit there. It's very good at identifying a certain type of learner. It's not necessarily good at identifying a gifted learner. I know some people that have scored 99s on the test and I would not say that their children

are particularly bright. They're bright kids, but I wouldn't say they're out there brilliant—I'm sure that they will do well in the world, but they're not geniuses by any stretch.

As for her own son, she explained, "I do think he's very bright, but I think most parents think that about their kids." When advantaged parents "play the game" that other similarly advantaged parents are playing by prepping and testing their children for G&T, but do not get placed in the G&T program that they desire, there is a mismatch between their sense of "place" versus their "placement" in the school and larger system. This leads advantaged Gen Ed parents to question the definition of giftedness in this context (bright vs. smart vs. gifted), the measures the DOE uses to label some students G&T and others Gen Ed, and the competition of getting a G&T seat at TCS. Kelly's story illustrates that there are factors beyond test scores—for example, needing to get a 98 or 99 for first time students, sibling priority, and so on, that go into the competition for a G&T seat.

Denise, a first grade Conflicted Follower in the Gen Ed program, questioned the whole idea of labeling a four-year-old "gifted" because she implied that most children in *City Limits* are being prepped for the G&T test. She said, "I wouldn't say anybody who pulled a bunch of kids out of the G&T program at [TCS] are like, gonna be the next Bill Gates or a rocket scientist, ya know? I think probably the majority was prepped for it. I don't think a kid can be truly gifted. I think a kid can be a faster learner."

When asked how she would define giftedness, Denise answered: "I think definitely different than the DOE does. Their definition is who can do really well on this test by being prepped. I actually think it's someone who has an ability to do something extraordinary, like if a kindergartener can do algebra or geometry or compose music. It certainly isn't what the Department of Ed's standards are." Advantaged parents with children in the Gen Ed program thought the name "gifted" should be saved for children who have exceptional talents or abilities, beyond test taking ability, not children who get a certain score on a standardized test when they are four years old.

Even the nine G&T Defenders in this book, whose social status is somewhat legitimized by their child's placement based on one test score, also question the gifted label in this context. For instance, Carrie, who has a first grade child in the G&T program, questioned the use of G&T tests for children so young because it reflects their advantaged backgrounds, "At four years old? No. I'll do it because that's the system and I was working through the system, but I just don't think that it adequately measures giftedness." When asked why she feels that way, she explained, "I know that there's probably parents who don't test their kids. They don't know, or they don't bother or whatever.... I see that there's a broad range of ability in the Gifted and Talented class, too."

A strong theme to emerge from the parent interviews is that parents feel that testing children so young—before they start formal schooling—is unfair because the test scores reflect more than just their intelligence. It also reflects their parents' cultural capital exchange, through test prepping, and so on, and whether or not they sign their children up to get tested. Carrie and other parents attribute the "broad range of ability" in the G&T program to the test preparation that children are being exposed to before the test, and the fact that siblings of G&T students get priority and only have to receive a 90th percentile score for admission. Jessica, a Conflicted Follower with children in both programs, points out that there are very different levels of ability in the Gen Ed classrooms as well, from children who technically passed the G&T test score cutoff to children who did not attend kindergarten and cannot read yet. Jessica says even though she does not like the sibling policy, she loves what it has done for TCS because "there are more 98s and 97s in our Gen Ed class than there is in the G&T class because you only need to score a 90 [if you're a sibling] to get into the G&T." Ultimately, advantaged parents, like Carrie, admit that they "work" the G&T system to get their children into the high-status G&T program.

Meanwhile, parents with children in the Gen Ed program question their child's placement the most because even when they follow the "rules of the game" that other similarly positioned parents follow, they are *not* placed in the appropriate program for someone like them. Therefore, the interview data shows that advantaged Gen Ed parents resist their placements and attempt to work the system to their advantage—with some being more successful than others—by prepping and retesting their children for the G&T, even if they say they do not believe in the gifted label in this context, feel bad about prepping (because it was "cheating" and they were not "supposed" to do it), or testing children so young. One aspect of this larger theme about the ways that parents question the measures used to define "giftedness" is that their definition of being "gifted" is very different than how the DOE defines the term (e.g., someone who scores above the 90th percentile on the G&T test). In fact, parents believe their children and other students labeled "G&T" are "smart" or "bright," but they would "never in a million years" call them "gifted."

Deconstructing the Construction of Giftedness
For instance, Lauren, a kindergarten Gen Ed Conflicted Follower, thought that passing the G&T test score cutoff was more about test taking skills than actual intelligence. She explains how she would define giftedness: "Probably a kid who's got like an IQ off the charts and could probably be like a kindergartener who could probably do like third grade stuff. That to me is gifted. The Gifted and Talented test that they give them, it's, you know—you probably have to be bright to do it, but you also have to be a good test-taker."

Lauren went on to say that her son scored a 94 on the test and that even though he technically passed the 90th percentile cutoff score and was guaranteed a seat in a gifted class (just not at TCS because it was not a high enough score), she did not believe her son was "gifted." In fact, she would never "in a million years tell anyone that he was gifted." She said, "I think they have it named improperly. It should be like 'accelerated' classes or something, but gifted to me, like I said, is somebody whose IQ is off the charts and who's like playing piano without looking at music and that type of thing. That's gifted to me. (Pause). And I think a lot of parents feel that way."

Despite parental attitudes about the G&T label, the validity of the G&T tests and the definition of giftedness, most of the White Gen Ed parents in this book who originally got their children tested for G&T in kindergarten retest them for first grade G&T admission. Advantaged parents retest for G&T admission even if they are not completely sure if the program is academically or socially "better" or they are happy with the Gen Ed program. In this way, going through the G&T admissions process is conflated with being a good parent because, as Lauren explained, "that's what you do" to "give your kid every advantage" in the system, which is not only perceived to be beneficial because of the students that you are surrounding yourself with in the G&T classroom, but is also thought to benefit students for their future middle and high school placements.

Lauren's quote relates to Annette Lareau's concept of "concerted cultivation" in which she explores how different social classes interact with institutional settings like schools.[4] Lareau found that middle-class parents are more proactive and "assertive" when interacting with school professionals by making sure that their children have certain opportunities no matter what. Applied to this book, advantaged parents use their "concerted cultivation" when they get their children tested and retested for G&T, because as Lauren replied, "that's what you do." Lauren and other Gen Ed parents in the book said that they felt pressure to retest their children because other parents were doing it and the G&T program was perceived to be "better" in terms of the people, even if, they were not entirely sure what was so different academically between the programs because the curriculum is the same and the teacher quality varies (see chapter four).

One reason that parents thought the G&T test results were "skewed" in New York City and favored White, more advantaged children was because most parents were apparently preparing their preschool children to take the tests by paying for private tutors or using costly test prep materials, which is what advantaged parents have been doing for years to get their children into highly selective middle schools (fourth grade standardized tests), specialized high schools (SHSAT), and colleges (SAT prep).

G&T Test Preparation—"I Did Do It, and I Feel a Little Bad about It"

In fact, while test prepping has become ubiquitous among families of older students trying to get into competitive private schools, selective middle schools, specialized high schools and colleges, advantage parents in this district prep their preschoolers for the G&T kindergarten admissions test, not only to pass the 90th percentile cutoff score needed if they are a sibling, but also to get the highest score possible if they are the only or first child admitted to the school. And, even as they consider the gifted label and measures as socially constructed, so too is their sense of what they need to do to give their child "every advantage" in the system by securing what's perceived to be the "best" education alongside other advantaged families like their own.

According to the interview data, 31 out of the 41 advantaged parents, or 76 percent, admitted that they did some kind of test prep activities with their children. Parents in the younger grades said the only reason they prepped their children for the G&T tests—either at home with workbooks or by hiring a private tutor—was because they knew that other parents were doing similarly. Basically, they argued that if they chose not to prep, their child would probably not get into the program because other children had been prepped. Claire, an upper-class G&T Defender with two children in the G&T program, questioned how "fair" the G&T admissions process was when she said, "And I still question whether or not it's fair because there's so many kids that test really well. There are kids that are getting 96 or 97 on these tests and don't get in because the cutoff is like 98 or 99 for G&T admission into TCS."

One mother referred to the test prepping as "a dirty little secret" in the school. Jessica, a first grade Gen Ed parent explained that "cognitively" she believed that her daughter was a better fit for the G&T program but if, as she said, "I don't do anything to help her prepare for it and every other child is preparing for it, then she just automatically could not get in because she doesn't have that preparation. So I did do it, and I feel a little bad about it, but it was a conscious decision and I feel like it was one I had to make" to get her into the G&T program.

Furthermore, Jessica said she feels that the difference between the students who get into the G&T program and the ones who do not depends on whether they were prepped or not for the test, which she said is just the "status quo these days." She also said that technically you are not "supposed to prep" and on all the DOE documents it says that if the proctor believes that your child was prepped, then they can stop the test. Nevertheless, even though she felt that it was "cheating," she tutored her daughter anyway to give her that chance for what was perceived to be a better education.

What parents said over and over again was that the more advantaged parents in the system are tutoring their children for the G&T test not only to get a passing 90th percentile score, but also to also achieve the highest score possible so they can get into the most popular schools like TCS. Although one of the DOE's goals with the G&T policy change was to admit a more diverse G&T population, test prepping and the extra advantages that White families have in the system result in the G&T classrooms across the city actually becoming more White. The DOE's shift from a more decentralized system in which individual schools used multiple criteria and had the power to choose a more diverse G&T population, to a centralized admissions policy that relies on a single score on a standardized test (see Table 1.1) favors more advantaged children in the system. In fact, the percentages of Black and Latino students in G&T classrooms have dramatically decreased since the policy change in 2008. These segregative patterns echo what many gifted and talented scholars have already warned about, namely that using an "entirely test driven admissions process will only exacerbate the problem of equity and racial imbalance" since it is very hard to identify lower-income, minority children as being "gifted" using tests alone.[5]

Lillian from the introductory vignette reiterates this point:

> I mean, because people have figured out how to take the test.... the whole point, I think, for the G&T was to create more diversity... but you're not getting diversity really. You're still getting the highly educated parents with, you know, *those kids going to those schools*. You're not really finding a gifted and talented—it's, yes, the kids are smart, but it's not because of anything other than their background probably, and what they're exposed to... yeah,

my son's smart, he's highly driven, but again if your child's not exposed to a lot of these things, they're not going to do well on the test.

This preparation for the G&T tests serves to privilege the more advantaged parents in the system even more and contributes to the social reproduction of the system. Betsy, an upper-class second grade G&T Savvy Negotiator whose son was in the Gen Ed program for kindergarten and first grade admitted that she paid a private tutor to prepare him for the G&T tests. She explained, "A lot of the wealthier parents pay to have their kids tutored or else, you know, they just are providing the kind of stimulation that works well with testing. Not that these other [Gen Ed] kids aren't bright it's that, you know, they're not necessarily—they didn't get verbal stimulation or whatever it is, that helps them test well."

Kathy, an upper-class fourth grade G&T Defender said that she did a lot of preparation for the G&T tests with her daughter. She joked that "leading up to the test, every night before bed, we'd play these little games where I make the block stack and she'd make the block stack and all this stuff. And then she took the test the next day, and that night she's like, 'Well, are we playing our game?' And I'm like, 'No, we're all done with that!' (Laughs). 'The game is over!'"

Lauren, a Conflicted Follower with a son in the kindergarten Gen Ed class admitted that she tutored her son before he took the G&T test for first grade: "Do I think tutoring helped this year? Kind of a little bit. I think maybe a little—had I done—I did it like four sessions. You know, I really didn't do it. The only reason I did it was because my son's teacher said it's important when they get older. She said, yes, it's really important for disciplinarian reasons in the older grades that they should be in G&T. So then I kind of freaked out a little bit." So, not only do parents know that other parents like them are prepping and retesting their children for G&T, but apparently teachers are also advising certain Gen Ed parents that they should retest for G&T because of the behavior problems in the Gen Ed program when students get older. This test prepping feeds into the anxiety and pressure that parents face regarding their children's placement in TCS and future school placements. Although Jessica said G&T test prepping is considered "cheating" and parents feel "guilty" about it, they do it anyway to give their children educational advantages in the form of G&T placements.

Mara Sapon-Shevin's research on G&T programs ties into the findings here about the reasons parents gave for retesting for the G&T program. Sapon-Shevin's qualitative case study examined a suburban elementary school that implemented a pullout program for gifted education once a week.[6] The students were from similar racial and SES backgrounds, but for those students that were left behind in the Gen Ed classroom there was lower academic expectations and self-esteem. Sapon-Shevin interviewed 11 parents and found that having their children go to the G&T classroom was a way to avoid the disciplinary problems in the regular classroom. Parents explained that "there is a lot of status attached to [G&T]," and their children "felt honored, special, smart, valued, and acknowledged" by being included in the G&T program.[7]

Even as the Gen Ed classrooms in the younger grades are becoming more racially/ethnically and socioeconomically mixed because more White families from the neighborhood are choosing the Gen Ed program now (the G&T programs remain mostly White), advantaged parents maintain the segregation between programs since most of them retest their children every year and eventually get them into the G&T program by the time they enter the second grade or leave the school. The next section describes another factor that plays a part in how parents make sense of where their children belong within the school—namely how parents make sense of their children's sense of the structures and the negative stigma related to their children's intelligence and academic self-concept if they do not secure a G&T spot.

How Parents Make Sense of Their Children's Sense of the Structures

Another reason why most advantaged parents with children in the Gen Ed program retest for G&T placement is because they do not want their children to feel "less smart" because of the Gen Ed label that they are given. Parents are worried about their child's academic self-concept, because, as one parent said, the G&T or Gen Ed label "sets kids up for who they think they are as a student especially when it's purely divided by racial lines." As explained in chapter two, there is a stigma of the Gen Ed label in terms of parent involvement. Parents also referred to the "stigma" of the Gen Ed label in terms of children's academic ability—for example, being "pegged as one of the not-so-smart kids" compared to the G&T students, which served to reinforce for parents where their child belonged in the system and contributed to the contradictions that emerged if they were not "in their right place" in the status hierarchy. In other words, Gen Ed parents felt a judgment about their child's intelligence based on their score on a standardized test. On the other side, G&T parents were also concerned about their child feeling "better than" the Gen Ed students if they found out about their "G&T" status and their placement within the school. This finding shows how parents make sense of their children's sense of the structures and, in turn, how that might affect the ways in which parents talk about G&T versus Gen Ed and their sense of place within the structures.

To illustrate, Kelly, a Conflicted Follower and incoming kindergarten Gen Ed parent, described the differences between the G&T and Gen Ed classrooms and what she worries about by having her son in the Gen Ed classroom. She said, "Everyone in the G&T class is either White or Asian. There are very few White children in the Gen Ed classrooms and it was mostly Hispanic. That's the way it is. I actually like diversity, so I don't have a problem with it from that perspective—but what I do worry about is that he will pick up on it at some point and feel pegged as one of the not-so-smart kids." Therefore, despite the fact that she likes diversity, Kelly worried about the "stigma" of the Gen Ed label, not just for her in terms of parent involvement (chapter two), but also for her son who might figure out what the G&T and Gen Ed labels mean and feel somehow less smart because he's in the Gen Ed program.

This relates to a recent study by Maika Watanabe, which connects the tracking and G&T literature and explores how the social construction of ability affects "G&T" and "Regular" track placements in a North Carolina high school.[8] Watanabe discovered that students start to internalize the "hierarchical" labels that are placed on them, which affects their motivation levels. Furthermore, teachers treat students differently, based on their track level, by giving more attention and higher expectations to the gifted track students. Applied to the TCS context, labeling students G&T or Gen Ed can also affect teachers' treatment and expectations of students and, as one parent replied, "Sets kids up for who they think they are as a student"[9] (see chapter five). Additionally, because the G&T label is so clearly divided by race and class lines, it can result in a visual image of "Whiteness as giftedness."[10]

The Gen Ed program, on the other hand, is perceived as the program that contains the "not so smart" kids with more severe behavior problems.[11] According to parents, this perception of what the Gen Ed label means is expressed by their children in different ways. As one G&T Defender, Cecelia, explained, there can be a perception with the students that the Gen Ed class is considered the "dumb kid's class." This feeling of being less smart can also create conflict and misunderstandings at home when siblings are placed into two different academic programs. Margaret, an upper-class Savvy Negotiator with children in both programs, explained that since her older son was already in the G&T program, she did not want her younger daughter who was placed in the kindergarten Gen Ed program to have the "stigma" of being in the Gen Ed. She explained that her son mistakenly believed that his sister was in "Special Ed" because she was not in G&T like him:

> Even the label of it is just, you know, "Gifted and Talented." I mean, any child at any age, at five years old, understands those words. And Gen Ed, you know, that's like—I don't know, Gifted and Talented definitely has the ring of being the special class. Like [my son] at one time said something like, "Well"—he asked if [his sister] was in Special Ed. He just didn't know, he didn't know what the difference was. And I don't think [my daughter] has an awareness yet that she's in a different program. But it just bugs me so much that she is, and—well.

Later in the interview, when asked how she would define giftedness, she hesitated and said, "I don't know." But, when asked whether she thought the G&T tests adequately measure giftedness, she adamantly replied:

> Not at all. I think that every kid has the potential to be, you know, to be great and to be a great student and a creative student and add a lot to their classroom, and I think dividing it up like that is really sort of dangerous... *because it sets kids up for who they think they are as a student* or—and especially like when it is purely divided on these racial lines, yeah, just, it adds this really negative culture at the school and it's divisive.

Despite Margaret's critique of the definition of giftedness and the use of a G&T test, she still used her cultural capital to prep and retest her daughter for a first grade G&T placement to avoid the negative stigma of the Gen Ed label. She embodied the G&T label because of her older son's placement in the program and her sense of where she belonged in the social structure. Margaret simultaneously resisted the label by being critical of the segregation and "negative culture" that the G&T program produced, and she reproduced the structures by retesting her Gen Ed daughter for G&T.

Tessa, a Conflicted Follower just retested her two older children for the G&T program and has a younger child going into the kindergarten Gen Ed program. When asked what she believed were the advantages or disadvantages of having two separate programs within one school, she responded, "I worry about singling kids out at an early age. I was very concerned about it because my son's not in [G&T] next year. They've got friends, I don't want them to think—I wouldn't want any kids to think that they're either special or that they're not good enough. I really struggle with the fact that it's highlighted at such an early age. But that's my biggest issue." She went on to say that she did not think that the G&T tests are adequately measuring giftedness, "they're measuring some kind of intelligence. I just think gifted is the wrong term. I mean they're smart kids...this is not Doogie Howser."

While Gen Ed parents do not want their children to feel "less than" the G&T students, on the other side, I also found that G&T parents, especially those with children in the higher grades, do not want their children to feel "better than" the Gen Ed students. In contradictory ways, advantaged parents all strive to be in the "better" high-status G&T program to be surrounded by other families like their own, yet they do not want their children to know which program they are in because of the status and stigma of the labels. Like Lillian explained in the introductory vignette, "I think kids figure it out that they're in one program and the other kids are in another so they feel somehow superior to those kids. I think that's all wrong, to start that at such a young age. And I also feel like kids—even if kids are faster with academics, it behooves them to be around kids that may not be so fast in a lot of ways. They can help those kids, they can learn from that." Another fourth grade G&T Savvy Negotiator, Caitlyn, did not want to tell her daughter that she was in the G&T program, even though she realized that she was in a G&T class, because "I didn't want her to think that the [Gen Ed] kids were lesser or something—I just didn't want her to feel like, 'I'm special, I'm smart, I'm a gifted person.' I think it's kind of a weird concept for a child. I don't think they can handle that really."

Although parents disagreed about when students figure out which program they are in, it is clear that children eventually do figure out that there are two different hierarchical academic programs within the school and can "feel" and even see the differences. Advantaged parents explain that students not only "see" the racial/ethnic segregation between programs, but they also realize there are academic and behavioral differences as well. Thus, it's not only about feeling a stigma from being in the Gen Ed classroom, it's also feeling "somehow superior" if you are in the G&T program that parents worry about for their children's academic self-concept. This feeling of either being smarter, superior, or special if you are in the G&T program, versus lesser than or inferior if you are in the Gen Ed program not only happens at school between students, but, as will be shown in chapter five, it can also create conflict at home in the same family.

The next section provides an analysis of the nine G&T Defenders who were more vested in the meaning and significance of the G&T program. This group of G&T parents with children in the younger grades had the least experience in the school or the Gen Ed program, and was found to internalize the G&T label based on their children's score on the G&T test.

Thus, contradictory attitudes emerge since their child's G&T test score gets legitimized as being reflective of their actual ability, even if it is also a social construction of their advantaged backgrounds. Their child's intelligence and ability gets legitimized by the test score, even if they do not necessarily believe their children are gifted or that the G&T admissions processi sf air.

For Some G&T Parents—"My Kids Are Good Enough to Be in G&T"

An example of how G&T parents internalized their child's academic ability based on their score on the G&T test was Cecelia, a kindergarten G&T parent, who said she was "thrilled" that her daughter got a "99" on the test and got into TCS's popular G&T program. She described her daughter as being "immensely gifted in a structural artistic way" and so she was "happy" that the G&T test "picked up" on her daughter's "particular type of giftedness." Furthermore, she said that there are a lot of "wealthy parents" in the G&T program and the "status" and "value" of the G&T label "matters to them, even though it shouldn't." In fact, parents estimated that they could save half a million dollars on private school tuition if their child passed the G&T test. Cecelia said, "I mean, it's just so insane. Like the score they get on this test, it's potentially worth like—the more I think about it—it's like a half a million dollars [for private school tuition], and it's like a three-year-old taking the test, when you calculate the number of years in school! It's just so crazy."

Although Cecelia's daughter ended up receiving a very high score on the G&T test, before she took the test Cecelia was not sure how she would perform. She told a story about practicing the G&T test with her daughter at home, and, on the day of the test, her daughter wanted to practice it one more time. She said she thought she had "totally blown it" when her daughter wanted to fill in the bubbles for the correct answers on the test, even though children do not have to, and that she colored in every bubble for each question. When Cecelia told her daughter only to fill in the bubble for the right answer, her daughter got mad and said she did not want to take the test anymore.

Throughout the interviews, Cecelia and the other G&T Defenders would internalize or "buy into" the G&T label since their child scored high enough on the standardized test to be offered a G&T seat at TCS. This legitimization occurred, even when these same parents going into the process said they did not believe their children were gifted or that the G&T test was fair because parents prep for the test. As Alyssa explained in the Introduction chapter, after some parents get their children's G&T test scores back, "Suddenly, you are what the test says you are." Therefore, if their child got a 98 or 99 on the test, their advantaged backgrounds get rewarded in the form of educational placements for their children.[12]

In fact, according to Gen Ed parents, there was a perception that most G&T parents in the school believed in the gifted labels that their children were given because of the "status" of the label. This perception was backed up by the history of the school separating G&T and Gen Ed students by skin color, which serves to further legitimize the academic identities and attitudes of White advantaged parents (and children) of being "smarter" or "better" academically because they were consistently placed in the separate, majority White G&T classes. This racial and SES segregation between tracks that has characterized the school since the G&T program was started in 1997, serves to reinforce for parents where their child belongs in the system (e.g., social boundary), and whether they should get them tested and retested for the G&T program (e.g., symbolic boundary) because that's where they feel they belong.

Anne, an upper-class G&T Defender with two G&T children in second and fourth grade, is an example of how G&T parents socially construct their child's ability and their place within the structures. Anne explained why she felt "pretty confident" that her older son would get into her "first choice" school, which was TCS's G&T program. He got a "99" on the test. Her younger daughter only had to get the 90th percentile for a G&T seat because she was a younger sibling, but she coincidentally got an "identical percentile" of 99 on the G&T test. Anne explains that she was not "anxious" about her daughter getting in since it was "unlikely that the second one wouldn't do well" on the G&T test, and "I don't think people were tutoring as much."

When asked to define giftedness, Anne replied that a gifted child would be "an abnormally smart kid [who is]...just able to learn at a young age behaviorally and sort of just, that ability to sit and listen at a younger age and follow directions at an early age often leads to that [G&T] label." She went on to explain in more detail who is labeled gifted in the school and who is not, which she implicitly relates more to students' advantaged backgrounds—in terms of race, class, prior preschool experiences, and parental support, rather than being a true reflection of a child's intelligence:

> I think it's—I personally don't think it's so much intelligence at this age as it is sort of support at home and hearing language in a way that it becomes more intuitive. It's just easier, I think, for some kids who have someone backing them up a little bit on this type of stuff because I think nothing they do at this age is rocket science. Every normal kid should be able to

learn this. [It's different] in a Gen Ed setting where not all of the kids have this support to get to where they could be and they don't have the preschool behind them to help them get to where they need to be.

Anne describes the people in G&T as "invested in their kids' education, so you're able to have a whole class of kids with that kind of support from people who are very engaged." In contrast, the Gen Ed program draws students from outside the neighborhood and "you don't always have kids who can get that [support] at home for loads of reasons, I'm sure. That makes it hard because it's hard for a six-year-old to be completely self-motivated."

Anne uses symbolic boundaries to distinguish between the G&T (e.g., children who have invested parents and support at home) and Gen Ed (e.g., children who did not go to preschool and do not have support at home) categories to determine where she and her children belong in the race- and class-based hierarchy. She also internalizes the G&T label that her two children are given, based on their identical 99th percentile score on a standardized test and clearly feels like her children are in the right placement because it fits with her advantaged background in the system.

One of the first comments that all nine G&T Defenders made during the interview was to announce their child's 98 or 99 score on the G&T test—providing evidence of how parents internalized the G&T label. For instance, Cecelia, a kindergarten G&T Defender, when asked what her school choice options were for her daughter, explained, "Well, first of all, she got a 99 on the test, so that opens up all the citywides to you, and plus the district... G&T's are all good, so you rank them all, you get one, you know? There's like no ifs, ands, or buts." She went on to explain that if she had not got her daughter into a G&T program, she would have moved out to the suburbs because private school was not, financially, an option for her family and she lived in a failing school catchment area.

For parents like Cecelia who lived outside TCS's catchment and did not have the Gen Ed program as a "fallback," getting into a G&T program was sometimes the only public school option in the city that they found acceptable to escape their "failing" majority Black and Latino zoned school. This situation created stress and anxiety for parents to have their children score high enough on the G&T test to be "in their right place" with other families like their own in the G&T program. Rosie, a first grade G&T Defender who also lived outside of TCS's catchment, did not originally think her daughter could pass the G&T cutoff score, but explained that she had her tested for G&T because she had to give her that "chance." Rosie was totally surprised when her daughter's G&T test results came back, and she found out that she got a "98...she was really 98.5 but they round down. Like I said, it blew me away. It was like one of those...moments in parenting where you're like—the success. You're like, "My child is gifted"—and you know—I called my husband—and you're like, 'I'm doing something right, what am I doing?' Because it feels good because there's so many defeating moments in parenting." Rosie's quote points to how children's high G&T test scores get conflated with good parenting.

Therefore, for these nine G&T Defenders in the sample who test their children for G&T to give themselves better options in the system, once they get their child's G&T test score back, it validates their belief in their child's intelligence and ability, and gives them validation that they are "doing something right" in terms of parenting. And, if parents are lucky enough to get their children enrolled in the G&T program of their choice, they are also more likely to be satisfied with their child's placement and "buy into" the distinctions between programs. Lauren, an incoming Conflicted Follower to the school, explained that after the G&T test scores came back some of her friends were saying:

> Well, I don't know, if she got into Anderson [one of the G&T citywide schools] it would be great but she got a 99 and the younger sibling would only have to get a 97 but then, what would it be like if the class was mixed 99 and 97? But the day before the tests, they wouldn't say that. And you can't h elpi t.

As Lauren explained, even if parents do not entirely believe their child is gifted, feel badly about getting them tested so young, or are bothered by the lack of diversity in the G&T programs, all of their earlier misgivings go away once they get their child's test scores back.

Their sense of place is constructed by internalizing the G&T label that their children are given, which matches their advantaged position in society. As Jessica, a first grade Gen Ed Conflicted Follower who was currently testing her second child for G&T, replied, "I think if the kid is in G&T, they really like it. If you're not in G&T, there's a little bit of pining and sour grapes." She went on to explain that the G&T students are perceived to be smarter because they scored high enough to get into the program, and even though she tries not to "buy into" the labels in the school, especially since her first child is in the Gen Ed program, to a certain extent she and other parents do. Jessica explained:

> As much as I try not to buy into it, and also as much as I hope my kindergartner will get into G&T because I think she is, I think she is the kind of kid that focuses a lot, and she really wants to learn. So I try not to buy into

it, but I have to say that I do. There's a little bit that's like, oh yeah, you know, *my kids are good enough to be in G&T*. And I don't really believe it, but you know, there's two baskets, and I mean there's a [G&T] basket and there's the other [Gen Ed] basket, so.

Although parents said that the G&T status "shouldn't matter," once their child gets a top score on the test they "buy into" the G&T label anyway because, as illustrated in the next section, it "connotes a certain level of achievement" or "value" for parents to tell other parents that their child is G&T.

The "Status of Being Chosen" for G&T

Parents said that the G&T label is a "value" or status that matters to many parents; even though they also admitted "it shouldn't matter." This illustrates the contradictory attitudes that emerge when parents are constructing their sense of place within the structures. For example, when asked if parents talk about the possibility that the G&T program could be phased out in the future, Cecilia, a kindergarten G&T Defender responded, "It's not a topic that's come up a lot, at least within my class's parent body. I think that people are very attached to the idea. I think it would take a lot to let it go because, of course, it's like value, which is like what you say, yeah, my child's in public school, but she's in G&T and there's a lot of wealthy parents in that school and I know that it matters to them, even though it shouldn't." In other words, the G&T label is particularly important when they are telling other parents outside of the school which program their child is in because it connotes a certain level of status—thus, matching their privileged position in society.

On the other side, like Jessica said above, for the Gen Ed parents who got their children tested for G&T but did not get into TCS's G&T program, there was a little bit of putting down the G&T program simply because they could not have it. Therefore, from the Gen Ed parent's perspective, they sense that many G&T parents "buy into" or internalize the labels and categories in the school, like the status and exclusivity of the program, and act like their children are special or better than the other children because of their score on the G&T test.

When asked what was the most important thing in her school choice decision, Tara, a third grade Gen Ed Reconciler said that teacher quality was the most important thing, "because I think that's what makes the class, not the actual program overall." As a follow-up question, Tara was asked if her reason for choosing TCS was different than other parents in the school and she said, "Yes, I think they [G&T parents] like the idea of having a separate program. Feeling like their kid is smarter or whatever the perception or terminology they want to use. I think they like that." Domenica, a first grade Gen Ed Conflicted Follower, also pointed out that although her and her friends do not "buy into" the labels, most G&T parents in the school do: "They actually feel that their kids are gifted if they get into the program. It's this whole competition kind of feeling, and once you're in the school—like in our school, it becomes a little segregated." She went on to say that she has a problem with the name of the G&T program "because I think the parents and the kids do end up believing they are actually geniuses, that their kids are special compared to the other kids."

Lisa, a Gen Ed Reconciler in the kindergarten Gen Ed program, explained that once G&T parents enter the school, "it feels like they're part of the G&T program but not of the whole school. They make it really— there is a difference. 'Yeah, my kid's in the first grade *G&T* class' versus some other person who will say 'She's in first grade'. They really make the emphasis that it's not the same as the rest. But it's the parents, because the kids don't know that [at least in the younger grades]."

The parents with children in both programs were able to compare firsthand the academic and social differences between programs since they had experienced the two different sets of teachers, students, and parents. Melissa, a Savvy Negotiator with children in both programs, when asked if she's heard anyone critique the G&T program within the school said yes, that the principal would rather not have two programs, as well as some teachers who do not see a "need" to have a G&T program because it "causes more rift than anything else." Melissa goes on to say, "I'm sure there are some parents who would hate to see the G&T go." When asked which parents felt that way, she responded, "the parents who have children in the Gifted who would never consider putting them in the Gen Ed. But it's tough to know until you've been at the school for a long time and you know, or until you do the Gen Ed and you realize that it's not that big of a difference [academically]."

The G&T parents that Melissa is referring to, who would never consider putting their child in the Gen Ed, have those attitudes, according to Melissa, because they have no direct experience with the Gen Ed program, parents or students. The Gen Ed advantaged parents could sense that the G&T parents thought they were better or that their children were smarter compared to the Gen Ed families, which served to exacerbate the feeling of being second best in the school even, as will be shown in the following chapter, when parents tried to downplay the academic differences between programs.

The next chapter explores how parents are making sense of and adapting to the changing demographics in the Gen Ed program as it is becoming a more "acceptable option" for White and higher-income families. In the context of a school that enrolls advantaged White parents on both sides of the G&T/Gen Ed boundary line, parents develop contradictory attitudes between who they are, where they believe they belong, and where they and their children are placed in a segregated two-track school.

Chapter Four
How Parents Recreate and Reproduce the Boundaries

Alice is a White, upper-class mother with three children. She and her husband moved to TCS's neighborhood 14 years ago because they had friends there. Alice found out about the public schools because a woman in her apartment building "took the plunge" and sent her children to public schools and was really "happy." Growing up, Alice had attended excellent public schools in the Midwest and replies, "I really believe in the public school. I'm not a private school kind of person. I like the diversity. I like that the PTA and parents work really hard to provide extra enrichment kinds of programs...so that we can, you know, we feel like they're getting the things that they might not otherwise get in public schools."

Alice described other people in her social circle, including most of the parents at her children's preschool, as having a "knee jerk reaction that if you're in a certain income bracket, they didn't even consider public school." Nevertheless, she decided to enroll her oldest daughter in the G&T program at TCS and explained, "The people I knew who had gotten in [G&T] were really smart. They're probably on par as smart or smarter, at least at that time, than a lot of her friends from [preschool] who had gone to private school. So I thought I'm not losing anything as far as intelligence or how quickly these kids pick up on anything by being in a G&T program." Alice's daughter has since graduated from TCS and is now enrolled in middle school. She shared that when her daughter started at TCS there was only one other family in her apartment building that sent their child to public school, but now it's really changed and most people choose TCS over private school.

When it was time for her two younger sons to start kindergarten, Alice said she did not really consider other schools even though she was pretty sure they were not going to pass the G&T test because they were "totally disinterested" in the G&T workbook that she tried to practice with them. It ended up that her one son scored a 94 on the G&T test and because of sibling priority (from his sister), he was accepted into the G&T program for kindergarten. Her other son, however, did not make the 90th percentile score for siblings and was placed in the Gen Ed program for kindergarten. Alice had him retested and had made the switch for first grade.

When asked to describe the school, Alice explains that the two "programs, they really don't have different curriculum. It's just the pace maybe, the stage which they go through." She also explained that her kindergarten son's Gen Ed teacher was the same teacher that "my daughter had for kindergarten for G&T." According to Alice and other White Gen Ed parents, this particular teacher has taught both G&T and Gen Ed for kindergarten and teaches the "kindergarten class like a G&T class" regardless if it's Gen Ed. Alice says that the "whole make-up" of the Gen Ed class has changed a lot from when her daughter went through the program seven years ago because the White "neighborhood kids" did not want to go the Gen Ed route, and they did a lot of "busing in" from outside the district to fill those seats.

Alice makes a point to say that TCS was not a "neighborhood school that was going anywhere... [because] none of the neighborhood kids wanted to go there. It's not a wealthy enough environment like [the other disproportionately White neighborhood schools]... where those are in fairly high real estate areas where you got a middle-class population and everyone's fairly similar, and you know, they have parent involvement in 'spades' and 'bring in lots of money.' We don't have that many—we have a small group of parents who are involved. It's getting better, but you need that population base to really fill a public school that's going to be able to offer the extra stuff that the DOE is taking away. So that's what the G&T program did for [TCS], it brought in all the parents who wouldn't otherwise be there. And that's honestly I think why G&T started for many of these schools, it's to keep the parent base, the local parent base in the school... and no matter how much I like the parents in [my son's] Gen Ed class, and they're sweet, they're not really involved with raising money, for helping out, you know, at different functions at the school. I never see them."

Alice goes on to say that she likes that the school is "diverse" but that the "G&T classes are honestly not that diverse" especially in terms of "minority diversity," and it's just "too bad." When asked whether Black and Latino parents get their children tested for G&T, she responds by saying that "they just register for Gen Ed." She leads the G&T school tours, and the "people on the tours are the parents who have options... for G&T or private and want to consider all of their options." This points to how the G&T policy favors the most advantaged parents and sorts the least able out of the system. She attributes the reason for the Gen Ed parents of color not being involved in the school as a "culture" thing because it is not in their "mindset" to "go out and try to raise money for the school...it's just a different point of view."

The highly involved advantaged parents, on the other hand, include "some Gen Ed but primarily G&T" parents who are usually not working, "and look, in this city, it's very tough just to live in it, so they're probably slightly wealthier families...and they also have the skills, a certain skill set. You know, a lot of them went to college, grad school, the ones who are fantastic at a lot of these things are people who are lawyers, they have writing skills, you know, we have a lot of people from the arts, but they still have writing skills, they can write grants...you need a certain basic ability to be able to write...and you have to have—you have to have the time to do it and a desire to. You know, and just the realization that everything you do is helping your child...if you don't raise money our kids are not going to have all of these extras that are important." In this way, Alice's biggest "frustration" with the G&T and Gen Ed program at TCS is "the lack of parent involvement" and the lack of effort from other Gen Ed parents that you have to raise funds in the Gen Ed classes, which she believes is the key for "success" in the public system.

At the end of the interview, Alice explains how the school culture has changed now that more White, neighborhood families are choosing Gen Ed: "First of all, one of the rules is we don't talk about G&T versus Gen Ed in the school, you know, that there's a difference in the programs...or is your kid in Gen Ed? Is your kid in G&T? You know, you try to say what class they're in or whatever. You don't really talk about it with your child. You don't—because you try to minimize any sense of, you know, difference, especially with parents. If they're in the Gen Ed they're pretty sensitive. So we didn't really talk to people about did you have your child tested or what was their test score, and so that's—you know, I didn't really talk about that with families in the Gen Ed." She hopes "it's common sense. Why would you go around saying, 'My kid is da-da-da.' It gains you nothing except hostility."

Although Alice feels that the segregation between programs is "too bad" and she "appreciates" the diversity that her son experienced in the kindergarten Gen Ed classroom, she does not believe that the G&T program should be phased out. The problem is that "most of the people who are in G&T are not in the catchment...and the out of catchment kids are mostly all G&T people and those are the parents who are working to keep the standards up." She says, "Again, it's all economics and who comes to the school. We're in a—our catchment falls...the school has the parents who send their kids to private school and we have low income housing—you know, generally, they don't have extra income to put into the school, and the DOE is taking even more money out."

Thus, in a relatively short period of time, the distinctions between the G&T and Gen Ed programs shifted from one "based on skin color alone" to a more complicated overlap between the two programs, with the Gen Ed program attracting more advantaged, White families from the neighborhood to fill the Gen Ed seats. Instead of busing in Black and Latino students from outside the district to fill the Gen Ed seats, the school is busing in more White students across the district to fill the G&T seats. This demographic shift in the Gen Ed program is evidenced by the school's overall White student population increasing from 46 percent of the total in 2008 to 59 percent in 2014.[1] Meanwhile, the Black and Latino student population has decreased steadily in the school from 48 percent to 25 percent. As more seats in the Gen Ed program are being filled by White, advantaged students from the neighborhood, fewer seats are available for Black and Latino students who live outside of TCS's attendance zone (see Table 1.5 in chapter one).

This chapter, like the prior two chapters, shows how contradictory attitudes develop within advantaged, White parents in different ways depending on their child's grade level and placement within the structures. In this moment of recreating the boundaries, parents considered the "diversity" in the Gen Ed classrooms (meaning more White students) as a "positive thing" in the school and a sign that the school could (and should) phase out the G&T program. Regardless of the positive benefits of "diversity" in the younger grades, the boundary between G&T and Gen Ed in the upper grades is still being reproduced. White Gen Ed parents who said they would support a move by the school or the system to phase out the G&T program altogether, still retest their children for G&T to give their children what they consider to be the "best" education alongside similarly advantaged families like their own.

Meanwhile, these same parents with children in the Gen Ed program who are retesting for G&T *also* say that the G&T program is still "needed" at TCS in order to attract the right "kind" of "G&T" parents to the school (e.g., as Alice explained, advantaged, White parents who live outside TCS's catchment). They realize that without these G&T parents, the school might not be able to attract highly involved parents who donate time and money to the school, which also improves the reputation of the school.

In fact, the G&T Defenders in the younger grades (see chapter three), who internalized their child's gifted label, were the most adamant about not wanting the G&T program to "go away" because they thought their child's G&T placement was appropriate. G&T parents who lived outside of the catchment also did not want the G&T program to be phased out. They worried that if there was no G&T program they would not be able to go to TCS anymore because they were not zoned for the school (which was also a concern brought up by incoming G&T parents at the G&T school tour). They rationalized that their children were being exposed to school-level diversity and were concerned about the segregation that still existed within the school and across the programs (see chapter two), but still did not want to see the G&T program phased out. Thus, contradictory attitudes emerge when they simultaneously "see the vision" of being "one school" instead of two should the G&T program be phased out, yet they do not want to "see the G&T program go" because it attracts high-quality families.

This chapter also provides evidence of the multiple ways that advantaged White parents adapt to the changing boundary lines in a school where White students are being placed into two different hierarchical programs. Parents with children in the G&T programs, in particular, developed strategies to make all parents in the school feel like they were part of the same school instead of two separate ones. Alice, along with other G&T parents, spoke about a silence or ambivalence about the two programs in the school and a tendency to "downplay the differences" by saying that the curriculum is the same in both programs or the teacher matters more than the program. As Alice described, they follow these "unspoken rules" in order to be "sensitive" to advantaged White Gen Ed parents (especially parents with children in both programs) and to hide the existence of the two programs from their children. While some parents follow these rules, particularly parents who have been in the school the longest and are critical of the structures, others do not. One upper-class kindergarten G&T Defender named Claire said, "When the new kindergarten parents come in," they are a little "naïve" and will openly ask other parents which program they are in and talk about it in front of their children. She said that there is a "political correctness that you don't ask that question" because "you want to say 'we're all in the same school.'"

The school itself has also adapted to the changing demographics, as one parent said, by "working hard to make it an equitable place and make it good for all the students" (see also chapter five). As Alice points out, the principal moved one of the "best" G&T teachers in the school into a kindergarten Gen Ed classroom. She felt she most likely made this decision to appease White incoming parents into the Gen Ed program as well as parents with children in both programs, some of whom had the same teacher for their older G&T children. In fact, Lisa, a kindergarten Gen Ed

Reconciler, said that having that teacher in Gen Ed "helped the morality of the school knowing that there was a good teacher in there."

Yet, even when parents attempt to downplay the academic differences between programs and say they appreciate the diversity that their children are being exposed to in the Gen Ed classrooms, the parents with children in the Gen Ed program still reproduce the boundaries between programs when they decide to prep and retest their children for G&T. According to parents, most of the retesters eventually switch to G&T or leave the school. This becomes an increasingly important issue to advantaged White parents as their children get older and enter the grade levels in which the Gen Ed program becomes more non-White. At the same time, by minimizing the academic differences, G&T parents question whether what they are getting is any different than what the Gen Ed are getting.

Unlike other disproportionately White neighborhood schools with no "projects," parents believe that as long as TCS enrolls a critical mass of lower-income students of color, as well as more advantaged students like theirs, they "need" two separate programs within the school to keep the boundaries intact. Ultimately, it is through advantaged parents' boundary maintenance that we can uncover the contradictions in their sense making between what they say they want and need in a school, where they believe they belong, and where their children are actually placed in the system.

Recreating the Boundaries: How Advantaged Families Who Choose the Gen Ed Program Are Changing What the Boundary Line Means

According to parents, even though the G&T program remains majority White, the segregated atmosphere between the two programs in TCS has slowly been breaking down over time because the Gen Ed program is admitting more White students from the neighborhood. This demographic shift in the Gen Ed program is seen as a positive development in the school. Prior to 2008, students were seemingly placed in G&T and Gen Ed "based on skin color alone." White, advantaged parents who are now choosing the Gen Ed program, including the parents with children in both programs, are recreating what the boundary line means. The Gen Ed has transitioned from one that historically enrolled Black and Latino children, to a Gen Ed program that started to enroll "successful" White "neighborhood" families and younger siblings of G&T families living outside of the catchment.

As noted in earlier chapters, *before* this demographic shift occurred, the racial segregation was very stark between programs. According to parents' accounts, enrollment in the K-2 Gen Ed classrooms was roughly 30 percent White[2] and growing, as more and more White parents made the choice to enroll their children in their neighborhood public school even if their child did not get into the G&T program. As parents explained, the sharp racial distinctions between the G&T and Gen Ed programs for students in grades 3–5 remain, since White families prep and retest their Gen Ed children until most of them eventually switch to the G&T program or leave the school.

G&T parents in the older grades said they never would have chosen the Gen Ed program for their children when they were in kindergarten because of the segregation. Tanya, a first grade Gen Ed Reconciler who lives in TCS's attendance boundaries, described how older women from her neighborhood told her that TCS was not a place where you would have sent your [White] children back in the 1980s or 1990s because it was a segregated Black and Latino school. Similarly, in an informal conversation with a White parent who lives a block away from TCS, she said that she "wished" she could have sent her daughter to kindergarten at TCS back in 2003 because of the location, but it was not an option because students were segregated in the G&T and Gen Ed programs. According to parents of children currently enrolled in the school, the diversity in the Gen Ed program is seen as a positive development of the school and a sign that the G&T program could (and should) be phased out now.

"The Recession Did a Lot for That": The Changing Boundary in the Gen Ed Program

As described in chapter one, there are three main reasons why the Gen Ed program is starting to enroll more White, advantaged parents from the catchment area: there is overcrowding in the most popular, disproportionately White schools due to increasing family gentrification (especially schools A and B in Table 1.3, chapter one); the recession took a toll on household income; and the change in the G&T admissions policy. In addition, because there is an increased demand from the White neighborhood families into the Gen Ed program, TCS does not need to bus in Black and Latino students from outside the district to fill the Gen Ed seats.

Dana, a first grade G&T Savvy Negotiator, described why the Gen Ed program is starting to enroll more White families from the neighborhood: "The recession did a lot for that. A lot of people who would be sending their kids to private schools didn't. And then also a lot of people who would be moving out to the suburbs didn't because they were worried about their jobs and they couldn't sell their apartments, so it was a very different dynamic between the two programs."

In fact, starting around 2008, the economic recession hit New York City. According to parents, like Dana above, and the popular press, the bursting of the housing market bubble and the resulting economic crisis caused many *City Limits* parents to choose public over private schools.[3] This was the case not only for kindergarten admission, but also some upper-class private school parents, like Lillian in chapter three, started to enroll their youngest children into public schools because they could no longer afford private school tuition for all of their children anymore. This speaks to the changing attitudes of parents who thought they would choose private school or G&T programs and instead decided to "take a leap of faith" with TCS's Gen Ed program because other parents like them were making similar choices.

Kathy, an upper-class G&T Defender with a daughter in fourth grade, described her "whole take on the G&T program," which, she said, "people can be very critical of, but [TCS] was a failing school... in the middle of the projects that no one would send their children to before the G&T was started." She describes the demographic changes from when her daughter started in 2007 till now, and gives credit to the White G&T parents for making the school better and attracting neighborhood families:

> You look at the classes, when I started and when my daughter started, you could walk out of the classroom just based on skin color alone and know what class you were in. And that is the thing that none of us liked that was an issue with the school. But now it's not that way anymore, and it's a real accomplishment for the people that started the G&T program, because the transition happened after me. I mean, you know, I wouldn't have gone, I wouldn't have sent my daughter there to school, if there wasn't a G&T program. And now, by two years later, it has completely changed.

As a result of the demographic change, since 2008 the Gen Ed program has become a far more acceptable option for White, "upper, middle-class" families. But, as Jessica, a first grade Gen Ed Conflicted Follower, made clear, the "Gen Ed program itself" is not becoming more "acceptable" to White families in the catchment area, the "demographics are becoming more acceptable. I really think that's what it was." This points to the relationship between race and class and perceptions of public school quality when choosing schools and programs within them.

This new "diversity" in the Gen Ed classrooms in kindergarten through second grade, meaning more White students, is seen as a "positive thing" in the school because the segregation is diminishing. On one hand, parents with children in the Gen Ed program hoped the school would become a "true" neighborhood school that attracted more neighborhood (meaning

White) families and the G&T program would be phased out. Ironically, these same parents all strive to be in the G&T program themselves because they want to give their children what is considered the "best" education with similarly advantaged families like their own.

The Simultaneous Desire for a G&T Placement and for the G&T Program to Be Phased Out

As explained in chapter two, the advantaged Gen Ed parents in the younger grades stress the benefits of exposing their children to "real life" diversity, more because their actual classrooms are "diverse." For example, Tessa who is a Conflicted Follower with children in both programs, talks about her daughters' experience in the Gen Ed classroom. She said, "I like the diversity that my kids are experiencing, and not just ethnic but socioeconomic as well...And I think the kids are learning from—learning much more about different cultures and everything and they love it."

Although Tessa retested her daughters for G&T, she also questioned the reason for having the G&T program remain in place when she explained that "the climate has changed and you can have successful families in the Gen Ed, what's the advantage to having [the G&T] then?" She ended up getting her two daughters switched from the Gen Ed program that she liked so much because of the diversity, into the majority White G&T program because she thought her children were "bright kids" and wanted to provide them with the "best education that you can...within your means."

Tessa and other parents with children in the Gen Ed program embody contradictory attitudes. They are torn between their beliefs in diversity and phasing out the G&T program, but they also want to give their children what they consider to be the "best" education "within your means," which in this case is the majority White G&T program (that they also want to phase out). These contradictory attitudes emerge over whether G&T programs should be phased out or not because there are more White parents in the school who have had experience in both programs. These White parents do not see much of a difference academically between the G&T and Gen Ed classrooms—at least in the younger grades. This is contrary to the tracking/de-tracking research that found that higher-income, more educated White parents will vehemently oppose de-tracking reforms.[4]

Additionally, White Gen Ed parents question why TCS continues to offer a G&T program since there are more advantaged families from the catchment choosing the Gen Ed program now. They argue that the reason the DOE introduces G&T programs in certain schools is to attract middle-class White parents into the public schools. Because that is now starting to happen in the Gen Ed program, they no longer need the G&T program. These same parents believe that some educational systems "need" G&T programs because they are considered "failing" schools and they must "bring certain classes of people" into the school to make it better. At TCS, however, the demographics are becoming more similar between programs so the parents believed that they could phase out the G&T program. In total, 73 percent of all parents, or 30 out of 41, would support the phasing out of the G&T program. The parents who did not think the G&T program should be phased out are the G&T parents in the younger grades and those who live outside of TCS's zone because they have little experience with the Gen Ed program. But the majority did not believe the G&T program was "necessary" at TCS anymore, as Jessica, a first grade Gen Ed Conflicted Follower, explained:

> It's not that I'm against if they have gifted and talented programs. I just think that for our school, it's not necessary. The socioeconomic demographic of our school is so similar, there's just not that much difference between these kids. We're not trying to bring certain classes of people into this school to make it better. They used to have to do that. They don't anymore because that's who it is now, that's what the make-up, the natural make-up of the school is now.

A kindergarten Gen Ed Reconciler, Lisa, also said she did not see any "reason" for having the G&T program anymore:

> I think the reason for it has gone away now, like maybe when the schools were more diverse and you really wanted your children to be in a well-behaved class where the kids were more focused, then maybe it made a difference. But I don't think the reason for it being offered now, other than that they might lose some kids. But you know, if my kids do better in Gen Ed, if their classes are representative of what the whole school would look like, it would be fine.

The students that these parents said the school might "lose" are the G&T families who lived outside the catchment area, which is one of the main reasons that parents cite for keeping the G&T program. Lisa went on to say that "if the purpose of having a G&T program is to attract middle-class or upper-middle-class families into public schools, then it's 'working.' But if the purpose is to give advanced students an accelerated classroom environment, then it's not doing its job probably because the curriculum is the same." What parents do not mention are the "other" children they are losing when neighborhood White families are taking all of the Gen Ed seats—for example, the Black and Latino students from outside the district who used to be bused in. Over time, then, the G&T policy is "working" since the school is changing from a racially and socioeconomically diverse school to a disproportionately White and higher-income one.

Thus, Gen Ed parents like Jessica who advocate for the G&T program to be phased out because it is not serving a "purpose" in the school contradict themselves. Advantaged families are starting to choose the Gen Ed program and there is no "advanced specialty curriculum." Yet, they still retest their children for the G&T program anyway because that is where they feel they belong, in what's perceived to be the "best" education alongside other similarly advantaged parents like them. In this way, because there are two hierarchical programs to choose from in this school, White parents want to reconcile their placement by getting their children in the high-status G&T program that fits their privileged position, even if it contradicts with their belief in phasing the G&T program out.

These parents with children in the Gen Ed program also seemed hopeful about the TCS becoming a true neighborhood school, like school A or B, since it is attracting more "local" neighborhood families (e.g., not bused in) to the Gen Ed program. In fact, parents would talk about how the segregation between programs is getting better in the younger grades, which they thought was a positive development of the school. For instance, Elaine, a third grade Gen Ed Reconciler, compared how segregated the Gen Ed classrooms in her grade were to the Gen Ed classrooms in the younger grades, saying that more diversity in the younger grades is a good thing: "We kind of got the tail end of the bad part of it, I think we're the last grade that it's really, really split. I have a very good friend whose daughter is in second grade in Gen Ed and it's much more mixed in her Gen Ed than it is in mine. I mean that's good for the future parents that are coming in and the future kids."

For G&T parents in the upper grades, they also see the diversity in the Gen Ed program as a "positive thing" in the school because they are concerned about the stark segregation that they are experiencing between programs. Melody, a G&T Defender who has two children in the G&T program said that the "division" that the G&T has "caused in the older grades is not a positive thing." She believes "in the future" that there will be more White, advantaged families "who actually want to live here to be in the catchment." She said, "Like our apartment is going up for sale in two weeks. I'm advertising [TCS] and I'm seeing that as a positive thing, that it's in this catchment for a Gen Ed spot."

Chrissy, a G&T fourth grade Savvy Negotiator, compared TCS when she started there five years ago and now:

> When we first started...it was much different. There was a clear divide between the G&T and the Gen Ed. Frankly, it was a concern for us. It seemed like the haves and the have-nots. Throughout the years, however, it has changed. So the Gen Ed now in our particular school—in kindergarten, in first grade, even in second grade, are children that typically would have been in the G&T. They're the upper middle class. [This change] is a great thing for our school though, because we have parents that won't have that feeling of segregation, you have parents in both classes that are really pulling together to make the school a better place. So I'm thrilled for those lower classes. Didn't happen for my daughter, but it is—I believe it's a much better thing.

Although many G&T parents in the older grades thought the diversity in the Gen Ed classrooms "was a great thing" for their school because segregation between programs was diminishing, they did not necessarily want the G&T program to be phased out, especially if they lived outside of the catchment area. In other words, these parents still felt that they and their children were "in their right place" in the social hierarchy. They believed that the G&T program, as Melody claimed, "Still has its place" in the school. In fact, Melody said that when she was choosing kindergarten programs for her children, she never would have chosen the Gen Ed program at TCS especially for her oldest son in fourth grade because "there would not have been any blue eyed, blond hair children in the Gen Ed program before that."

There is also the issue of the status and advantages that parents perceive the G&T label will provide for their children now (in terms of peer effects and peer environment) and for future middle school and high school placements. When Tanya, a first grade Gen Ed Reconciler, was asked if she believes the G&T program will be phased out, she breaks down the two sides of the debate:

> I think it's a perception. If people think that without a G&T, my kid's going to then be on a bad road all the way through—the way that the New York Public Schools are set up, the fact that you have to bid at middle school and high school, the way the system is set up I think the perception is if the school doesn't have G&T, my kid's never going to get into a good middle school. I don't know. But if they phase it out and then the school has a good enough reputation just as a stellar school on its own, I don't think it's a problem phasing it out. It's really—everybody just wants the best thing for their kids, everybody just wants the better middle school and

the better high school. The way the system is set up, it just breeds this sort of weirdness.

Parents with children in the Gen Ed program seemed hopeful that TCS would be a true neighborhood school with no G&T program in the future—only accepting "local" students from the catchment area. They were also skeptical, however, that the G&T program would be phased out because, as Alice describes in the introductory vignette, it attracts the right "kind" of G&T parent to the school, from outside of the catchment area, who is highly involved and makes the school "better." In addition, they argued that there are still Gen Ed parents from the "project housing" sending their children to the Gen Ed program, therefore the G&T "serves a purpose" academically.

For these parents, they believed that as long as TCS enrolls a critical mass of lower-income students of color living within the catchment area, as well as more advantaged students like their own, they "need" the G&T program to keep the boundaries intact between "us" (advantaged parents) and "them" (lower-income parents of color who enroll their children in the Gen Ed program). Because of this boundary, White, advantaged parents in the Gen Ed program felt like they were in the second tier program if they were not with the similarly advantaged families in the G&T program.

Adapting to the Changing Boundaries in the School: "You Try to Minimize Any Sense of Difference between Programs, Especially with the Parents"

As a result of the changing demographics in the Gen Ed program, parents said that the school's culture has changed to be more sensitive to this new group of advantaged, White Gen Ed families. This is particularly the case for the parents with children in both programs so that they do not feel like they are in the "second tier" program. Because of these demographic changes, parents have created unspoken rules to try to "minimize any sense of difference" between the two programs. They follow these unspoken rules to diffuse the tension between the two sets of advantaged, mostly White parents who have their children in either, or both, hierarchical program(s). Additionally, they explained that they do not want their children to find out about the two different programs because, as described in chapter three, they do not want them to feel superior or inferior based on their G&T and Gen Ed labels.

Besides not talking about the two different programs, advantaged parents in the G&T and Gen Ed program will downplay the academic differences between programs by saying that the curriculum is the same or the teacher matters more than the program. G&T parents downplay the differences to relieve the tension between the two sets of advantaged parents within the school. The Gen Ed parents, on the other hand, downplay them to argue that the G&T program is no longer needed if the curriculum is the same and the demographics are becoming more similar between programs.

The Silence about the Two Programs within the School—
"If They're in Gen Ed They're Pretty Sensitive"

A strategy that TCS parents used to "minimize any sense of difference" between programs was not talking about which program their child was in or not discussing G&T test results, especially in front of their children. They felt it was better for their children not to know and it simply caused tension between the parents. Parents described how some incoming families will come in and be "kind of naïve" by just asking other parents which program they are in. There is a kind of political correctness that parents quickly learn, however, to make everyone feel like "we're all in the same school." Ironically, parents want a G&T placement and will prep and retest to get one if they originally get placed in the Gen Ed, but at the same time do not like the "division" and the feelings of superiority or inferiority that this two-track system creates in the school. There is also a perception that some teachers and administrators "don't like the fact that there's Gen Ed and G&T education." As a result, G&T is not talked about in the school and as one parent put it, "there's an ambivalence about the idea of G&T rather than an embrace of it."

As Alice explained in the introductory vignette, "One of the rules is we don't talk about G&T versus Gen Ed in the school, you know, that there's a difference in the programs. *You don't say, is your kid in Gen Ed? Is your kid in G&T? You know, you try to say what class they're in or whatever.* You don't really talk about it with your child. You don't, because you try to minimize any sense of, you know, difference, especially with parents." It was interesting that when Alice was asked later in the interview to talk more about the "rule" that you're not supposed to say "G&T" and "Gen Ed" in the school, she said, "Well it isn't a rule." She clarified that it's "unspoken" between parents. When I asked her how she knew about this "unspoken rule," she replied: "Somebody once said to me a long time ago, don't talk about it. I mean, you hope it's common sense. Why would you go around saying, 'My kid is da-da-da.' It gains you nothing except hostility."

While observing two TCS parents meeting each other for the first time outside of school, they used their child's grade level and room number as a code for what program they were in, for example "I'm [Cecelia] and my daughter is in K103." Outsiders and children who do not know which classroom is G&T or Gen Ed would not know the difference, but to insiders in the school, the parents are simply using code language to tell other parents which program they are in because they all know that "K103" is a G&T class. During the interview with Cecelia, she brought up the topic of the school's "culture" and said that she's "amazed" at the "distinctions" between the two programs. She explained, "Like I've noticed that a lot of the parents don't want to talk about it in front of the kids about who's in G&T and who's not and I think that there's at least a branch of the parent body that wants to eliminate it, but I don't know how that's going to go down." Cecelia said that it's not only parents in Gen Ed that would like to see the G&T program "go," it's some G&T parents as well: "Like there's a woman that we ride the bus with a lot, and her kids are in G&T, and she's definitely like, whenever we talk about it, we have to talk about it in code because she doesn't really want her kids to know about the difference, and then she was saying that eventually, she thinks it [the G&T program] will be eliminated, and she seems supportive of that." This type of activism by some parents is a sign that parents would support a G&T phaseout, even when their own children are in that program.

At the G&T school tour, one of the incoming G&T parents asked if children find out if they are in the G&T program. A PTA mother who has children in both programs, got up and adamantly responded that "parents outside the school use that language and ask whether your child is in G&T or not, and you say please don't use that language in front of my child, don't name the program, just say [the teacher's name]." Parents do not want their children to find out about the "difference," as Cecelia mentioned above, because of the feelings of inferiority and superiority that the labels connote, which parents worried could also affect their academic self-concept (see chapter three). Jennifer, a first grade G&T parent, described what was happening inside the school since the demographic shift has occurred:

> There seems to be a wind blowing—a vibe in the air—that some parents don't like the idea—they recognize that there is this division in the school and they don't like that. Some administrators don't like the fact that there's Gen Ed and G&T education. As a result of that, it's not talked about... I think people downplay it because there's a lot of kids that begin in Gen Ed, test and test and test to get into G&T.... So it's not something that people talk about. I never even hear the phrase in the school. People don't use it. So there's no sense of, "Let's have a meeting of all the G&T teachers and parents."

In fact, G&T and Gen Ed parents will further downplay the differences by saying that the curriculum is the same or the teacher quality is similar across programs—providing more evidence that what parents are looking for is not a G&T program per se. They simply prefer to be around similarly advantaged parents. Building off the findings in chapter three, the interview data shows that parents socially construct what the "best" education is for their children by where they believe they belong in this segregated two-track system than it is any objective assessment of the curriculum and teaching available in each of the two programs.

"The Curriculum Is Exactly the Same" in Both Programs

One way that TCS parents try to minimize the differences between programs and/or argue that the G&T program should be phased out is by saying that academically the two programs are similar because the curriculum is the same. The school choice consultant that many of these parents hire to help them navigate the school choice process, explained that out of all the schools that offer G&T programs, "[TCS's] G&T parents have been the most vocal in terms of saying 'I'm not sure what my kids are getting compared to the kids next door in the Gen Ed, what's making this a G&T program?'... They don't want the Gen Ed to sort of be the stepchild. But in doing so, they've made it less convincing to the families in G&T that they are getting something different by being in G&T."

The interviews with the G&T Defenders, in particular, showed how frustrated they were that there was "nothing specific to the G&T curriculum at [TCS]," especially compared to the citywide G&T schools that apparently work a grade or two ahead, like the "highly gifted" and coveted Hunter, Nest, or Anderson. This is probably due to the fact that the NYCDOE offers a vague definition of the purpose of G&T programs: "G&T programs aim to deliver accelerated, rigorous, and specialized instruction, aligned to Common Core Learning Standards... [that] supports the needs of exceptional students."[5] Some thought that their child could be challenged more, but there was no way to do that with the standardized NYCDOE curriculum, for example, the districtwide *Everyday Math* curriculum, and no specialized teachers to help the advanced students move ahead.

When asked what the difference is academically between the two programs, Dana, who has two children in the G&T program, replied,

> They have the same curriculum, they have the same workbooks. They're supposed to—the G&T, they expect them to go faster and go a little deeper,

but they're not working a grade or two ahead. Whereas at Anderson, they're expected to go a grade ahead in math and if you're not working a grade ahead in math, you get a tutor. Whereas at [TCS], if you could work a grade ahead in math, there's no opportunity to, which is a little like (laughs), I'm like take the five kids who can work a grade ahead and let them. But there's no reason for doing that, which I find a little—it would be nice to lett hem.

Tessa, who is a Gen Ed parent, just got her two daughters into the G&T for next year. She explained that she thinks the G&T goes into a little more depth than the Gen Ed program and that it's "more about the people that you're surrounding yourself with" than the curriculum. Tessa added that, "it would certainly be my hope" that her children would be more challenged in the G&T program, but she questioned, "If it doesn't, what would be the point of it?"

Kathy a fourth grade G&T Defender, who does a lot of school tours said that incoming parents will ask about the "G&T / Gen Ed mix and what do you think of that?" Her answer to parents is: "The curriculum is exactly the same [in G&T]. There is no advanced specialty curriculum. But what happens is that if everybody in [the G&T] classroom immediately nods their head when you say 'Henry Hudson was the first guy in Manhattan,' then you're able to move on to discuss what was life like on the boat with Henry Hudson, do you see?... but if you stop for behavioral reasons because somebody doesn't get it, you have to stop. To me, that's all you're getting out of Gifted and Talented." According to Kathy, G&T and Gen Ed students are learning the same things, but the pace is faster in G&T because there are fewer disruptions in the G&T class. Therefore, parents often spoke about peer effects and classroom environment, in this case in terms of student behavior and range of academic ability, as reasons why they strove to be in G&T.[6]

G&T parents want their child in the G&T program largely because of who else is in the classroom, not because of the curriculum, which is the same in G&T and Gen Ed. Coincidently, this is the same reason that Gen Ed parents give for retesting for the G&T program. Beatrice, a first grade Gen Ed Conflicted Follower, pointed out that the "biggest reason that you want your kid in the G&T program" is because of the "behavior problems" in the Gen Ed classrooms. She also thought that the separation between programs feeds the perception that G&T is getting something better, when in reality, she said, "the curriculum is the exact same." But, she noted:

> The perception of G&T and Gen Ed is night and day. And they don't ever intermingle in projects, Gen Ed and G&T, which I think is a mistake if the

curriculum is the same. The kids have no involvement with one another, so you're creating this perception with the kids and with the parents especially that they're doing something completely different when in reality they're not.... my feeling is if the curriculum is the same, why are you wasting all of this money on this "special program" when it's all the same supposedly?

Thus, for parents like Beatrice who have children in the Gen Ed program, contradictory attitudes emerge when they are critical of offering a G&T program that is not that different academically, but still retest their children to get into the G&T program that they say is "all the same."

In addition, parents with children in both programs agreed that there is no difference between programs when they compare their children's G&T and Gen Ed homework. Margaret, an upper-class Savvy Negotiator who could compare her older G&T son's kindergarten homework with her younger daughter's homework in Gen Ed, said, "What [my son] did in his G&T class, he had a notebook with these certain assignments. You know, very New York City programmed. [My daughter's] doing the exact same stuff, [in the Gen Ed] the exact same stuff, down to the same poems where they have to cut out and glue and circle the rhyming words and underline the verbs. It's all the exact same stuff." Even though they are doing "the exact same stuff" in Gen Ed, Margaret still decided to get her daughter retested for G&T because of the negative stigma of the Gen Ed label. Therefore, no matter how much parents tried to downplay the differences between programs, they still felt that the G&T program is the "better" program because of the people enrolled there. They retested their children for the G&T program because it is where they felt they belonged.

A fourth grade G&T Savvy Negotiator named Caitlyn could not explain what was different between the two programs in terms of the curriculum. She even argued that in some cases the teacher matters more than the program. She replied:

> I don't think [the curriculum] is [different] at all, because I remember asking, "Well, is it accelerated?" No, "Is it more in-depth?" I don't really know that it's that different, frankly.... Because when I've observed some of the Gen Ed classes, they're going very in-depth into things depending on the teacher. And they have some duds, but it's more because they have teachers that they can't get rid of frankly who have been there a long time, but they're terrible teachers. But they're in the G&T and the Gen Ed.

Thus, another way parents attempt to minimize the differences between programs is to say that sometimes the teacher matters more than the program since teacher quality varies across programs. Some parents, though, still thought the G&T teachers tend to be the better teachers in the school.

The Teacher Matters More Than the Program—"It's Not the Classroom, It's the Teacher that's Leading It"

As Caitlyn explained above, parents claim that sometimes which teacher you get is more important than the program because there are good and bad teachers in both programs. One teacher, in particular, was often discussed to emphasize that point. She used to teach G&T but now teaches Gen Ed in kindergarten because the principal intentionally moved her. Lisa said that moving that teacher "helped the morality of the school knowing that there was a great teacher in there... [my son's] teacher used to be a G&T teacher but she's Gen Ed now. The way she describes her teaching method is that, although it's a Gen Ed classroom, she teaches them as if it's G&T." This "phenomenal" teacher told Gen Ed parents that she used to teach G&T and still teaches her class that way, thus making parents feel a little better about their child's placement—at least for kindergarten. When asked for her opinion about the biggest difference that stands out between the two programs, Violet who is a Savvy Negotiator with children in both programs, stated: "I think it solely depends on the teacher because everything in each program is teacher-driven. And I have to say—my younger son is in the Gen Ed program, his teacher used to teach G&T and it solely depends on if they challenge them when they need it... So it's not the classroom, it's the teacher that's leading it."

Tara, who is a third grade Gen Ed Reconciler, explained that she retested her daughter for G&T every year because she felt pressure to do so because the G&T students are perceived to be getting a better education. The children are smarter and better behaved, and so on. She retested her daughter because other parents like her were retesting, even though she replied, "I was really happy with Gen Ed, I felt that she was getting a great education and she had great teachers. The teachers—one of her teachers did teach G&T before she taught her class and she was a phenomenal teacher. She went up five reading levels. So it really depends on the teachers." Although she was "happy" with the quality of education in Gen Ed, she retested her daughter so she could feel like she was in her "right place" given her advantaged background. Other parents explained that there used to be a "clear divide" between the good and bad teachers in the G&T and Gen Ed. But, as parents made clear, the new principal changes the teachers around every year. Colleen, who is a Conflicted Follower, with a kindergarten child being taught by a Gen Ed teacher, mistakenly said at the beginning of the interview that her son was in the kindergarten *G&T program* at TCS. After a couple of questions, however, she realized her mistake. She explained, "[My son's] teacher...used to be a G&T teacher but she's Gen Ed now. The way she describes her teaching method is that, although it's a Gen Ed classroom, she teachers them as if it's G&T. That's what I meant to say, sorry."

Advantaged, White parents from the neighborhood, including the parents with older children who had this teacher when she used to teach in the G&T program, requested her and felt better about sending their children into the kindergarten Gen Ed classroom if they got her. Parents downplay the academic differences and admit that there is no difference in the G&T curriculum. They even admit that some Gen Ed teachers are "good." Yet, they continue to spend hundreds of dollars on test prepping and retest every year to get into the so-called better G&T program simply to be surrounded by similarly advantaged parents and students.

It was also clear that however hard parents tried to hide the existence of the two programs from their children, according to parents, students eventually figure out about the two programs within the school. Parents said what stands out to their children the most are the racial distinctions and behavior problems that separate the G&T from the Gen Ed. Racialized tracking practices, as Karolyn Tyson writes, "influence students' perceptions of the link between race and achievement, their self-perceptions of ability, how they view one another, and where they think they and others belong."[7] At TCS, even when parents attempt to downplay the differences between programs and the principal switches teachers around, the categories and distinctions that are maintained between programs cause parents with children in the Gen Ed program to feel out of place in the race- and class-based hierarchy.

The Distinction Still Remains: "Why Are All the Brown-Skinned Kids in the Other Class?"

A concern that kept repeating itself during parent interviews was that many of the White advantaged G&T and Gen Ed parents did not want their children to find out about the two different academic programs in the school. As demonstrated in chapter three, G&T parents do not want their children to feel special or superior to the Gen Ed students. Alternatively, the Gen Ed parents or parents with children in both programs do not want their child (or themselves) to be stigmatized for being in the lower-status program. Even though the boundary line between programs is shifting now to include more White families in the Gen Ed category (in grades K-2), the racial segregation still remains in grades 3–5 because these same

White families are retesting their children for G&T. Both sets of White G&T and Gen Ed parents were bothered by the segregation and perception of difference that still remains between programs, especially when their own children realize where they are placed within the hierarchy.

Denise, a first grade Gen Ed Conflicted Follower, said the biggest distinction that still remains between programs is the level of diversity (meaning a mix of racial/ethnic backgrounds): "I kinda feel like when you're standing in the playground and they bring down the first grade classes, and you watch them come down, *the G&T classes are a much less diverse group of kids than the Gen Ed class.* Clearly, that's the most visible thing." The "visible" differences between programs still exist, even though there are more White students being placed into Gen Ed, because the G&T program remains majority White and parents retest for G&T. For instance, Kelly, an Incoming Kindergarten Gen Ed parent said about getting her son into the G&T program, "Yes, I would have liked him to get into a G&T program, but he's going to be fine. He's a smart kid—he's going to do fine wherever he goes, especially because he has parents that are supportive. I've heard some mixed reviews as the grades get older. Like, after third grade I've heard it starts to get a little bit—I guess people move out or whatever? I don't know why, but one of the parents told me that it starts to get a little bit questionable.... There's fewer kids in the program that make it as good."

Betsy, an upper class second grade G&T Savvy Negotiator, whose youngest son was in the kindergarten and first grade Gen Ed program before switching over to G&T, explained that retesting for G&T is a "problem that exists in the school" because "people do what I did and they'll send their kids to the Gen Ed program for kindergarten, for first grade, for second grade, but we haven't really had—and maybe this is changing, I hope so—those families stay through the upper grades. They tend to leave, either to switch over to the G&T or maybe leave the city or maybe go to a different school." Betsy said you can just see the difference between classrooms because "there's a lot more diversity in the lower grades than there is in the upper grades. And by diversity, I mean like there's more White kids." Betsy implied that because White parents do not want to be the minority in the Gen Ed classrooms in the upper grades, they retest for G&T until they eventually get in, leave the city, or go to a different school.

Ironically, White advantaged parents strove to be in the G&T program and prepped and tested (and retested) their children because that's where they felt they belonged, but did not want their children to know about the two different academic programs in the school. This is tied to their contradictory attitudes in terms of who they are (e.g., someone who believes in diversity and is concerned about the segregation and the G&T label), where they believe they belong (e.g., with the other parents and students like them in the higher status G&T program) and where they are placed in the segregated system. As described above, some parents will even use code language in front of their children in order for them to not hear the G&T and Gen Ed labels used. As one mother said, it's a little "idealistic" to think that students do not realize where they are placed in the system especially when the racial segregation still remains. These students are getting tutored to take the tests, and some parents still talk about it in front of their children.

At the G&T school tour, incoming G&T parents also seemed concerned that their children would figure out which program they were in. The principal and the PTA parents leading the school tour assured them that students do not know about the two programs until they are older. In fact, the G&T parent giving the school tour said that her son did not figure it out until fourth grade.

The majority of parents were considerably more skeptical. They believed their children would figure out which program they are in early on, especially because first and second grade students have to retest for G&T within their own Gen Ed classrooms and so many of the children are being prepped for the G&T tests—sometimes by professional tutors. Rosie, a G&T Defender in first grade, said: "I try never to talk about it in front of her, but it happens. People ask, like, 'Oh, so you're at [TCS], is it G&T or Gen Ed?' It's nothing we've ever talked about. I know by the time she's in fifth grade she'll clearly know what it is—or fourth grade. There's no way she's not. I remember when I would tour schools and I would be like—I would ask the parents, 'What about your...', 'Oh my kids don't know, they don't know the difference.' And you want to be naïve and believe it, but—and yeah maybe in kindergarten and first grade they don't know, and maybe in second grade but they're going to know." As Margaret, a parent with children in both programs, explained "even the label of it is just, you know, 'Gifted and Talented.' I mean, any child at any age, at five years old, understands those words. And Gen Ed, you know, that's like—I don't know, Gifted and Talented definitely has the ring of being the special class." Another parent joked, "How gifted can they be if they do not know which program they are in?"

According to parents, however, even if students do not know about the *academic* distinctions between programs, they do notice the behavior and demographic differences between classrooms. Dana, who is a G&T Savvy Negotiator, said that her oldest son "noticed by second grade" that there were more behavior problems and more "brown-skinned kids" in the Gen Ed class. He asked her, "Why are all the brown skinned kids in the other class?" When questioned whether parents try to downplay the differences between programs, Dana explained,

> It depends on the parents. I know Gen Ed parents who talk about it all the time, and then G&T parents who, if somebody says, "What school do you go to?" they say, "My kid goes to G&T at [TCS]." It's like they need to say that. I never say it. I don't want my kids to say it. I don't want there to be a difference. That's a little idealistic.

Chrissy, a fourth grade G&T Savvy Negotiator said if she could do the school choice process over again she would not choose TCS's G&T program because students know the "differences" between programs. Instead, she would have chosen a neighborhood school with no G&T program: "Looking back, I do think I don't believe in the G&T versus the Gen Ed. Looking back, I don't think that children—my daughter knows that there's a difference between her class and the other class. And I don't think children need to know that when we're trying to teach everybody, children especially, everybody's equal, and then to clearly say 'You're not equal in school.' I don't know if it's necessary to have that."

Not only do students notice the racial segregation between the Gen Ed and G&T classrooms in terms of race/ethnicity, they also notice the behavior differences. Anne, an upper-class second and fourth grade G&T Defender said that what her children notice the most is that "the kids are better behaved [in the G&T program] but other than that, I don't think they would tell you 'We're smarter than the other kids' or something. They wouldn't—they certainly would never say that. They'd know that the kids behave a little better in their [G&T] classes. They'll comment on the kids' behavior." In addition, Melody, a G&T Defender with two children in the G&T classrooms who said her older son did not figure out the differences until fourth grade, said that he noticed the behavior issues in the Gen Ed classes, and made a point to say "that's the only thing he noticed."

Even when parents and the principal assure incoming parents that students do not know about the two different programs, it seems that students figure it out at some point during their elementary school career. Despite the silence surrounding the two programs, parents said that the difference that stands out to students is the behavior problems and skin color that divides them into two sets of classrooms. These divided classrooms can lead to stereotypes and stigmas of academic inferiority and superiority (chapter three). In this way, by using G&T programs to track students, it teaches children that segregation is still acceptable and being practiced inside schools.

The lingering segregation in the school is what makes the newly diverse Gen Ed classrooms such a positive experience for the Gen Ed children in grades K–2 and a positive development for the school. Regardless of the positive benefits of *diversity by default* in the Gen Ed program, though, parents continue to retest for G&T and the upper grades remain very segregated by race, class, and academic ability. The interview data show that despite the silence about the two different programs in the school, parents and students still see and feel a difference. Gen Ed parents feel like they are missing out on something by not being in the G&T classes with other parents and students like them, therefore they prep and test their children for G&T, which serves to reproduce the boundaries and the cycle of segregationc ontinues.

Reproducing the Boundaries: Why Parents Believe the G&T Program Is Still "Needed"

According to the interview data, the advantaged, mostly White families all strive to be in the G&T program to be around other similarly advantaged families, even if they also believe that the G&T program at TCS could (and should) be phased out eventually. The White, advantaged parents with children in the Gen Ed program, including the G&T parents in the older grades who have experienced the school's culture longer, agreed that the G&T program could be phased out, *in theory*, because the demographics between the two programs are becoming more similar. They said that the reason the DOE introduces G&T programs at certain schools is to attract middle-class parents from the neighborhood, and since that had been accomplished to a certain extent at TCS, they could phase the G&T program out. *In reality*, however, these same parents would not want to see the G&T program go because it attracts the right "kind of caliber of parents and students" to the school.

A good example of this contradiction within parents over whether they thought the G&T could be phased out occurred when Betsy, a second grade G&T Savvy Negotiator, said during the interview that she sees "the vision and it would be great if we could have the same kind of caliber of parents and students without having the G&T because I would love it if we could just be one school. But I don't think we're there yet," because it takes time to build up a good reputation and the "problem is right now, a lot of our kids come from out of our zone, you know, so a lot of those kids—it's not just about the kids but it's the parents, those parents are the ones who really do a lot for the school. So if you just went cold turkey, I think the character of the school would change a lot." But, later during the G&T school tour, when anxious incoming parents asked if the G&T program would eventually be phased out because they have younger siblings and they live outside of the catchment area, Betsy, who was one of the parents giving the tours, did not hesitate when she said "as long as G&T exists, we will have it" at our school. Understandably, in front of these incoming G&T parents, the vision of becoming one school by phasing out the G&T program was lost.

Lisa, a kindergarten Gen Ed Reconciler, thought that having the G&T program in the school "creates too much animosity between two groups, or a feeling of being better because one is in the program...parents that are in the G&T look at some of the parents that are not like 'Oh, my son got in.' It's a weird feeling." When asked if she heard anything about the G&T program phasing out, Veronica who is a Conflicted Follower with children in both programs said, "Yes, we [parents] talk about the environment, about the two programs in one school, how happy children are in the school." As Lindsay, a Savvy Negotiator with children in both programs, explained, though, parents are "concerned about this kind of system, but a lot of the parents defend having a G&T program. I think they like it."

Lauren, a kindergarten Gen Ed Conflicted Follower said she did *not* believe DOE officials would phase out the G&T program at TCS, and she would support that, because "they attract a great group [of parents] and why fix what's not broken...I don't think they'd want to upset it." Later in the interview, however, she brought the issue up again when asked what she would change about the G&T policy by saying, "I would do away with the G&T programming if it would not disrupt, if it would mean that they were going to bus [Black and Latino] kids in again, no, they need to keep it. But if it would not mean that, then I think it would make everybody's lives easier. But some parents wouldn't want it [the G&T program] to go away, so I don't know." In this way, White, advantaged parents with children in the Gen Ed program or G&T parents in the older grades seemed conflicted between wanting the G&T to be phased out because of their belief in diversity and concern for segregation, but also not wanting the G&T program to "go away" because of the advantaged parents the program attracts.

Reasons for Keeping the G&T Program—to "Elevate a School"

Parents in the G&T, Gen Ed, and those in both programs contradicted their earlier argument that the G&T program could (and should) be phased out in the school, by saying that the G&T program is still needed in order to attract the right type of parents and students to the school, increase the school's reputation because of the parent involvement, and create distance from the "other." This is the same argument that supporters of G&T programs use when they say that they "are crucial for middle-class parents seeking refuge from low-performing neighborhood schools."[8] In fact, one way that the district seems to be attracting White parents into "failing" public schools is by opening up G&T programs at schools with a majority of students of color, like TCS did 20 years ago. The school choice consultant explained, "Of course [school A] and [TCS] were not schools anyone [meaning White, advantaged parents] went to before the G&T was there" because they were majority Black and Latino schools.

As Kathy, a fourth grade G&T Defender, responded, "I believe that G&T programs can elevate a school and then they can be phased out and the school will stay a great school, you know?" In this way, parents believed that the G&T program "pulls the school up" because they attract the right type of parent—one who has money to donate and gets involved in the PTA, which in this case are the majority White, higher-income parents. Then, the theory goes, once the school gets a better reputation because of who is enrolling their child there and what they are doing for the school, then parents from the neighborhood will want to go to the school regardless of whether there is a G&T program or not. TCS, apparently, is in the middle of this transition. More White families are starting to enroll their children in the Gen Ed program, but instead of staying in the Gen Ed program they all retest for G&T and attempt to cross over the gifted/non-gifted boundary. Parents were also conflicted about whether TCS's G&T program should be phased out or not because there are still lower-income parents of color enrolling their children in the Gen Ed portion of the school, which causes the rigid boundaries between programs to remain intact.

One White incoming parent to the Gen Ed program named Kelly explained why she thought G&T programs within schools improve the overall "quality" and reputation of the school, especially schools that enroll a majority of students of color, such as school J (pseudonym), which just started a G&T program. She replied:

> [School J] has a very keen and motivated principal and assistant principal who are extremely interested in improving the quality of the school. The way to do that is to get the G&T kids there and to get the money from the G&T parents and to get them involved in the school because it doesn't have a very active PTA. It doesn't really have that kind of reputation. As a result, it doesn't attract the kids there that it needs. So moving it there was a good move... and the question is how long do you keep it there before you move it some place else and improve those schools, too?

According to some parents, by adding a G&T program at school J, DOE officials are hoping that White, middle-class parents from across the district will choose the separate G&T program and eventually the entire school will improve, just like what is starting to happen at TCS. As Kelly states, "G&T kids" and "G&T parents" are in reference to the mostly White and/or higher-income parents from across the district who will make the school better by being more involved and donating money. In this way, the symbolic boundaries between "us"/"G&T" and "them"/"Gen Ed" are clearly defined by the White, advantaged parents in this segregated school system, which then translates into social boundaries that allow this group of parents to use their uneven cultural capital exchange to gain access into high-status G&T programs. Therefore, even though Kelly wished that the G&T program at TCS would be phased out now because her son got into the Gen Ed program and she was fearful of the "stigma," she also thought adding G&T programs in certain schools that enroll a majority of students of color is a "good move" because they would attract the right type of "G&T kids" there, which will improve the reputation and the quality of education.

Courtney, an incoming parent to the G&T program who lives outside TCS's zone, when asked if she heard that the G&T program would be phased out, replied, "What would happen to me? I wouldn't be able to go there anymore because it's not my zoned school?" She went on to explain why she thought school A's (see Table 1.3 in chapter one) decision to phase out their G&T program and school J starting a G&T program at the same time was not a coincidence. "I mean they said [school A was phasing their G&T program out] because they had more regular [or Gen Ed] applicants, and they ran out of actual physical space for G&T, which may be true. But I also feel like it's a good way to get [school J's G&T program] to work better. So they're spreading the wealth a little."

Proponents of G&T programs, like Courtney, argue that if G&T is "working" to attract White families into the public school system and improve the schools, then why would the NYCDOE phase the G&T programs out? Yet, TCS has maintained a segregated G&T program for nearly 20 years, and there is no end in sight. This book argues that using G&T programs that rely on a single standardized test score for admission is bad practice because it favors advantaged, mostly White parents in the system and results in second-generation segregation. In fact, the tracking and de-tracking research, much of which was conducted in the 1980s and 1990s, provides an abundance of empirical findings on the negative effects of tracking in secondary schools—educationally, socially, and psychologically—and the strong relationship between track placements and students' background characteristics, especially race and social class.[9] This ties into the main point of the school choice literature—namely that there are consistent patterns of racial and SES segregation when parents can influence school placements, use their unequal cultural capital exchange to get their children into higher-quality schools of choice, and there are no diversity measures to balance the schools.

Because advantaged parents buy into and embody the structures to a certain extent—for example, using self-contained G&T programs to attract other White, higher-income families, they believe that TCS's G&T program is still "needed" not only to attract the right kind of families, but also to create distance from the "other." Not surprisingly, G&T parents such as Courtney who live outside of TCS's catchment area, or 11 out of the 16 G&T parents that were interviewed, make this claim the most. This position makes sense since they would *not* have been able to choose TCS if there was no G&T program.

The G&T Program Still "Needed" at TCS Because of the Demographic Differences
Another reason that G&T parents gave for keeping the G&T program at TCS was the racial and socioeconomic diversity of the student body. Oftentimes, parents would compare TCS to other schools in the area that are disproportionately White with no G&T, particularly GT2 (which is currently phasing out their G&T program—See Table 1.2 in chapter one), school A, and school B (See Table 1.3 in chapter one), by saying that these other schools can go without a G&T program because their student body is demographically more similar than TCS's and they do not have public housing in their zones. As Anne, a second and fourth grade G&T Defender who lives outside of TCS's catchment, replied:

> I think that's the only way parents with kids who are invested in their education will go [to Gen Ed] is if it's the same way as [school A] or [school B] [e.g. are located in a higher income neighborhood with more White students]. I just think that's a hard task when you have—I just think the makeup of the neighborhood is different and the zone is different than we have... I don't know of any housing projects in [those schools]. I think that sometimes families are struggling more in our school to do basic things and it's hard to then sort of give the kids the support that they might get when you're not struggling for the basics. So I think that makes it a little easier as far as those other programs go.

Anne and many other G&T parents who lived outside the catchment area said that because there are housing projects and lower-income students in TCS's catchment, as well as more advantaged families like their own, they need two separate programs within the school. In this way, parents use the boundaries to imagine who they are by imagining who they are not, whether it's comparing TCS to a school that recently phased out their

G&T program or a disproportionately White neighborhood school with no G&T.

It was clear that parents did not think G&T programs are necessary at schools that are disproportionately White and higher-income "with no projects next to them...because it wouldn't be serving a purpose." But, parents agreed that having a G&T program at TCS makes it a better school because it attracts the right kind of G&T parents, who mostly live outside the catchment area. In other words, if you got rid of the G&T program, you would risk losing those highly involved parents from outside TCS's zone.

Although some of these same White, advantaged parents would rather the school be all Gen Ed and "a true neighborhood school," like other disproportionately White and higher-income schools in their district, many explained that having the White parents and lower-income parents of color within the same school means you need the separate G&T program. Kathy, a fourth grade G&T Defender who also lives outside TCS's zone, when asked what the advantages to having a G&T program were, explained:

> When you have schools like ours that have projects in them, and these are people who want the best for their children, just everybody wants—there's nobody that doesn't want the best for their child, that's life. But you don't have, when you're working, you and your husband, three jobs and your kids are latchkey kids and there's not a book in your house because you can't afford it, it's not the same as having two parents that have advanced degrees who have read every book about how to raise children, and by the time you start elementary school, you can practically read. It's not the same and it's not fair to try to compare them. But if you can do the best that you can, which I think G&T is helping, then why isn't that a good thing?

In other words, since the public housing in TCS's catchment "bring in a different type of population," the G&T program is still wanted and needed to separate the two different sets of children who come from different backgrounds. Kathy's quote also relates to the social and symbolic boundaries that parents use to define "us" and "them" categories. For example, when Kathy refers to the parents who are "working three jobs" and the "kids are latchkey kids" versus parents who have "advanced degrees" and "have read every book about how to raise children," it is clear how parents use symbolic boundaries and a cultural deficit framework to sort their children into the high-status G&T programs where they feel they belong.

In the next chapter, TCS is revisited three years after the original study to explore how 18 parents experience(d) the Gen Ed program for their children's education. It includes follow-up interviews with eight White parents from the original sample who had their children in the kindergarten or first grade Gen Ed program in 2011 to see how the school has changed. It also includes a first-time interview with a White Gen Ed parent in the fourth grade. The findings show that these White advantaged parents are continuing to use their cultural capital to test prep and secure a G&T seat because of the perceived G&T advantages and the stigma of the Gen Ed label, with six out of the eight parents switching their child to G&T or leaving the school. Parents had less of a critique of having the G&T program and phasing the program out now than before because there is more competition to get a G&T seat.

Additionally, a comparison group of nine Black and Latino mothers who enroll their children in the Gen Ed program at TCS were interviewed regarding their perspective of the two different programs, parents, and children in the school. The Gen Ed parents of color believe that G&T is used as a tool for segregation, status, and power within the school. They question the definition of giftedness in this context because parents are tutoring for the G&T test, and they have limited information about schools from their social networks or preschools.

CHAPTER FIVE
"The Only Thing They Got out of This Is Segregation": TCS Revisited

Mercedes grew up in the Dominican Republic and moved to New York City when she was 18 years old. When she came to the United States she learned English, and was accepted into college. Mercedes earned a degree and currently has a part-time professional job. She has two children enrolled at TCS in the kindergarten and fifth grade Gen Ed program. She lives in a rent-stabilized apartment in a building in which "the only people that go to public school are me and the super. Everybody else goes to private because there's a lot of money in the building." Mercedes explains that it is really expensive to live in "this neighborhood" and that many Spanish people live in small apartments with their parents.

She starts off the interview by saying how "crazy" TCS is, because "if you walk into a school, it's 1950's segregated, Blacks and Whites. Eventually they're going to have two doors, Whites through here, Blacks through there, you know what I mean? What are they trying to do? That is strange to me." She believes that the White parents like the status and exclusivity that the G&T label affords them in the school, which creates this boundary between parents and students. Mercedes explains that White parents who start in the Gen Ed program will invite her daughter to birthday parties, but as soon as they switch over to G&T the parents and children act like they are "so special" and they "aren't friends anymore." She said, "I don't blame the kid for that. I blame the parents. It's the parents. Like there were two little girls that stopped talking to my daughter and the mothers knew they were friends. I'm sure the mother said something, 'You're in G&T now, you don't need to talk to those kids.' What changed? That's so strange. My daughter told me. I said, 'she doesn't say hi to you'? She doesn't even look at my daughter." When asked if the parents act that way too, she replied: "Yes, that mom used to talk to other moms when their kid was in Gen Ed, and her daughter went to G&T. She doesn't even say hi. Not even hi. Isn't that weird? . . . It's the parents. How can you do that? And how kids walk into a room and don't even acknowledge somebody? And they walk around like they're better than you."

Additionally, Mercedes said the White parents would use their power in the school to request the "best" teachers. She recalled a time when she was sitting in the office with a Jewish mother who wanted her child's teacher switched. This mother told Mercedes, "I'm going to go in the office and change it, blah blah blah." Mercedes remembers how "confident" the mother seemed: "I don't know if she got it done, but she felt that she could do it. And [this mother] said, 'I know people in broadcasting, I can get things done'. And I was like, huh, interesting." Mercedes said that all the "White parents" get the best Gen Ed teachers too, especially in kindergarten. Another parent told her that if she does not get the Kindergarten Gen Ed teacher who used to teach G&T, that Mercedes should "fight it because... all the White parents are getting" her. This is the same teacher that the former principal switched to Gen Ed to appease the White families who were entering the Gen Ed program.

Mercedes also brings up the symbolic boundaries that parents use to categorize people into groups based on race and class. When asked to describe the parents in the school in more detail, she responded: "Somebody assumed because I'm Spanish that I lived in the projects. I never even walked into a project. I don't know anybody that lives in the projects. So that's why when people talk about it like that, I get a little offended because I'm like, you don't know. You can't put everybody in that circle just because they are a certain race or whatever, even though I know a lot of Dominicans that just live off of that [food stamps or housing]. That doesn't mean that all do." She said that when people try to relate her to other Spanish people, "(a) I wasn't born here; (b) I didn't grow up here; and (c) my family all has college degrees." She said that it is just so weird that people "assume right away." Mercedes also said that her youngest daughter is really fair-skinned and that people will ask her if she is the "babysitter" even though her daughter is calling her, "Mommy, mommy, mommy." She explains that the Dominican Republic is so mixed in terms of race and skin color and that she "never saw color until I came to this country and people started asking me, "Where are you from? What is your accent? I'm like, why all these questions? I never in my life experienced anything like that, and then the older I get the more that I see it because, you know, you get older, you pay more attention I guess."

The Gen Ed Black and Latino, lower-income parents in this book also question the measures used to define giftedness in this context, relating giftedness to whether or not students were tutored. Mercedes explained that while she *did* have her oldest daughter tested in preschool for G&T, she got a really low score. Therefore, she did not bother getting her youngest daughter tested. When asked how she would define giftedness, Mercedes said: "People were so obsessed, paying $2,000–$3,000 for a tutor. I'm not paying it. Even if I had it, I wouldn't pay it. And that's the thing; all of the G&T kids train. All of the kids in G&T, some of the parents can afford it. They have grandparents that can afford it. They pay for this. But that's not G&T." Mercedes also had a different conception of the definition of G&T. She believes that her oldest daughter, who does not need tutoring or help with homework, should be labeled "gifted." "I don't help her with homework. She's on her own. You're talking about G&T? She's G&T. She does her homework. I don't check her homework. I don't even know she does her homework because I told her that's her responsibility.... I already went to fifth grade, so I already did that. I'm not going to do it again. If I started helping out with her homework, who's doing the homework? Me.... I said, whatever you don't understand, ask your teacher because I'm not a teacher." This example of not helping with homework confirms White parents' perceptions of the cultural differences in parent involvement between White parents and "immigrant" parents. It also relates to Lareau's concept of "natural growth" or the tendency of working class and poor parents to rely on the school or teachers to have more authority over their child's educational experiences.[1]

In terms of school choice, the Black and Latino parents in this book generally have limited information about their school choice options in the system, particularly when you compare the social networks of information of the White parents. Even if White parents work full time, they know other parents at the school who keep them informed about school choice and other school news. In comparison, Black and Latino parents just assume that they go to their assigned neighborhood school, as Mercedes explained: "You have a kid, you send them to school. I didn't know you had to jump through hoops to get a kid in school... If I knew better I would have tried somewhere else, but I had no idea." Similarly, Althea, an African American mother who grew up on Long Island, said: "I had one child and I had no clue of anything. I'm like 'So what do you do next?' because like I said, I came from a place where— this is the elementary school you go to, this is junior high, this is the high school.... So what do I know? I didn't know you had 50 million schools in New York City. I'm like, 'What is this? This is ridiculous.' Very stressful."

While advantaged parents try to get as many options as they can and have back up plans if they do not get into their preferred choice, Black and Latino parents face many barriers to the school choice process. These obstacles include having difficulty obtaining school choice information from their preschools and social networks, navigating the separate, online applications and deadlines, and attending school tours. Mercedes said she was the only Latino parent at a recent middle school tour and "This [area] is not all Jewish and Irish. There's a lot of Spanish." When asked why she thinks Latino parents are not going to tours she replies, "Because they're not communicating to the people properly and that's a way to get the people out. Not everybody has the luxury to stay home and not work, so if you're working and you're not getting all of this feedback and people telling you, you don't know." She recalls the time when one of her friends called her to tell her about a middle school tour. Her friend said, "You need to sign up for the tour," and Mercedes said, "I didn't even know! She said to me, 'Sign up because all of these White people are taking the spots and you're not going to be able to get one.' That's exactly what she said to me! So I said, okay. Let me sign up. But if she wouldn't call me, I would be in the dark and then the time would come and I wouldn't even have a school for my daughter." By having one friend who tells her about school tours, Mercedes has more capital than a lower-income family with fewer social ties.

The other point that the parents of color made clear is that the negative effects of second-generation segregation are placed squarely on the shoulders of the students, not the parents. When asked how she would describe TCS to someone who is not familiar with the schools or programs, Mercedes said: "It's New York City, and a kid that doesn't have blue eyes and blonde hair should not feel out of place. This is New York City. We are so mixed." She recalls an "incident that just happened, one of the General Ed teachers was not in school so they divided the class. They sent some of the kids to the G&T. This little girl, she's really Spanish but she's really dark, so when she came out of the class she felt so out of place. She was like, 'I was the only person of this color in that class.' To me, it's so strange that only Caucasian kids are in G&T." Mercedes believes that the reason they have G&T at TCS is "to divide the kids...it's really sad because it's so divided." She questions "Why are you taking the opportunity from other kids? That's just not fair." She also said that the Spanish or Black boys in the school are "always targeted. They have a problem in behavior or learning, but it's their culture...Spanish people are very strong and very loud...But if people start pointing at you that you have a problem, eventually you're going to believe it." Parents of color described the school's culture as being very divisive between the haves and have-nots, not only for parents in terms of parent involvement, but also for students who may not feel a sense of belonging in their school. They may start to internalize their "less than" status or label because they are not in the "smart kids' class." Ultimately, parents of color did not enroll their children in the G&T program because their children did not score well on the G&T test (if they got them tested), they did not know about the program before they applied, and/or they did not want to be the only person of color in the G&T classroom.

As an addition to the book, nine Black and Latino parents, including Mercedes, were recruited to participate in in-depth interviews in order to explore their perspective of the two programs, parents, and students within the school. The parents of color come from different race/ethnicities, cultures, and socioeconomic backgrounds and have their children enrolled in different grade levels and programs at TCS, but are mostly in the Gen Ed program[2] (see chapter one and Table 5.1). Two African mothers who lived outside of TCS's catchment also had experience in both programs because their oldest child was accepted into the G&T program and their younger child(ren) were in Gen Ed. The parents of color believe that G&T is used as a tool for segregation, boundary maintenance, status within the school.

Table 5.1 Black and Latino parent sample

Name	Race/Ethnicity	SES	No. of Children	School Program	Referral	Zoned School
Mercedes	Latina/Dominican	PT Job; Some College	2	Gen Ed	Jessica (Classroom Network)	Zoned School
Maria	Latina	PT Job; Some College	1	Gen Ed	Melissa (Classroom Network)	Zoned School
Sofia	Latina	PT Job; Some College	1	Gen Ed	Mercedes (Classroom Network)	Zoned School
Ana	Latina	FT Job; No Degree	1	Gen Ed	Carrie (Pre-K Network)	Zoned School
Althea	African American	FT College Student	1	Gen Ed	Margaret (Classroom Network)	Zoned School
Amara	Black/African	PT Job; College-Educated	1	Gen Ed	Jessica (Email sent to the whole class)	Out of Zone
Brianna	Black/African	FT College Student	3	Both	Althea (Classroom Network)	Out of Zone
Tammy	African American	FT Job; No Degree	1	Gen Ed	Ana (Classroom Network)	Zoned School
Deana	African American	FT Job; No Degree	1	Gen Ed	Maria (Classroom Network)	Zoned School

They question the definition of giftedness in this context because parents are tutoring for the G&T test, and they have limited information about school choice from their social networks or preschools.

Using G&T as a Tool for Segregation, Boundary Maintenance, and Status

Like Mercedes explained, Gen Ed parents of color believe that the G&T program is being used as a way to "divide" TCS students by race and class. Ana, a Columbian, working-class mother who lives in the neighborhood, believes "the real problem is the lack of diversity." She said it is not just the feeling of segregation with the students that is bad, but the parents can "feel" it too. When asked about parent involvement in the school, Ana replied: "It's segregated. There is no communication because they are into their G&T thing. Even with them, you can feel that it is different... It's a problem because it just doesn't feel like a community."

Amara, an African lower-middle-class mother who lives outside the catchment area and had an older daughter graduate from the G&T program and a younger daughter in Gen Ed, explained that it is the "area" of TCS that "makes the segregation" because "you have across the street from [TCS] a 2 bedroom apartment, for $5,000–6,000 dollars, and there's projects right here, and brownstones and both have to come, they cannot say no to come to the school and that's why all this income level are here... and it's this big divide." Amara said that she wishes her youngest daughter would be in G&T, like her older daughter used to be, because of the "stigma" and the feeling in the school that "one side is better than the other." Yet, she also said that being on the G&T side as the only Black family was also "bad" because of the "feeling" of segregation: "It's segregated and when you are in the [G&T] class and you are the only one as a parent sitting in G&T and everybody's looking at you like... like that is so bad. Like the way we grew up in Ethiopia, I never see that kind of thing I don't know, I come here and my husband has to tell me again and again and again, I mean I know it is, but because I don't grow up here and I don't know that feeling, so for us it's different." When asked about the advantages and disadvantages of having the G&T program in the school, Amara replied: "Nobody gets advantage of that, except they [White parents and students] are together, they are by themselves, that's what they want and that's how they do it. The only thing they got out of this is segregation."

When asked what is the biggest thing that stands out to her between programs, Althea, who is an African American mother living in public housing with a son in Gen Ed, responded: "What do you want me to say? Most of the G&T are White children. It's just hard for me to believe that there's no Black or Spanish G&T. That's weird to me. I think it's insane because I know some really smart kids. I don't get it." She explained that all the White parents who may have started out in Gen Ed, "You come next year, and they are all in G&T and I'm like, how are they all in G&T?" Her theory about why White G&T parents who can afford private school choose G&T instead is because: "Okay, we're not paying for private school because there's three of you guys, so mom can stay home and dad can just work. So since we're not paying for school, which is like $100,000–125,000, mommy doesn't have to work and we can get two summer homes and go on lots of vacations. We can stay home and just have a great life with you guys and go to PTA make sure you guys get into G&T and live happily ever after. That kind of thing."

Symbolic Boundaries Parents Use

Parents of color said that parents use race and class to determine where other parents belong in the school and larger social system. This phenomenon happens even when parents' initial perceptions about whether parents are in the G&T or Gen Ed are wrong because, as was illustrated in chapter four, White parents can be in Gen Ed now. Because the segregation between programs has been like that for decades, White parents and teachers assume White parents are in G&T, even if they are on the Gen Ed side. As Prudence Carter writes, "A school's sociocultural context...fosters a system of meanings in which students and educators create and reproduce in-group/out-group boundaries, which are likely to be associated with the degrees to which all students are fully incorporated into the academic setting."[3] In TCS, it is also the parents who are affected by the "us" and "them" boundaries and their sense of belonging in the school. This pushes White parents to retest for G&T to feel in their right place, and perhaps deters Gen Ed parents of color to test for G&T because they would be the only person of color in the G&T classroom. This boundary maintenance is evident in the student-student and parent-parent interactions within the school (e.g., codes, behaviors, and expectations), including how Gen Ed students and parents of color experience the academic and social stigma and segregation.

This boundary work happens in the reverse, too, when Black students are enrolled in G&T. Amara noticed how teachers would use race and class to make assumptions about her oldest daughter' placement in the school, since she was "the only Black girl in the [G&T] classroom." She said that the first thing G&T teachers say at parent teacher conferences is how "well-behaved" and "well-mannered" her daughter is, and seem surprised that she entered kindergarten already knowing how to read, like it was "a big deal." When asked if the teachers are comparing her daughter to other children or what they are implying, Amara said, "No it's Black and how she behave...it's not about the academics, they talk about how your child is mannered, da da da." She remembers how other G&T parents in the school would act surprised, and even question her if she was volunteering for something when they found out her daughter was in G&T. Amara said that parents would use code language to see where she belonged in the school by asking who her daughter's teacher is, and even then, act like "Oh really, are you sure?" She explained, "Everybody of course doesn't think I'm in the G&T because...even if I say I am, they're like Ohhhh you are? Who's your daughter? And I'm like it's OK, I understand.... You get used to it." Thus, because White students were always in G&T and Black and Latino students were in Gen Ed, Amara said, "It's hard to change things."

When asked to describe the G&T parents in the school, Amara said that most of the G&T parents are really wealthy and "look like they are really proud" of their G&T status in the school: "I mean we go to school with these kind of people and sometimes it really makes them mad to share their money with us, but if we are liberal we shouldn't, you have it, you should give it away." But, she said because the majority of White advantaged parents, and not the Gen Ed parents of color, are the ones who are donating "$2,500" a year to hire the teaching assistants in the classrooms, and many Gen Ed parents cannot afford that, they act "obnoxious...sometimes it's really scary, they stand in a group in the morning, you go to PTA meetings and if you ask a question, they're like, 'Who are you?'" In this context of G&T programs as the answer to keep the middle class invested in New York City public schools, not only do low-income families of color get marginalized and undervalued in terms of parent involvement efforts for school improvement, in TCS, students of color also get segregated in lower-status Gen Ed programs. This segregation can affect future opportunities and outcomes, and result in stigmas of academic inferiority based on skin color and placement in the school.[4]

Question the Definition of Giftedness

Parents of color in this book overwhelmingly believe the G&T students get G&T seats because most of their parents paid for test prep, which is unfair and not a true measurement of their ability. Brianna, an African, lower-middle-class mother with children in both programs, said even though she does not believe in test prep, "One problem of course is some have money, you can make your child ready to pass the test." Amara replied, "From what I heard" most G&T parents "pay a lot of money to prepare their kids" for the G&T test. She asks "If you needed tutors and you have to go to Kumon [a tutoring company], how are you in G&T? I'm like, when you take the same test and you are in the special group, but you need more time to finish your work? You are not a G&T." Althea stated that she knows G&T students "that really shouldn't be there. Their parents prepped them good enough to get in, but they can't keep up and the parents are always complaining."

Brianna, when asked if she prepared her children to take the G&T tests, replied: "I never do that, but I do make him ready for school. I never knew you should prepare your child to get into G&T because I believe the gifted child is supposed to be naturally—if you expose him, you can get more I believe, but at least he should have his own talent, gift and talent." When asked whether she believed that the G&T tests adequately measured giftedness, Brianna explained, "I don't believe the G&T program is working as it's supposed to be. So I thought to myself, why should I make them ready? Why should I pay that much money to make my child ready, pay $100 per hour?"

In terms of test prep for future educational placements, Amara explained, "The same thing is happening now" with fourth grade tests for middle school and the seventh grade test scores used for high school admissions. She said other parents are paying $1,000 for a test prep after-school workshop for high school tests. Amara joked, "Do you know how many pairs of shoes I can buy for $1,000?" But her daughter keeps saying to her, "'Mommy all the kids are doing that class'... each one of [her friends] has 2 tutors twice a week and then they have the class twice a week and whoa, do you know how much the tutor costs? $150 an hour, that was the last thing I asked, I said excuse me, no way! What are you going to give for $150? A friend of mine got a cheaper tutor for like $85 and I thought, that's not cheap, and I was like $20 then I'll hire her, that's when I'm like no...that's a lot of money." Thus, one reason G&T parents get into the high-status, high-quality school options is because they can afford to test prep.

When asked about the future of G&T at TCS and the possibility of phasing the G&T program out, Amara adamantly replied, "There's no way we're going to...parents would fight it." When asked if parents would fight because they believe their children are gifted, she said "They know...every single one of them, and I know if [my younger daughter] passes she's not gifted, she got 89, she's a very good student, but gifted is a totally different program, gifted is when you're up and above, if you need a tutor then you are not gifted, you're a good student, you need guidance, but you're not gifted." Ultimately, Amara believes TCS needs to either change the name of the G&T program, or better yet, phase the program out and mix the students in the classroom.

Effects of Second-Generation Segregation

Cassie, a White advantaged parent with a son in the Gen Ed program, explains in the second half of the chapter that the effects of second-generation segregation are on the students who start to internalize their less-than status. Mercedes's vignette also points to the feeling of segregation and the sense of not belonging in the school if you do not have blond hair and blue eyes. Amara recalled a time when her G&T daughter came home and said that one of her White friends told her they could not be in the same program because of the color of her skin: "Mommy, my friend said we are not in the same program because the Black kids are bad. I'm Black, how come I'm good?" Amara said, "What do you say to that? Okay. Of course she has her ups and downs but we're never like, 'Oh, ay ay ay.' We don't do that. We just, like, so what? And one time, her friend said—she came home and said, 'Mommy, my friend said I cannot be in her club'—this is second grade—'because I'm Brown.' I said, 'Her loss honey, her loss.'" Thus, according to parents, because of the segregation and the hierarchical G&T and Gen Ed labels, students can feel out of place in the school and the classroom because of their skin color. They also sense the academic and social stigma of being perceived as smart / not smart that results from their label.

Brianna, a Black parent with two younger daughters in the Gen Ed program and an older son in the G&T program, provided a sad portrait of how children within the same family can perceive their academic self-concept because of their different G&T and Gen Ed educational placements. She explained that having her three children in different programs "creates an emotional conflict" between them. In her eyes, "I wouldn't say one is quicker than the other." But, her children "feel the difference" because parents at the school talk about the two different programs in front of them and her older son acts like "I'm better than you guys."

Therefore, Brianna said she has to assure her children that they are "all the same," but they "still don't understand why they are in different programs." The labels make students "more conscious" of the division. Brianna stated that her daughter asks, "What's that mean, Mama? This Gen Ed and G&T?" She said, "Especially my middle child, she's in the Gen Ed program and she feels unhappy and insecure. I try to convince her, even though [your brother] is in G&T, it doesn't mean he's smarter, but again I try to tell them that you can achieve in your own way. But still, there is conflict." Brianna went on to say that she would prefer if both the programs did not exist at TCS and if she could she would switch schools because of how divisive it is, especially in her own family. She replied,

"*They don't understand, but still they do understand.* Emotionally, they feel themselves on the inside, why am I here? Why is my brother in a different class? Is there something wrong? They don't know, but still they feel it." In other words, they sense the stigma and the inferiority that the Gen Ed label connotes.

Brianna described her own education in Eritrea, Africa as being much different than that in TCS because they brought together nine tribes and it was not segregated: "I would say it's a natural environment with a lot of kids, but we have different attitudes and culture, from all areas. I would say I was blessed to be part of them because I believe I had more experience than people who live here in the city... So many different people, different attitude, even though it was one country you have different experiences... [but] all the same education." If she had the chance, she would change the G&T program at TCS because it creates a "big gap" in the school. Brianna believes it would be a "better environment if they mix up all the kids... one child can benefit from the other child. It's better if they can have help from each other. From here, but also from all people, especially New York City, more diversity, so it's good to see very mixed cultures." Althea described her school choice process: "I decided by what kind of kids were there. Was it multi-cultural?... How many different kinds of kids? With these kids—no. Too many of those kids—no. Too many of these kids—no."

The message is clear that what the majority of parents in this book want is the best education for their children in a diverse environment. Yet, they have very few diverse, high-quality school choice options to choose from to escape their segregated neighborhood school. In the second half of the chapter, eight White parents who had their children in the kindergarten or first grade Gen Ed program in 2011 were reinterviewed to see what changes had occurred in the school over time.

TCS Revisited

Jessica is a White advantaged mother with three children currently enrolled in both programs at TCS. When she was interviewed in 2011, her oldest son was enrolled in the first grade Gen Ed program and her middle daughter had just been tested for a G&T kindergarten spot. She tested her oldest son to be in the G&T program in kindergarten and first grade, but he missed the test score cutoff by one or two points each time. Jessica said she does not believe that "at four [years old] you know if a child is gifted and talented" because there are so many other outside factors that could affect their performance on the test. And even though Jessica tested her son for G&T, she does not think "he deserves to be in a G&T program. I don't think that's kind of his make-up. But I also see other kids that are in the G&T program who come home with my son to play and I can't see any difference at all, nothing...in the homework...[or] in writing or cognitive skills."

During the time of the first interview, Jessica was placed in the "Conflicted Follower" group because she had decided *not* to test her son again for second grade G&T because she recognizes that her son is not "super-studious." She reasoned that "it's elementary school" and she wants her children to have that balance between "having a childhood and learning the skills to be good learners." Jessica explained, "I think life is hard enough as it is and I think they are growing up in a very high-achieving city and, you know, I just don't want to take that [their childhood] away from them yet." She believes that children develop in different ways and does not want to push or "fight" with her son every night to do homework if he is not ready to handle it.

Contradicting her previous statement, when reinterviewed again three years later, Jessica, who would now be considered a "Savvy Negotiator," said she retested her son for G&T every year until third grade (the last year you can retest for G&T) because "the truest benefit to me in G&T is you have less behavioral problems...that was my biggest reason for wanting to get [my son] out of the Gen Ed program." She related the behavior problems in Gen Ed to being able to sit and focus on the G&T test, implying if you can do that, then you can pass the G&T test: "Often there are more discipline problems in the Gen Ed program than there is in G&T because if you think that somebody can sit down for an hour and a half to take a [G&T] test, they must be able to have some focus if they're doing well in it. That's how I look at it." The other advantage of being in G&T, according to Jessica, is that G&T students seem better prepared to take the fourth grade standardized tests that are used for middle school admission's decisions. Jessica, like other parents with children in both programs, decides to retest her children for G&T, not because she believes her children are "gifted," but because of classroom behavior, parent involvement, and future educational opportunities.

During the initial interview, Jessica also brings up the reason why they institute G&T at certain schools and that if the Gen Ed program in the younger grades was as "non-diverse" as it is in the older grades, she would not want her son to be in that program. Jessica explains, "That's where you saw the reason why there is a G&T because they were trying to pull in different kids into the classroom and it's actually—I mean, I don't like it. I really wouldn't want my kids at that point to be in a G&T class that is so non-diverse and the other classes are so diverse. But you don't see that now in the lower grades." And, what bothers Jessica the most about the two different programs is the negative stigma of the Gen Ed label in terms of parent involvement and children's perceived academic ability. For that reason, she explains that she prepped her middle daughter for the G&T test before kindergarten, even though she thought it was "cheating." Jessica added that it's just the "status quo these days... I think that a lot more kids are getting prepped for it than not." Jessica also thought that "cognitively" her daughter was a "better fit for G&T," and that she was being a little "naïve" when her son went through the testing about how many other parents are prepping their children. When asked why she thought her daughter belonged in G&T, she answered: "Because I think she really wants to learn... I think you just—you know how to pay attention, you know how to sit still, and you just have an internal need to or desire to be focused and learn, and she's that kind of a kid... she asks me questions all the time."

Jessica uses her cultural capital exchange to get her daughter into the G&T placement, where she felt her family belonged, by prepping her child for the G&T test. Jessica said that the first thing she did was get information about test prepping from another pre-k parent who hired a private tutor for "an hour every week for months and months." She said that learning that process was "such an eye-opener to me, that's when I started thinking maybe I should do something too." When asked how she found out about the tutors, she said a friend referred her to a private school teacher who makes house visits. Jessica paid for "four lessons," which consisted of coming in and playing "games with my daughter. That's really what it was all about, just grouping things, asking questions so that she would think a certain way, and so that when she sat down and, you know, these tests are long—I think it's almost an hour... that you're sitting in there and four-year-olds are—they don't have very long attention spans." She rationalized her choice to prepare her daughter by saying that if she did not prep her it would "put her at a disadvantage if she never had done it at all, and all these other kids I felt were doing it."

Jessica also describes other factors beyond test scores that determine track placement. For example, Jessica explained that in her son's first grade Gen Ed classroom, there were five or six children that technically tested into G&T. They could not get a G&T seat at TCS, however, because they did not have high enough scores, especially if they lived out of zone. The siblings took the seats first "and they decided not to go to a different school. So they quote-unquote could be in G&T but they're not in that classroom. So I think at our school, I don't think it makes any sense. I understand why there's a G&T program, and I think for some schools it makes a lot of sense. I kind of wish it would go away at our school because I don't like the distinction, and I think that the kids that maybe don't learn as well could benefit from the kids that are faster learners." Jessica points out that there are very different levels of ability in the first grade Gen Ed classroom from children who technically passed the G&T test score cutoff to children who did not attend kindergarten and cannot read yet. Jessica says even though she does not like the sibling policy, she loves what it has done for the school because "there are more 98s and 97s in our Gen Ed class than there is in the G&T class because you only need to score a 90 [if you're a sibling] to get into the G&T."

At the time of the follow up interview in 2014, Jessica's oldest son is still in the Gen Ed program, her middle daughter is in G&T, and her youngest child is in Gen Ed. Although she preps and continues to retest her children for G&T, Jessica does not believe there are many "advantages" to having G&T at TCS because the "socioeconomic makeup" of the children in the younger grades is now so similar. In 2011, she asked, "At one point does it not make sense anymore to have a whole separate basket of kids that are supposedly super learners or whatever, you know, gifted?" She also questioned what that division or label does to the Gen Ed children's "self-esteem or ego" when they get older and find out which program they are in. Near the end of the interview in 2011, she says that she has been "hearing that maybe they will take [G&T] out eventually... parents are talking about it in the respect that they've heard from administration that they will probably cancel it."

The second part of this chapter includes data and analysis from follow-up interviews with eight White parents, like Jessica, who had a child enrolled in the Kindergarten or first grade Gen Ed program in 2011, and allows the reader to explore how the school has changed over time. It also tracks decisions made by these parents to switch their children to the G&T, leave the school, or choose to remain in the Gen Ed program. Additionally, this section includes an interview with a White Gen Ed mother named Cassie, who was not in the original sample. The findings show that despite the shifting demographics in Gen Ed, White parents are still retesting for G&T with six out of the eight parents either switching to G&T, or leaving the school (see Table 5.2). In fact, these parents are continuing to use their cultural capital to test prep and secure a G&T seat because of the perceived advantages of the G&T label and the stigma of Gen Ed.

Table 5.2 White parents who were reinterviewed in 2014

Parent	First Interview (2011)	Second Interview (2014)	G&T Status?
Jessica	1 child in Gen Ed	2 children in Gen Ed; 1 in G&T	Retested, but did not switch to G&T
Melissa	2 children in both; 1 in middle	1 child in Gen Ed; 1 in middle school; 1 in HS	Retested, but did not switch to G&T
Margaret	2 children in both	1 child in G&T; 1 in middle school	Yes, switched to G&T in 1st Grade
Lauren	2 children in Gen Ed	2 children in G&T	Yes, switched to G&T in 2nd Grade
Lindsay	3 children in both	2 children in G&T; 1 in middle school	Yes, switched to G&T in 1st Grade
Caitlyn	1 child in G&T; 1 in middle	2 children in G&T; 1 in middle school; 1 in HS	Yes, switched to G&T in 1st Grade
Tessa	3 children in both	2 children in G&T; 1 in middle school	Yes, switched to G&T in 3rd Grade
Kelly	1 child in Gen Ed	1 child in G&T	Yes, switched to a different G&T program in 1st Grade
Cassie	N/A[a]	1 child in Gen Ed	Retested, but did not switch to G&T

[a] Cassie did not participate in the original study. She was recruited when revisiting the school because of her experience as a White Gen Ed mother.

Less Talk about the G&T Program Phasing Out

Fast-forward three years and the discussion about phasing the G&T program out, that Jessica spoke about in her initial interview, is pretty "silent" because of the change in school leadership, and how popular and competitive the G&T program at TCS has become over time. As Jessica explained in her follow-up interview in 2014, "There had been talk about [the G&T phase out] years ago, but lately I've been hearing that it will probably be here for awhile." Britt, who has three children in the G&T program now, replied, "I have to say that the administration seems very silent" on this issue. Similarly, Kelly, a parent who left the school for another G&T program, said, "the segregation between programs may be a peripheral concern now that the seats are so few and far between because so many of the seats at [TCS] are going to siblings... and people are maybe looking past that because they're just happy to get a G&T seat, especially if you live near me [in a certain neighborhood] because the schools up there are terrible, so if you live up by me you're happy to get a [G&T] seat at [TCS], no worries about the segregation! (Laughs)."

The principal at TCS has changed three times in three years and the current leader does not seem to have the same vocal critique of offering the G&T program that the former principal did in 2011. Back in 2011, it was well-known that the principal was "not a huge fan" of the two programs at TCS because of the segregation and the tension that it caused within the school. The former principal reportedly was "deliberately moving teachers around, putting some of the strong teachers in the Gen Ed program" to appease White advantaged parents entering into the program. Instead of phasing the G&T program out, the current conversation is focused on keeping the two programs intact and making them more "equitable." According to Jessica, the administration is "really trying to operate like it is one school where there isn't those divisions... In fact, when they give tours a lot of times parents are really concerned and have a lot of questions about the G&T program and the administration is always very clear in pointing out that the curriculum is the same between the two programs." This is the same concern that was brought up by incoming G&T parents at the G&T school tour in 2011. According to parents, in the current era of an increased focus on standardized testing and the Common Core, the administration's main focus is bringing up test scores, and less focus is placed on the school climate.

Another reason for the silence about phasing the G&T program out is because TCS is the "top" G&T choice for *City Limits* parents now. This is the case because the other G&T program (School GT1) that was popular to advantaged parents decided to phase their program out in 2012. Parents explained that the other two G&T programs that the district offers are not as popular among White families because the Gen Ed portion in those schools is majority Black and Latino. Lauren, who has both of her sons in the G&T program now, said in some schools with G&T programs "that pull from the projects, it is not an option for everybody because some people are like, 'Oh great, they're giving me a G&T spot in a school where my kid's going to be a huge minority.' I don't know that that's an option for parents that are buying into the G&T program, you know what I mean?" Nevertheless, one parent named Kelly, who lives in TCS's catchment and was originally going to choose the Gen Ed program at TCS, decided instead to retest her son for G&T. She ultimately chose one of the lower-status G&T programs in the district because he was not being challenged enough in the Gen Ed classroom. When asked about her decision between Gen Ed at TCS and G&T at another school, Kelly replied: "Well, I don't know at the time I felt like [TCS], it's so funny because at the time [TCS] was very segregated by G&T versus non-G&T and I just didn't really like that *feeling*, but now I'm on the opposite end of it (laughing) so...I still don't like that feeling either, the feeling of segregation, but this program seems to work out better for him."

When probed on what the "feeling" of segregation is like in her school, Kelly said, "You can notice it just in terms of the class composition...you certainly sense it in the conversations that you overhear walking into the school and the language parents use with their children, I feel like the parental communities are very defined by classroom, which I think it would be nice if the parents would get together more as a grade level and just more as a whole school community, too." She also said what attracts parents to this particular G&T program is that it is known for being an "entry point" into the G&T middle school program, "which everyone is concerned about." On the other hand, what detracts parents from choosing the school is that it "pulls heavily from the housing projects into the Gen Ed program, and that's where the disparity between Gen Ed and G&T comes in, because these kids are all the low-income kids, and that's where the supposed segregation comes in because it feels like part community school and part selective school." When asked whether she thinks the G&T program will be phased out over time, Kelly answered, "No, I can't see that happening because [TCS's] scores are still very mixed and these schools draw from public housing, and that's not going to go away...[GT1] could phase their program out because they do not have public housing and demographically it was probably much easier for them to phase it out."

Another White parent, Cassie, who has a child in the Gen Ed program despite testing him for G&T every year, said that the reason they put G&T programs in the schools is to provide an "incentive" for White wealthy parents who could afford private schools. G&T is also there, according to Cassie, "to encourage income inequality. I'm totally serious. It's reverse bussing, back in the day. It's reverse desegregation." Initially, when Cassie moved into the neighborhood, she did not know that there was a G&T program and just registered her son for Gen Ed. Cassie quickly realized there was this "hierarchy" between parents and students, however, and had him tested for first grade G&T. He did not get a high enough score for TCS so he was offered a placement in another school farther away. She said, "I started getting really mad that he was not in G&T." The difference she sees the most between programs is the academic peer effects in the Gen Ed classroom: "What's happening is—I mean, this sounds like snobbery and it's so not meant to be but it kind of—I'm finding [my son] sinking to the level of these kids that I want him to stay the hell away from."

Because she does not like the "segregation" and the way they "label the kids" to make them feel "superior or inferior," she wishes that they would "mix" students up in the classrooms. Cassie said that even the after-school programs are segregated because the YMCA program is free and "basically all kids of color," while the "musical theatre and karate" classes are "very expensive." She said you even have to "pay to be in the school play." This creates a racial and socioeconomic divide even after school. She said that there are some "scholarship kids" in those classes, but "even scholarship kids have to pay something."

When asked if she has heard anything about the G&T program phasing out, she replied: "There are murmurs sometimes saying it shouldn't be here. There are quite a few people who don't like that there's no parent involvement whatsoever in the Gen Ed classes. It has been noted and there is a major financial divide. It has been noted. There are quite a few people who don't like the snobbery. It is just plain snobbery." She related the G&T parents as being the parents who "rule the school, they're the mean girls." Cassie adamantly believes that G&T programs are implemented because the DOE wants to attract White parents into the system. She explained that "if every kid took the G&T test," like the Regents test, and it was not something you had to apply for, "it would no longer fulfill the rich White parents' need to feel special and set apart...Bottom line it's all about the segregation." Cassie also believes that the effects of second-generation segregation are felt more by the Gen Ed children: "All of the Gen Ed kids are painfully aware of it. All of the Gen Ed kids know that they are second-class citizens." She gives an example by explaining that G&T children go on field trips all the time, while the Gen Ed students are left behind, and "We always run out of basic supplies and they're just overflowing with things that they don't even know what to do with. It's really such a tale of two cities. Yes, they're right here. Right here across the hall from each other. Oh, it's very sad."

In terms of the differences between the G&T and Gen Ed parent involvement, Cassie said she's "burned out" by always being the class parent that does everything. When asked why the other Gen Ed parents do not participate or volunteer, she explained, "I think they feel so alienated by the school that they just don't care. Now, a lot of them are just people that work 17 jobs to keep a roof over their heads and those people I have no resentment toward whatsoever. They're working 17 jobs to keep roofs over their heads and that's fine. I get that. I don't expect them to donate time or money or effort at all. But others, they just—I think that they just are divorced from the school because the school is divorced from them. I don't blame them." Because G&T parents donate the most time and money to the school, there is a perception that they are more valuable to the school—leading to Gen Ed parents feeling marginalized and undervalued. And, even though the resources from parent donations are supposed to be evenly distributed across programs, according to parent accounts, G&T parents still donate the "fancy printers," "air conditioners," and "rugs" to their child's G&T classroom, even when they're not supposed to.

According to parents, administrators are attempting to "level the playing field" between programs by having a shared supply closet for teachers, cross-aged reading buddies from different programs, and mixing G&T and Gen Ed classes when they go on field trips, because, as Jessica said, "everybody wants the kids to know each other." The parents and the administration have even discussed changing the name of the two programs to make it less of a "stigma." Margaret, who is an upper-class White parent with two children in the G&T program since her youngest daughter tested into G&T in first grade, said that the PTA has discussed changing "the language" of G&T because of the stigma and that there's been "talk about switching it but no real solution has come up." She believes that "it will always be clear that there's two different [programs] and one is considered more advanced somehow. Even if they changed it to the A program or the B program, at least it's not 'gifted and talented,' you know? Just that is so offensive." Jessica also would like to see the G&T and Gen Ed labels changed:

> I'm hoping that the school is still thinking about changing the name of G&T because it just seems like it's—I think it adds to the stigma. I think if you tell somebody that they're in General Ed and that somebody else is in Gifted & Talented, I think it just sounds—it makes the problem seem bigger than it is.

When asked if that is something the school can change, Jessica replied, "They've batted it around a little bit and I think the principal seemed open to it. I don't know if it's really going to happen anytime soon. There are parents that are going to be against it. I find that kind of interesting." Changing the name of the G&T program, though, does not address the core problem of within-school segregation that the system maintains.

Margaret said that at PTA meetings last year "there wasn't a ton of time spent on [whether the G&T program should be phased out], but I would say a lot of people who served on the PTA were very pro-having it phased out. But then I also know a lot of people talk so openly about it and ask as a first thing, 'Is your daughter in the G&T?' which I find really jarring. I found it particularly jarring when [my daughter] was in Gen Ed. It's sort of weirdly personal." She went on to say that some parents are "too invested in who are in the G&T versus who are not, elite or something, especially the new incoming kindergarten families are very into whether they're in G&T or Gen Ed." When asked what she thought was the biggest issue or concern facing the school today, Jessica replied, "I think as a parent, I still would like to see less concern or anxiousness among the parents about which program the child is in. I think that's a little bit of a hurdle that I'd like to see—I think that's actually more parental than the school. I don't know." Thus, the status of the G&T label continues to matter to parents, particularly the incoming parents, even though it shouldn't.

Parents continue to rationalize that a school that "pulls from the projects" needs a G&T program because as Lauren, whose son switched to G&T in second grade, explained, "It keeps the middle class and those are the ones that give the school hundreds of thousands of dollars. I'm sorry, but that's the way it works." Instead of phasing the program out and risk losing the highly involved parents that are attracted to the G&T program at TCS, parents said they should open up more G&T programs because there are so many students who make the 90th percentile score but do not get into TCS because their score is not high enough or because siblings take their spots. Lauren replied, "I feel like the system is broken because there aren't enough G&T slots [at TCS]. How dare you let your kid get a 98 and not give him a slot? You know what I mean? That is not okay. Move it up to 95 or higher or whatever you need to do. Move it up but make sure you have ample seats for everybody. That's absurd."

As already mentioned, Cassie, took the opposite side when she said White, advantaged parents would *not* want to expand the G&T program and make it more diverse because of the status and exclusivity of their child's G&T placement. She explained, "Ultimately, it's because of the money. The money is in the rich White parents that they want in the schools. Those rich White parents would not feel so inclined if all of those 'other people' took the test too and some of them even got in. You know I'm right." In other words, schools want G&T programs to attract the parents with money who will donate to the school. Parents want G&T programs because of the status, exclusivity, parent involvement, and resources that G&T parents bring to the school.

Parents are less inclined to advocate for phasing the G&T program out, however, because the G&T program at TCS is more popular and there is more competition to get a G&T seat. There is also still a perception that a G&T placement is a "feeder" for the better middle schools and high schools. Instead, they advocate for different things now to make the programs more equitable, including targeting a more diverse G&T student population, changing the name of the G&T program, or creating more G&T seats for students that qualify. That said, some parents are still very bothered by the segregation that exists and would rather see the G&T program go away because of the stigma of inferiority and superiority that it creates. At the same time, though, they also like the status that the G&T label affords them and fear the stigma of the Gen Ed label.

Reasons for Retesting for G&T

Even when parents critique the G&T program and attempt to downplay the differences between programs, they still feel that the G&T program, parents, and students are better. Jessica, who has two children in Gen Ed, said, "I retested my [youngest] daughter. I retested my son every year up until third grade because he always missed it by a point or two, so I just figured I would. I retested my youngest this year but I really knew I shouldn't. I just did it.... Just because." Although White, advantaged parents appreciate the classroom diversity in the Gen Ed classrooms and wish the G&T would be more diverse, they still choose to retest for G&T. They do this primarily because of the peer effects, parent involvement levels, and the academic or social stigma of the Gen Ed, and less about the academic differences, because the curriculum is the same. To illustrate, when asked what her biggest misconception was about the two different programs, Britt, whose youngest son tested into G&T in second grade, explained: "I think I thought it would have been much more advanced than it even was. To me, again, this was really just more about the group of people that were grouped together and stuff and moving forward but it wasn't like they were splitting atoms in the classroom, you know? I was picturing really pushing the kids and kind of pushing them to new levels, but it's a public school so there's also limits on what you can learn."

Instead of phasing the G&T program out, some parents believed that they should try to do more outreach and admit a more diverse G&T population into the school. When asked about the "diversity" in the Gen Ed classrooms compared to the G&T, Britt replied:

> It's really important to me. You don't get it in the G&T program as much. That's a shame I think. I don't know if it's promoting the G&T program to different ethnic or socioeconomic groups. It's not even like ethnic diversity. It is socioeconomic diversity. To me, that's super important, too. I love the fact that you'll get a college professor's kid, but you'll also get the superintendent of the building next door. It's a really good thing I think from the beginning, and honestly, the population that we have in the G&T program—it's expensive to live in the upper west side. It's no different really than you get, it feels like, in private school, which is—I'm not complaining about it but I actually really did like—I'm glad my kids were able to experience more of that [diversity] early on [in Gen Ed].

Again, White advantaged Gen Ed parents say diversity is really important to them and appreciate the *diversity by default* that their children experienced in the Gen Ed classrooms. Yet, apparently what was more important than exposing their child to diversity was the stigma of the Gen Ed label, particularly if their other children were in G&T.

As the school is becoming more popular to White, higher-income families over time, parents continue to praise the "true diversity" in the school because more and more White "neighborhood families" are choosing the Gen Ed program at TCS even if they do not get the G&T program that they prefer. In other words, the boundaries between programs are being broken down because there are White families on both sides now (see Table 1.5 in chapter one). Jessica, who now has two children in Gen Ed and one child in G&T, said, "Because the school is so popular now and you have to get a 99 in order to just get a spot, there's so many kids that score into the G&T that are in the Gen Ed classes now. It's kind of nice because now we really do have true diversity in all of the classes that we didn't have before, so that's kind of a good thing." In this way, she is using the term "diversity" to mean more White students in what was historically the majority Black and Latino Gen Ed program, while the G&T classes remain majority White.

When probed on what Jessica means by all the classes have "true diversity" now, she responds: "Actually it is a little disheartening. I'm just thinking about what I see in my kindergarten and first grade classes and there is I'd say *less diversity*. But it's truly a neighborhood school, so they really do pull from the demographics so I'm kind of interested myself that it isn't as diverse because it should continue. This is a very diverse neighborhood so it should continue to be that way."

On the one hand, parents seemed very proud that TCS was becoming a true neighborhood school that attracts "neighborhood" White families, even though they are losing some of the racial and socioeconomic diversity that they also said they appreciate in the school, due to Black and Latino students no longer being bused in from outside the district. Yet, even though the school itself is becoming more White, and higher-income over time, parents still strive for the highest-status G&T option that they believe will give their children advantages now and in the future.

MiddleS choolP lacement

A main reason for retesting is because as their children get older, parents seem to be getting even more "stressed" about test scores, not only for G&T placement in elementary school but also for the high-stakes standardized test scores in fourth grade and seventh grade that are used for middle school and high school applications. For example, Jessica recalled one particular time when she felt that her son was at a disadvantage for being in the Gen Ed program. It happened during fourth grade when the teachers were preparing students to take the tests that "really count" for middle school placement. She told a story about how there was this "fabulous" fourth grade G&T teacher that was chosen by the administration to run an after-school test prep program for the fourth grade tests. Jessica said that all of the G&T parents thought their child should be with this teacher because they were in G&T, and all of the Gen Ed parents also wanted their child to be assigned to her class. But, apparently the G&T and Gen Ed students were randomly assigned to the two different teachers and mixed together. Jessica said she had a parent come up to her,

> really upset at the way that the teachers were chosen, and I said, "We didn't have anything to do with that, that was administration, we just gave them the program." She said to me, "Well, my son is really smart and he's with all of these dummies in Gen Ed." I just looked at her and said, "You realize my son's in Gen Ed?" And she goes, "Oh, I'm sorry, that's terrible, I didn't mean it that way." I'm just like, whatever. Honestly, it didn't upset me but I was slightly appalled that someone would make that comment. I didn't take it personally, but I just thought, really? Do you walk around with this cloud of thinking that your son is really that much smarter?

This quote speaks of the stigma of the Gen Ed label and the entitlement that some G&T parents embody because their child is located in what is considered to be the highest-status program. Jessica admits that an advantage to being in G&T is that "generally the kids in G&T do go to better middle schools," but she thinks it's more about the student than the program they are coming from. Other parents, however, thought a G&T placement guarantees entry into the "best" middle schools because students have higher academic self-esteem. Their stronger academic peers are also pushing G&T students and the teachers are better for preparing students to take the fourth grade tests that are used for middle school applications.

For instance, Britt thought that G&T provides extra advantages for middle school placement and adds to children's confidence that they can get into the better schools, when she said "It does give kids a heads up, too. It's like, that's my whole thing and that's why I want them to have it. You don't want to be called a B-student from the beginning, you know? It's not a question in [the G&T] class that you're going to go to the [G&T middle school] program or one of the good ones. Don't worry about it, you know? We'll make sure that you're fine." Britt also felt that there was "something missing and stuff that wasn't taught" in Gen Ed. She said she was supplementing more at home and "spending more money on tutoring them" when her children were in the Gen Ed program: "I think if my kids had been in the Gen Ed program—especially for me who works as much as I do, I would have had to be much more involved and on top of it and had to take off [from] work more. I think they've kind of done that for me" in the G&T program.

Parents also said that fewer people are leaving the city or switching to privates now, which they say causes more anxiety and competition around G&T and fourth grade tests for middle school placement, too. Margaret explained that for the fourth grade standardized tests, "the school didn't provide anything and people got tutors. [My son] got a tutor for the last two months or something. A lot of the families I know had tutors. Not all of them. It was sort of a dirty secret to have one—it feels unfair." Kelly said, "For the fourth grade tests everybody tutors, which bothers me to no end because I don't want to do it." This is another example of how parents had to compromise their values by choosing to prep their children for admission into the high-status schools and programs where they felt they belonged. When asked what she believes are the advantages for the G&T program now and in the future, she replied, "Honestly, the biggest advantage is that it seems to be a feeder for the better middle schools, which then seems to be a feeder for the better high schools and better colleges, so it's sort of the 'if you do this then you get that,' playing the game part, and the better teachers tend to be in the G&T classrooms." Similarly, when asked if being in G&T helps them with the fourth grade tests for middle school, Cassie said "Of course," because they are being "coached" to take the G&T tests and then "they get more and more practice with the standardized tests" and "It's all about the standardized tests."

In terms of the seventh grade tests for high school placement, Margaret replied, "Seventh grade is this really stressful year. People are concerned about the tests for this year. It's for the good district [high] schools that people want and they're competitive to get into. The specialized [high school] tests, that'll be next year [for my son]. These days everybody tutors for it. It's par for the course."

Being in G&T "Where All of the Smart Kids Are"

The parents who had (or still have) children in both programs, like Tessa, Lauren, Margaret, Kathy, and Jessica, explain that it is especially high stakes for their Gen Ed children to switch over to the G&T program because their siblings are in G&T and they see it as a social and academic stigma. For instance, during the first interview with Jessica, she questioned what effect the labels can have on Gen Ed children's "self-esteem or ego" when they get older and find out which program they are in? In the second interview, she answered her original question by telling a story about a time when her son came home and told her that one of his G&T friends said that they were moving to the next grade level in math, but that "you guys wouldn't do that because you're in a different class." She said that night he was "struggling with some homework and we had a conversation and he's a really low-key kid, he doesn't really get upset, but he did. He got really upset. He said, 'Well, if you wanted me to work so hard, you should have put me in G&T because that's where all of the smart kids are.' I actually told the principal about it because I wanted her to know that these kids do absorb those differences."

Britt said, "I really hate the label. I don't know that it's great for kids to think that 'I'm in the gifted program' and stuff. And what I've heard too—and this is the other thing I was worried about with [my son in Gen Ed]—is that it becomes—it's less of an issue in the lower grades, but it really is more of a stigma. Kids just realize it when they get to the fourth and fifth grade and I didn't want him to feel from the beginning that he was a C student because that's not the case at all." She remembered her daughter talking about other students who did not get into the gifted program saying comments like, "'I don't know why she didn't get in because she's smart.' Like it's implying that kids aren't smart if they're not in the [G&T] program...and also again it's visually very clear too, which I think is nuts." By using G&T programs to attract White families into the public schools, which results in second-generation segregation, White students learn a hidden curriculum of privilege and superiority. Black and Latino students, on the other hand, learn inferiority instead of cross-cultural understanding and equality.[5] It is true that the G&T programs technically do their job to attract White families and desegregate public schools at the building level. But, the question remains, what is the cost to students and families who enroll their children at TCS when the within-school segregation causes academic and social stigmas and a school culture that is divisive and non-inclusive?

Other rationales parents gave for retesting for G&T included the behavior issues in the Gen Ed classroom. Lauren explained the behavior issues in her son's first grade Gen Ed class: "The teacher didn't have control over the classroom because there were 4 or 5 kids that were just acting up." Because of that experience, she said that she "paid thousands of dollars for [G&T] test taking." As a result, her son went from an 86 in first grade to a 90 in second grade. Yet, she still said she was not sure "if the tutoring helped at all, you know what I mean? Maybe it would have—he would have got a 90 anyhow. But we had to do something!" She replied that if he did not get into G&T they were going to leave the city and go to the suburbs. She also said that her son "started to notice [that he was in Gen Ed]. He said, 'Mommy, I want to be in a class like [my brother] with all the smart kids.' You can start to notice, right? So he got in by the skin—he got a 90, and he had sibling pull. His next year, second grade was fabulous. He had a great teacher. She told me his confidence just went through the roof." Lauren thought that having her son in the G&T with other "super smart kids ... forces you to rise to another level so I do feel like surrounding yourself with smarter people makes you smarter."

Using similar arguments for retesting for G&T, Tessa who is a Conflicted Follower with two daughters in G&T and a younger son in Gen Ed retested for G&T three times before he finally got a seat for second grade. When asked why she decided to retest her son, Tessa replied:

> I knew he was a bright kid. It's just the way he speaks and everything. He understands things.... especially with his sisters being in it, I really did see it as a stigma. And I didn't love it enough, but I just think it was more about you play to the level of your competition. I think it was just more about the kids that were in the class. *It was never even a question not to because I think it's a huge advantage*, you know, and I think it preps you for middle school testing and everything, too. (Emphasis added)

In this way, White advantaged parents use their cultural capital to tutor their children for the G&T test and have back up plans to leave the city if they do not get into the school or G&T program that they desire. While White parents have school choice options and back up plans, the majority of the parents of color in this book are not aware of their options and just enroll their children in their neighborhood school. This goes against the argument that school choice advocates make that more choice levels the playing field and gives less advantaged parents a better chance of getting into a high-quality school.

The next and final Conclusion chapter describes how the policy context that parents are operating within creates the status distinctions between schools and programs in the first place, and further, how policies could be implemented to combat the segregation that the system maintains. The Conclusion discusses the implications of this research, critiques of the system, and offers policy recommendations based on the findings from this book.

CONCLUSION

PUTTING INTEGRATION (BACK?) ON THE
EDUCATION POLICY AGENDA

New York City is known for its incredible racial/ethnic and socioeconomic diversity. It is also notorious for being the third most segregated school system in the country.[1] This segregation occurs both between schools and within schools that house self-contained G&T or dual language programs.[2] Gary Orfield, a civil rights scholar, writes about the condition of New York City school segregation in a recent UCLA Civil Rights Report, stating, "This is ultimately a discussion about choice. Choice can either increase opportunity and integration, or increase inequality and stratification."[3] The parent interview data has shown that using G&T programs to attract White families into the public school system can, by default, desegregate schools, but can also result in "desegregation without integration,"[4] academic and social stigmas, marginalized parent communities, and a divisive school culture between the haves and have-nots. Over time, this practice can also result in a more White and higher-income school overall, as White catchment students enroll in the Gen Ed program and Black and Latino students are no longer bused in to fill the Gen Ed seats.

This book's main argument is that the core problem of offering G&T programs at the elementary school level is flawed. By using a single test score for admission and by assuming all parents will apply for testing and use school choice to gain access to G&T programs, the NYCDOE is not necessarily identifying "gifted and talented" students. They are simply identifying advantaged students in the system. *City Limits* school choice program is "color-blind" because its central goal is to maximize parental choice and not to integrate schools. As Gary Orfield cautions, when you rely upon a deregulated school choice system with no "civil rights standards" in place,[5] like New York City, it leads to an increase in inequality and stratification between and within schools with G&T programs.[6]

In the current post–civil rights era, New York City district officials could learn from the parents in this book about how within-school segregation operates, the social construction of giftedness, the ongoing debate about G&T tracking and best practices, and the role of social reproduction and boundaries in maintaining educational advantage. In fact, this case study in one elementary school goes beyond individual parents' choices by highlighting how the G&T policy and the sociocultural context shape the distribution of opportunities and create the status distinctions between schools and programs. In other words, within this policy context, many parents said they would prefer to enroll their children in diverse schools that have strong educational programs. But because of the lack of such options available, they continue to make choices that privilege their children and perpetuate the status quo. They choose disproportionately White schools and programs because it matches their privileged position in the larger society and prevailing messages about worth, value, and opportunities in an environment in which parental anxiety runs high regarding their children's future in a competitive society.[7]

Jay MacLeod writes about this relationship between individual choices and the larger context of inequality: "Individual choices matter and make a difference, but the stage is largely set."[8] In fact, parents on both side of the G&T / Gen Ed boundary felt that the New York City "system is set up to split people into groups, White, Black and Brown," thus, they use their uneven cultural capital exchange to "game the system" and get their children into the high-status G&T options. They are permitted to do this because of the DOE-dictated admissions criteria for gifted programs, especially the standardized G&T exam that has historically resulted in disproportionate numbers of White and Asian students passing the cutoff score; the extra prepping and tutoring for the standardized G&T tests that higher-income parents can afford and others cannot; the separate G&T classrooms located in particular school buildings that enroll a majority of lower-income students of color in the Gen Ed program; the unequal preschool opportunities, and so on.

By studying how White advantaged parents make sense of their children's placements in a segregated school context, this book illustrates how they either navigate the status associated with giftedness or the stigma of the Gen Ed label by rationalizing and reconciling where they belong. G&T parents justify their situation by promoting the fact that their children are being exposed to school-level diversity. Gen Ed parents, however, are getting *diversity by default*. In fact, the desires of advantaged parents to have their children educated in a "diverse" setting, conceptualized at the school or classroom level and meaning different things to different parents, gets reconstructed depending on their child(ren)'s placement(s) in the school. On the other side, Gen Ed parents of color see the school and the G&T program as a tool for segregation, status, power that is unfair, and takes opportunities away from their children. The G&T program also creates a situation in which the White students are thought of as the "smart kids."[9] This is the perfect opportunity to phase segregated G&T programs out by targeting the Negotiators, Followers, and Reconcilers in the system who have experience in both programs and have to negotiate their better than / less than status. Schools like TCS that are enrolling White students on either side of the boundary continue to foster misunderstandings and an divisive educational environment for parents and students within the school.

The question remains that if "diversity by choice" was a viable option for parents,[10] would more parents choose that option and could these boundaries between parents, students, schools, and classrooms come crumbling down? Is there political viability to bringing together the competing ideals of free market choice and social mobility on the one hand, and democratic equality and diversity on the other, by providing more high-quality, diverse, and de-tracked school options?[11]

What Can and Should Be Done?

Gary Orfield rightly points out that when school districts do not make "integration a goal, it cannot happen."[12] Therefore, if NYCDOE officials are interested in eliminating second-generation segregation within schools that offer self-contained G&T programs,[13] and setting the policy agenda to school integration, there are two options to consider moving forward. These include keeping G&T programs and identifying a more diverse G&T student population, or phasing G&T programs out to create more diverse school settings. If G&T is to remain within schools that also house Gen Ed, there needs to be more equitable methods for the identification of gifted learners. In fact, the parents in this book overwhelmingly believe that the G&T test that the district uses to define giftedness is more about students' advantaged background characteristics and whether or not they were prepped for the tests, than any accurate measure of a child's intelligence. In this context, it is also about whether or not parents send their children to high-quality private preschools, are informed about the G&T admission's process, and sign their children up to take the G&T test in the first place.

DiversifyG &T

Research has shown that the relationship between tracking and gifted education, as it intersects with the use of standardized tests, will most likely result in a "gifted identification problem." Disproportionate numbers of White, higher-income students are enrolled in G&T classrooms and Black/Latino low-income students are in lower-tracked classrooms.

Indeed, scholars have advocated for a better way to identify gifted students, especially low-income minority students since they are underrepresented in gifted programs.[14] The National Association for Gifted Children (NAGC) states that "one test at a specific point in time should not dictate whether someone is identified as gifted," therefore identification should occur over time.[15] NAGC recommends using multiple instruments for G&T identification, including objective (standardized tests and grades) and subjective (nominations, teacher observations and ratings, and portfolios) measures. Researchers have found that there are certain approaches that are more effective in identifying gifted students who are from lower-income families, including "curriculum-based assessment," "portfolio assessment," "open-ended teacher referrals," and "conceiving of identification as a process, not an event."[16] While *City Limits* did try to use teacher recommendations along with test scores for G&T admission in 2007, it only lasted one year because of advantaged parents' complaints over teacher subjectivity. The following year is when the centralized G&T policy began, which created less diverse G&T programs.

Therefore, policy officials should rethink the use of a single test score when children are in preschool for G&T admission, wait to test students for G&T later in elementary school, and provide more outreach about G&T options to preschools that serve lower-income students to help offset the advantages that middle- to upper-middle-class parents possess in the G&T application process. While these recommendations might "marginally increase equity and diversity" in the short term, they will not attend to the "problematic idea at the core of many G&T programs—namely that elementary school children need to be segregated by ability, when such 'ability' is likely to reflect primarily the privilege and experiences conferred by socioeconomic status."[17] According to a recent *New York Times* article, The New York City Council is considering one piece of legislation and two resolutions to address school segregation, including the use of multiple criteria for admission to the Specialized High Schools, requiring the DOE to provide critical data relevant to the demographics of schools and school districts in an annual report, and moving from a "neutral stance" on achieving school diversity to an active "policy goal."[18] While these are all noble first steps on the path to school integration, none of these address the racial disparities that result from the use of a single test score for G&T admissions.

Phase G&T Out

A second option to consider is one that will address the core problem of G&T segregation—by race/ethnicity, class, and academic ability. This option would phase out segregated G&T classrooms in neighborhood schools that also offer Gen Ed. Mara Sapon-Shevin, a leading opponent of G&T programs, has argued for dismantling G&T programs and implementing more inclusive, differentiated curricula and teaching to diverse learners (G&T students included) based on the inclusive special education model.[19] For instance, Sapon-Shevin writes: "Gifted programs are implemented for students for whom educational failure will not be tolerated (generally the children of the White, privileged parents) and are enacted in ways that leave the general education system untouched and immune to analysis and critique."[20] In a more recent writing, Borland explains that even if more lower-income minority students were placed in G&T programs, the "problems persist" and that "effective education and equitable education can [not] coexist with gifted education."[21]

Instead of using separate G&T programs to attract advantaged families into public schools, which inevitably leads to segregation between tracks, school officials—here and elsewhere—should consider "de-tracking" the G&T programs by creating heterogeneous classrooms where "gifted" and "non-gifted" students learn side by side in "gifted for all" culturally responsive learning environments. This approach uses the Schoolwide Enrichment Model (SEM) devised by two gifted education professors, Joseph Renzulli and Sally Reis.[22] In fact, when the current New York City school chancellor was an elementary school principal, she decided to phase out the G&T program at her school and replace it with SEM.[23] Since then, two other schools in Park Slope, Brooklyn have phased their G&T programs out as well. Wells & Serna contend, "If a school does away with separate classes for students labeled 'gifted' but teachers continue to challenge these students with the same curriculum in a de-tracked setting, the only 'losses' the students will incur are their label and their separate and unequal status."[24] Thus, de-tracking the G&T and Gen Ed programs is key to closing the opportunity gap in New York City elementary schools.[25]

School leaders have an important role to play in shaping and enabling second-generation school practices, like tracking, ability grouping, and the misplacement of students in special education.[26] School administration, teachers, and parents also have the power to develop strategies to be more inclusive across G&T and Gen Ed parent boundary lines—for example, not allowing unfair classroom donations to the G&T classrooms. Further research could explore principals' perceptions of their agency around organizational structures and school culture, political barriers to enacting change, and ways they could increase equity within schools through de-tracking and teacher professional development.[27] The attention should be shifted from a narrow focus on standardized testing (including the G&T tests) to a more inclusive approach that uses heterogeneous classrooms and high expectations for all students using the SEM approach. For instance, a principal in Durham, North Carolina, David Snead, noticed that Black students comprised only 7 percent of G&T identification compared to 98 percent of White students in his elementary school that was 30 percent White and 70 percent Black. This resulted in achievement gaps between White and Black students.[28] He decided to investigate the problem and found that teachers were the gatekeepers of the G&T identification process. In order to close the achievement gap in his school, he created an "Exploratory Guest Program" in which Gen Ed students that showed "potential" for G&T could be exposed to the challenging G&T curricula; he set "early expectations" by ensuring all kindergarten students be at a certain reading level before first grade; he hired a teacher for one-on-one reading and math tutoring; and he had teachers participate in diversity training that would help them to better identify talented Black students.[29]

As a result of Snead's approach to desegregating Southwest Elementary, from 1999 to 2003 the achievement gap between Black and White students was "virtually eliminated."[30] His success was transformed into "Project Bright IDEA" curriculum in North Carolina, which is targeted to K–2 classrooms and uses "gifted for all" teaching methodology. Students are randomly assigned to Bright IDEA classrooms and have higher G&T acceptance rates compared to other students at the school. This experiment shows that "universalizing access to G&T-quality curriculum" can have equitable effects by race and class. It also illustrates the powerful learning opportunities that can happen when all students are held to high expectations and given challenging curricula. Halley Potter, an education policy researcher at The Century Foundation, advocates for shifting neighborhood schools with self-contained G&T programs to SEM "one school at a time."[31]

The underlying notion is that what White advantaged families *want* and *need* are separate and unequal spaces for their children's education.[32] Although, there were hopes that the current New York City school chancellor would "overhaul" the G&T system, she apparently also believes in the power of G&T programs to attract certain "communities" into the system. The chancellor was recently quoted in a *New York Times* article as being pro-G&T programs: "What exists right now is serving the purpose of communities, and I have no intention of touching it," even though before her tenure as chancellor she believed in mixed-ability classrooms.[33] The assumption is that if the NYCDOE phased the G&T programs out, there would be massive White flight from the public schools. Yet, that does not seem to be the case since many White advantaged families are bothered by the segregation, do not "buy into" the G&T label, cannot afford private school or a move out to the suburbs, and will downplay the differences between programs—particularly since the curriculum is the same. Although some advantaged parents in the *City Limits* School District will probably choose separate, predominantly White G&T programs as long as they exist, there is a growing group of advantaged parents in the system who might choose otherwise. If New York City policymakers would create more viable racially and socioeconomically diverse schools and programs within them, they could capitalize on parent critiques about the segregating effects of G&T programs.

There is also a growing uneasiness from parents about the anxiety and pressure that they are placing on their children to perform well on the high-stakes standardized tests that the NYCDOE requires, not only to get a 98 or 99 for G&T in elementary school, but also for middle school and high school placement decisions. Amara, an African mother with experience in both programs at TCS, described the situation:

> I don't understand the pressure we give to our kids these days. It's getting worse, sometimes I feel like as a parent we are the ones doing this, we push our kids so hard, so much, sometimes I'm afraid we are going to push them down and they are going to fall off the cliff, these kids are with us 24/7, and then there has to be a limit, we push, we push, and we don't do it for ourselves we have to do what the kids want because they want to impress uss o much.

Policymakers should stop relying on a single test score for admission into selective schools/programs that serve to advantage White families even more. This should be an important goal for gentrifying cities like New York City, while helping to provide more equitable educational opportunities for all children. As schools like TCS become more "diverse" in the Gen Ed program, meaning more White students, and boundaries are slowly being broken down over time, it is the perfect opportunity to appeal to advantaged parents' ambivalence between diversity and exclusivity, as well as their discomfort with the "dichotomy" built up within schools with G&T programs. Kelly, an Incoming Parent to the Gen Ed program in 2011, who now has her son in a G&T program, explained:

> I have very mixed feelings about testing them so young for these things. I wish that it could be a little bit different—I either wish they would get rid of G&T entirely, or that they would establish more gifted schools like Anderson and devote more resources to those seats and kind of pull it out of the neighborhood schools and in a specific area where there isn't this dichotomy built.

There is an opportunity there to stop the cycle of social reproduction in schools with segregated G&T programs by phasing the programs out and making G&T a non-option (except for in the citywide G&T schools), and making *diversity by default* in the Gen Ed program, diversity by choice instead.

Create and Promote Diverse Schools

An option for policy makers to consider, then, would be to create and promote more racially diverse, non-G&T schools such as the highly popular district-wide (unzoned) schools with separate application processes and distinctive themes. In fact, there are currently two unzoned schools in this district that have long waiting lists of White advantaged children. These schools are diverse at the classroom level and are popular school options for advantaged families. The new unzoned schools should be new schools that are located in more racially and socioeconomically diverse neighborhoods—possibly as overflow schools to relieve some of the overcrowding in the most popular, disproportionately White schools. This option, though, relies on a diverse group of applicants to apply to each school. Therefore, schools would need to advertise their program to attract a diverse group of applicants.

Another step for policymakers and school administrators is to change the perception of what the "best" education looks like in this context—from disproportionately White and higher-income schools and programs being the best option, to schools that are celebrated for their diversity. Amara, an African mother who had experience in both programs at TCS, said "I think for a school to be a good school you have to mix it, for me I'm a Black mother, I don't want to be in a predominantly Black environment, at the same time I don't want to be in all White, I want a mix." *City Limits*, as well as other school districts in New York City and across the country, could follow in the footsteps of two of Brooklyn's Community School Districts (CSD), 13 and 15, who jointly devised a "pro-diversity admissions rule" because of gentrification and overcrowding in certain neighborhood schools.[34] CSD 13 and 15, with the help of a nonprofit organization called New York Appleseed, advocated for the DOE to use a lottery application process that uses a formula to ensure that 35 percent of students at each school would be from "disadvantaged" backgrounds, meaning English Language Learners and students who receive free and reduced price lunch.[35] While the Supreme Court PICs[36] ruling limited the use of race as the sole criterion for student assignment policies, school districts are still permitted to expand the definition of diversity to include other diversity measures particular to their community context to integrate schools.[37] For instance, the Berkeley Unified School District uses a "diversity code" to maintain racial diversity in its schools based on a student's geography. The "diversity code" uses neighborhood location to calculate the percentage of students of color and socioeconomic status in each "planning area" when parents are choosing schools.[38]

Using students' geography and expanding the definition of diversity could work in the *City Limits* district since it is gentrified with a mix of affluent neighborhoods, several public housing buildings, an enclave of recent Latino immigrants, and several subsidized or rent-stabilized residential buildings. This diversity, though, is not reflected in the schools—with the most popular schools with disproportionate numbers of advantaged students being overcrowded. Just like they did in Brooklyn with the NYCDOE's approval, this pro-diversity option would entail eliminating existing schools' catchment zones and opening them up for district-wide enrollment. This option could appeal to TCS parents who want to expose their children to "diversity" or at least not be in the minority in their zoned school while maintaining socioeconomic and racial diversity and not allowing low-income students to be pushed out by changing demographics. Some CSDs have also discussed the implementation of a controlled choice program to diversify schools, which would eliminate zoned schools altogether and use an algorithm to place students in schools based on SES and other factors. Controlled choice programs have had success in Cambridge, MA and Montclair, NJ, and could be a viable option for *City Limits*.

Like the unzoned schools that draw students from the entire district, another way to achieve diversity in this district would be to create magnet school options that have racial/SES integration as their main goal. Magnet schools receive federal or state funding and offer special programs or themes (like art, drama, or science) to attract diverse students from different neighborhoods. Since the 1980s, several CSDs, including *City Limits*, have received funding to open magnet programs. However, they have not followed through with the primary goal of desegregation largely because of the lack of commitment from the DOE to desegregate schools. Unlike some cities, like Hartford, Connecticut, that have successful magnet programs,[39] those in New York City have not lived up to their potential.[40] The US Department of Education is emphasizing the benefit of diversity in its competitive magnet school funding process. These magnet school programs could use multiple criteria for admission, like interviews, observations, and teacher recommendations, to admit a diverse student population. This option, though, does not fix the problem of segregation in the neighborhood schools. Therefore, magnet school programs would need to be carefully designed so as not to make neighborhood schools more racially and socioeconomically isolated by only attracting the more advantaged parents.

The parent interview data strongly suggest that more undivided and diverse school options would ultimately be what many advantaged parents are looking for (even if they have their children enrolled in the G&T program), as evidenced by their contradictory attitudes about where their children belong in a school with two hierarchical programs. This is particularly true for parents who have had experience with both programs and realize that there is not much difference academically between the two programs. The irony is that the history of the city's public school system has been to use the separate and unequal G&T programs to keep White, middle-class families from leaving the public schools. But, as Caitlyn, a fourth grade White parent, explained: "I do get the sense that the average person is just looking for—they don't necessarily want a G&T program, they just want a good basic education for their kids. And I think in New York there are such extremes. I feel like it's hard just to find a middle of the road—[school A in Table 1.3] is that way, but ya know, if you don't happen to live in that zone then you have to make it work."

G&T Critiques

There is evidence beyond this research that more New Yorkers are questioning the validity of these separate and segregated G&T classrooms. For instance, The *New York Times* ran a piece on G&T programming that criticized the New York City school system and other urban districts for using G&T programs to "help prevent White flight from the schools" and that the use of standardized tests for G&T admission "tends to skew the programs toward children from Whiter, and wealthier families."[41] The article also cites a G&T parent who said that the reason G&T programs are majority White is not the "result of anyone's bad intentions." Instead, this G&T parent said that it is a "result of people committed to a system that can never work if the objective is diversity" because, like this book also found, White, affluent parents pass along their advantages to their children in the form of G&T placements.[42]

New York Magazine ran a cover story criticizing the City's G&T policy for testing children at too early of an age because their IQs are unstable and their scores can change dramatically depending on the type of test used, how comfortable the child is with the tester, and other environmental factors.[43] Additional changes have been made to the types of G&T tests used each year, tests that the DOE claims would be harder to prepare for, none of which address the narrow criteria being used in selecting students or the racial separation that these programs create within schools that have them. In another local news article, the author cites a national specialist in gifted education as saying that an "entirely test driven admissions process will only exacerbate the problem of equity and racial imbalance," since it is very hard to identify lower-income, minority children as being "gifted" using tests alone.[44]

In fact, the research findings contained in this book strongly support phasing out G&T programs across the district with 73 percent of parents, or 30 out of 41 parents, saying they would support a G&T phase out. This is the case because of how uncomfortable they are with the ongoing segregation between programs, their critique of the validity of the G&T tests, and their definition of what giftedness means in this context. Parents believe that all children have gifts and talents that should be recognized and nurtured in schools. Classrooms should be mixed with higher-ability students that can help the lower-achieving students succeed. The parents with children in both programs, in particular, best articulated their belief that the "gifted" label is socially constructed—relating "giftedness" in this context more to students' advantaged backgrounds and G&T test preparation than their true intelligence—because they stated that they did not believe one of their children is more "gifted" than the other.

Research has also shown that, on average, low-SES children are less prepared to start kindergarten than their high-SES peers.[45] Sean Reardon found that for children who started kindergarten with higher-level skills, the achievement gap between Black and White students got wider as they progressed through school.[46] These findings have important implications for using high-stakes G&T tests on four-year-olds to determine if they are "gifted" or "not gifted," specifically for those children who attend a high-quality, private preschool that bestows on them clear advantages that other children may not receive. In fact, parents said that certain private preschools will do test prep practice in school to prepare children for the G&T tests.

New York City's new Universal Pre-K (UPKNYC) campaign is a step on the right track to help combat the disparities in students' school readiness. Under the new mayor's leadership, the DOE is now offering universal preschools that are free to all families so students come to school better prepared to start kindergarten. If all students start kindergarten with higher-level skills, this could be one way to narrow the achievement gap as students progress through school. In fact, parents in this book spoke about how much money private preschool costs ($15,000–30,000 per year), and how difficult it used to be to get a universal pre-k seat in one of the neighborhood schools in their district because of the lack of available seats compared to the demand.

The research findings in this book illustrate the subtle, micro-level mechanisms that create, perpetuate, and exacerbate racial segregation and inequality in education. The findings suggest the limits (and dangers) of deregulated, "color-blind" school choice policies that favor advantaged families and consistently lead to second-generation segregation. It also reveals the ambivalence that advantaged parents themselves feel about being part of these privileging processes and programs. In highly diverse school districts across the country, like Rockville Centre, New York or Morristown, New Jersey, school leaders, parents, and educators take pride in their district's diversity—saying that students are learning so much more about our increasingly diverse society when they are learning side-by-side with racially, socioeconomically, and culturally diverse students. Instead of teaching students a hidden curriculum of White privilege and superiority and Black and Latino inferiority in tracked classrooms,[47] diverse school districts across the country should put desegregation and integration [back?] on the policy agenda to prepare children for a global society andg reatere quality.

Notes

Preface and Acknowledgments

1. Lareau, *Unequal Childhoods*.
2. Roda and Wells, "School Choice Policies and Racial Segregation"; See discussion of the study in chapter one.
3. See Borland, "The Death of Giftedness"; Gootman, "Children Face Rejection by Neighborhood Schools in Manhattan"; Saulny, "Gifted Classrooms Will Soon Use Uniform Test, Klein Decides."
4. Maia Cucchiara helped review an article submitted for publication in the American Educational Research Journal—Social and Institutional Analysis, which is based on chapter two.

Introduction   Maintaining Their Advantage

1. All names of districts, schools, and participants are given pseudonyms to ensure confidentiality.
2. The terms "G&T" and "Gen Ed" are used because those are the labels that parentsu sed.
3. SeeS tillman, *Gentrification and Schools*.
4. Losen, "Silent Segregation in Our Nation's Schools"; Oakes, *Keeping Track*.
5. In this context, "advantaged" parents tend to be the White, higher-income families. See Bifulco et al.'s use of the term, in "Public School Choice and Integration."
6. Roda & Wells, "School Choice Policies and Racial Segregation."
7. Demerath, *Producing Success*; Cucchiara, "Are We Doing Damage?"
8. Mickelson," SubvertingS wann," 216.
9. Meier, Stewart, & England, *Race, Class, and Education*; Mickelson, "Subverting Swann."
10. Carter, *Stubborn Roots*.
11. Ibid.
12. Aja, Darity Jr., & Hamilton, "Segregated Education in Desegregated Schools."
13. Arum & Beattie, *The Structure of Schooling*.
14. During the time of the study, the student scores from the Otis-Lennon School Ability Test (OLSAT) and the Bracken School Readiness Assessment (BSRA) were weighted and averaged to produce one score. If the student scores above

the 90th percentile, he or she is guaranteed a spot in one of the G&T programs in the district.
15. See Borland, "The Death of Giftedness"; Borland, "Gifted Kids Deserve Better"; Sapon-Shevin, *Playing Favorites*; Sapon-Shevin, "Equity, Excellence, and School Reform."
16. Staiger," Whitenessa sG iftedness."
17. Sapon-Shevin, *Playing Favorites*.
18. Watanabe, "Tracking in the Era of High-Stakes Accountability Reform."
19. Because the district G&T programs are so popular and so many students make the 90th percentile cutoff, for admission into the most popular programs like TCS, students need to get a 98 or 99. To apply to citywide G&T programs, students are required to get a 97 or above and are admitted by lottery.
20. Gamoran, "The Variable Effects of High School Tracking."
21. Mickelson, Bottia, & Southworth, "School Choice and Segregation by Race, Class, and Achievement"; Oakes, *Keeping Track*.
22. See Oakes, Wells, Jones, & Datnow, "Detracking"; Rubin, "Detracking in Context." The tracking and de-tracking research provides an abundance of empirical findings on the negative effects of tracking in secondary schools—educationally, socially, and psychologically—and the strong relationship between track placements and students' background characteristics, especially race and social class.
23. Wells &S erna," TheP oliticso fC ulture."
24. Mickelson, Bottia, & Southworth, "School Choice and Segregation by Race, Class, and Achievement," 268.
25. Gootman, "Children Find Rejection by Neighborhood Schools in Manhattan."
26. Tyson, *Integration Interrupted*,6 .
27. Mickelson," SubvertingS wann."
28. Haimson & Kjelberg, "NYC Schools under Bloomberg and Klein."
29. See Borland, "The Death of Giftedness"; Borland, "Gifted Kids Deserve Better"; Sapon-Shevin, *Playing Favorites*; Sapon-Shevin, "Equity, Excellence, and School Reform."
30. See Sapon-Shevin, *Playing Favorites*; Staiger, "Whiteness as Giftedness"; Oakes, *Keeping Track*; and Margolin, *Goodness Personified*; Margolin, "A Pedagogy of Privilege."
31. Sapon-Shevin, *Playing Favorites*,3 3.
32. See Posey-Maddox, *When Middle-Class Parents Choose Urban Schools*; Cucchiara, *Marketing Schools, Marketing Cities*; Johnson & Shapiro, "Good Neighborhoods, Good Schools"; Holme, "Buying Homes, Buying Schools"; Lewis, *Race in the Schoolyard*; Kimelberg & Billingham, "Attitudes Toward Diversity and the School Choice Process"; Roda & Wells, "School Choice Policies and Racial Segregation"; Makris, *Public Housing and School Choice in a Gentrified City*; Sattin-Bajaj, *Unaccompanied Minors*.
33. Makris, *Public Housing and School Choice in a Gentrified City*.
34. See Stillman, *Gentrification and Schools*; Roberts, "Gentrification and School Choice."
35. Raschka," RejectingG &T";S tillman, *Gentrification and Schools*.

36. Hyper-segregated schools are defined as schools with more than 90 percent children of color. In the "City Limits" school district, there are 9 out of 19 schools that fit into this category. For some parents in the sample who live outside of the school's catchment, these are the zoned schools and they are using the G&T program to escape. Two neighborhood schools are considered racially and socioeconomically diverse and are very popular with White advantaged parents.
37. In the "City Limits" school district, out of 19 schools, 3 offer dual language and 3 schools offer G&T.
38. Charter schools in this district also tend to be hyper-segregated. An exception is one charter school that attracts some White, higher-income families.
39. Each family is assigned to a zoned public school based on their residential address. Other school options include public schools outside of their zone if there are seats available. Gifted programs require parents to get their children tested the fall before they start kindergarten. If students score above the 90th percentile, they are guaranteed a seat in a district G&T program. If they score above the 97th percentile, students become eligible for the citywide G&T programs. Unzoned schools draw students from across the community school district. There is one unzoned school in the City Limits district and it requires a separate lottery application. Charter schools are free public schools that also require parents to fill out an application and enrollment is based on a lottery. Dual language programs are self-contained classrooms within schools that enroll half English-only students and half that speak another language. The goal is for students to become fluent in both languages. See http://insideschools.org/elementary/gifted-a-other-options for more information.
40. At the time of the study in 2011, Asian students comprised 10 percent of the total student population (or about 50 students). Parents explained that most Asian families enroll their children in G&T at the school. While no Asian parents were interviewed for the book, this could be an area of future research.
41. Kershaw, "Agony on the Upper West Side over a Battle to Shift a Gifted Students'P rogram."
42. Demerath, *Producing Success.*
43. Bourdieu& P asseron, *The Inheritors*,4 96.
44. Bourdieu & Passeron, *The Inheritors*; Bourdieu, *Distinction*; Bourdieu, "The Forms of Capital."
45. Swartz, *Culture and Power*,1 91.
46. Lamont & Lareau, "Cultural Capital"; Bourdieu, *Distinction*; Bourdieu & Passeron, *The Inheritors.*
47. Ford, "Desegregating Gifted Education."
48. Bourdieu, *Distinction.*
49. SeeL areau, *Home Advantage* and *Unequal Childhoods.*
50. This book contributes to a smaller body of literature that has applied Bourdieu's framework to studies of race in the US context. See MacLeod, *Ain't No Makin' It*; Carter, *Keepin' It Real*; Wells & Crain, *Stepping over the Color Line.*
51. Lamont, *Money, Morals, and Manners*; Lamont & Molnar, "The Study of Boundaries in the Social Sciences."
52. Delale-O'Connor, "Drawing the Line," 2.

53. Barth, *Ethnic Groups and Boundaries*; Lamont, *The Dignity of Working Men*; Lamont; *Money, Morals, and Manners*; Lamont & Molnar, "The Study of Boundaries in the Social Sciences."
54. Lamont & Molnar, "The Study of Boundaries in the Social Sciences," 169.
55. Ibid.
56. This conception of diversity is different than what Jennifer Stillman found in her 2012 book, *Gentrification and Schools*. She found that White parents used the term diversity to refer to how many White children attend the school (p. 16). In comparison, the parents in this book used the term in different ways depending on their relationship to the structures.
57. Winerip, "Equity of Test is Debated after Children Compete for Gifted Kindergarten."
58. Gootman & Gebeloff, "Gifted Programs in the City are Less Diverse."
59. Haimson & Kjelberg, "NYC Schools under Bloomberg and Klein."
60. Gootman & Gebeloff, "Gifted Programs in the City are Less Diverse."
61. Ravitch, *The Death and Life of the Great American School System*,8 9.
62. Otterman, "More Preschoolers Test as Gifted"; Katch, "Gifted and Talented School Are Segregation by Another Name."
63. Holzman, "Gifted and Talented."
64. Borland, "The Death of Giftedness"; Sapon-Shevin, "Equity, Excellence, and School Reform"; Mickelson, "Subverting Swann"; Potter & Tipson, "Eliminate Gifted Tracks and Expand to a Schoolwide Approach."
65. Baker," Gifted,T alenteda ndS eparated."
66. Loveless, "The Resurgence of Ability Grouping and Persistence of Tracking"; Hess, "America's Future Depends on Gifted Students."
67. Oakes, *Keeping Track*,3 00.
68. Mickelson, "When Are Racial Disparities a Result of Discrimination?"; Lucas & Berends, "Sociodemographic Diversity, Correlated Achievement, and De Facto Tracking"; Oakes, *Keeping Track*.
69. Kohli," ModernD ayS egregationi nP ublicS chools."
70. Ford & Grantham, "Gifted and Talented"; ABCNY Report, "Ending Discrimination in Gifted Education in New York City Public Schools."
71. Ford & Grantham, "Gifted and Talented."
72. Oakes, *Keeping Track*, 184. Other cases related to racialized tracking include *Moses v. Washington Parrish School Board* and *McNeal v. Tate County School District*.
73. Tyson, *Integration Interrupted*,1 3.
74. Legal Defense Fund, "New York City Council Members Introduce Measures to Expand Access to Specialized High Schools."
75. Ibid.
76. Corcoran& B aker-Smith," Pathwayst oa nE liteE ducation."
77. Kohli," ModernD ayS egregationi nP ublicS chools."
78. Scott," SchoolC hoicea sa C ivilR ight."
79. Mickelson," SubvertingS wann,"2 41.
80. See Civil Rights Project, "Federal Education Policy Should Promote Diversity"; Mickelson, "Subverting Swann"; Frankenberg & Debray, *Integrating Schools In A Changing Society*; Burris & Garrity, *Detracking for Excellence and Equity*;

Wells et al., *Both Sides Now*; Wells & Crain, "Perpetuation Theory and the Long-Term Effects of Desegregation."
81. See Roda & Wells, "School Choice Policies and Racial Segregation."
82. See Orfield & Eaton, *Dismantling Desegregation*; Roda & Wells, "School Choice Policies and Racial Segregation"; Wells et al., *Both Sides Now*; Brantlinger et al., "Self-Interest and Liberal Educational Discourse."
83. See Brantlinger et al., "Self-Interest and Liberal Educational Discourse."
84. Wellse ta l., *Both Sides Now*.
85. Posey-Maddox, *When Middle-Class Parents Choose Urban Schools*,7 .
86. This figure was based on what parents told me, not what the NYCDOE or TCS provides because they do not break down enrollment numbers by G&T versus Gen Ed.
87. Holme, "Buying Homes, Buying Schools"; Brantlinger et al., "Self-Interest and Liberal Educational Discourse."
88. Gamoran, "The Variable Effects of High School Tracking"; Oakes, *Keeping Track*; Wells & Serna, "The Politics of Culture."

1   The Case: G&T Programs within New York City Schools

1. All schools are given pseudonyms to protect confidentiality.
2. Kershaw, "Agony on the Upper West Side over a Battle to Shift a Gifted Students'P rogram."
3. Kucsera & Orfield, "New York State's Extreme School Segregation."
4. Posey-Maddox, *When Middle-Class Parents Choose Urban Schools*,2 9.
5. The terms zone, catchment, and neighborhood are used interchangeably to mean the same thing. For instance, each student is automatically assigned to their zoned or neighborhood school, which is determined by their home address and which catchment area they live within. Although neighborhoods do not usually line up with school catchment areas, these words are often used synonymously.
6. NYCDOE Statistical Summaries: http://schools.nyc.gov/AboutUs/schools /data/stats/default.htm.
7. New York City Independent Budget Office Report, "New York City Public School Indicators: Demographics, Resources, Outcomes." http://www.ibo .nyc.ny.us/iboreports/2013educationindicatorsreport.pdf.
8. Otterman, "More Preschoolers Test as Gifted, Even as Diversity Imbalance Persists"; Fessenden, "A Portrait of Segregation in New York City's Schools."
9. Fessenden, "A Portrait of Segregation in New York City's Schools."
10. US Census Bureau, 2013.
11. Kucsera & Orfield, "New York State's Extreme School Segregation."
12. Resmovits, "The Nation's Most Segregated Schools Aren't Where You'd Think They'd Be"; Orfield, G., Kucsera, J., & Siegel-Hawley, G., "*E pluribus...separation?*"
13. Darling-Hammond, *The Flat World and Education*.
14. Kucsera & Orfield, "New York State's Extreme School Segregation."
15. Roda & Wells, "School Choice Policies and Racial Segregation."

16. Farkas et al., *Time To Move On*; Orfield & Eaton, *Dismantling Desegregation*; Wells et al., *Both Sides Now*; Roda & Wells, "School Choice Policies and Racial Segregation"; Stillman, *Gentrification and Schools*; Lacireno-Paquet & Brantley, "Who Chooses Schools and Why?"
17. NYCDOE,2 009/2010.
18. This is contrary to what Stillman found in her book on parental school choice in New York City. Stillman (2012) explains that the "Gentry parents" in her book "would never call" schools with G&T programs "diverse" (p. 121).
19. NYCDOE,2 009/2010.
20. UrbanBaby blog posts: http://www.urbanbaby.com.
21. Winerip, "Equity of Test Is Debated After Children Compete for Gifted Kindergarten."
22. Gootman & Gebeloff, "Gifted Programs in the City Are Less Diverse."
23. Haimson&K jelberg, *NYC Schools under Bloomberg and Klein*.
24. The five citywide G&T schools include The Anderson School in Manhattan (K–8), NEST+M (New Explorations into Science, Technology and Math) in Manhattan (K–12), and TAG for Young Scholars in Manhattan (K–8). In addition, two new citywide G&T schools with grades K–1 opened in Brooklyn—The Brooklyn School of Inquiry, and Queens—STEM.
25. Winerip, "Equity of Test Is Debated After Children Compete for Gifted Kindergarten."
26. Lareau, *Unequal Childhoods*.
27. Roda & Wells, "School Choice Policies and Racial Segregation."
28. See Borland, "The Death of Giftedness"; Gootman, "Children Face Rejection by Neighborhood Schools in Manhattan"; Saulny, "Gifted Classes Will Soon Use Uniform Test, Klein Decides"; Roda & Wells, "School Choice Policies and Racial Segregation," for evidence of the segregation within the schools.
29. NYCDOE,2 010.
30. Gootman and Gebeloff, "Gifted Programs in the City Are Less Diverse."
31. Gootman, "Children Face Rejection by Neighborhood Schools in Manhattan."
32. Wise," TooM anyG eniuses."
33. Insideschools.org, "Is a Gifted Program Right for Your Child?"
34. This example points to the various ways parents conceptualize the term "diversity" (see Introduction).
35. NYCDOE,2 009/2010.
36. Beginning in the 2010 school year, TCS will offer two G&T classrooms and three Gen Ed classrooms for incoming kindergarten children. The school took away their Universal pre-k program to add an additional Gen Ed classroom since more White, catchment families started enrolling their children inT CS.
37. http://www.townhouseexperts.com/.
38. http://www.nybits.com/apartments/.
39. www.Infoshare.org.
40. NYCDOE,2 010.
41. NYCDOE, 2008–2015.
42. Raschka," RejectingG &T."

43. O'Leary, "What Is Middle Class in Manhattan?"
44. Throughout the book, I note White parents' "upper-class" status to distinguish them from middle- to upper-middle-class parents.
45. See also Bifulco et al.'s use of the term, "Public School Choice and Integration." Like Lareau in *Unequal Childhoods*, I define the White parents in my sample as falling into the "middle-class to upper-middle-class" category since they all were either employed in a professional or managerial position and/or were collegee ducated.
46. Like Lareau in *Unequal Childhoods*, I classify parents of color as "working-class" because neither parent was employed in a middle-class job. In the two African households, the father was employed in a professional career and both parents were college-educated. The two mothers had part-time positions. Therefore, I classified those two families as being lower middle class.
47. Yin, *Case Study Research*; Merriam, *Qualitative Research*.

2   Striving to Be G&T "Because the People in It Are Just Like You"

1. I changed the name of the state where they were moving from, to ensure confidentiality.
2. Baker," Gifted,T alenteda ndS eparated."
3. SeeS tillman, *Gentrification and Schools*.
4. Lamont, *Money, Morals, and Manners*.
5. Bourdieu&W acquant, *Outline of a Theory of Practice*,1 7.
6. Lamont & Molnar, "The Study of Boundaries in the Social Sciences," 169; Barth, *Ethnic Groups and Boundaries*.
7. SeeK imelberg," BeyondT estS cores."
8. Holme," BuyingH omes,B uyingS chools."
9. See Posey-Maddox, *When Middle-Class Parents Choose Urban Schools*; Roda & Wells, "School Choice Policies and Racial Segregation."
10. See Brantlinger et al., "Self-Interest and Liberal Educational Discourse."
11. Staiger," Whitenessa sG iftedness."
12. See Brantlinger et al., "Self-Interest and Liberal Educational Discourse"; Saporito & Lareau, "School Selection as a Process"; Weiher & Tedin, "Does Choice Lead to Racially Distinctive Schools?"; Holme, "Buying Homes, Buying Schools"; Johnson & Shapiro, "Good Neighborhoods, Good Schools."
13. Holme," BuyingH omes,B uyingS chools."
14. See Cucchiara, *Marketing Schools, Marketing Cities*; Posey-Maddox, *When Middle-Class Parents Choose Urban Schools*.
15. Cultural deficit perspective puts the blame on an individual's culture and community for underachievement by using negative stereotypes and assumptions about low-income students of color. Because of this, institutional barriers in schools, such as tracking and segregation, are absolved from responsibility for the racial disparities that exist because the blame is placed solely on the

student and her/his family (see Valenzuela, *Subtractive Schooling*; Oakes, *Keeping Track*;D elgado-Gaitán, *The Power of Community*).
16. SeeL areau, *Unequal Childhoods*.
17. Crozier et al., "White Middle-Class Parents, Identities, Educational Choice and the Urban Comprehensive School."
18. Cucchiara, *Marketing Schools, Marketing Cities*; Demerath, *Producing Success*.
19. Posey-Maddox, *When Middle-Class Parents Choose Urban Schools*.

3 The Social Construction of Giftedness

1. Ic hangedL illian'so ccupationt oe nsurec onfidentiality.
2. The G&T Defenders in this book believe their children are gifted. The rest of the parents believe their children are smart or bright, but not gifted.
3. The "diverse" middle school that Lillian is describing has a total school enrollment of 60 percent White, 15 percent Black, 7 percent Asian, and 12 percent Latinos tudents.
4. Lareau, *Unequal Childhoods*.
5. Raschka," RejectingG &T."
6. Sapon-Shevin, *Playing Favorites*.
7. Ibid.,1 60.
8. Watanabe, "Tracking in the Era of High-Stakes Accountability Reform."
9. See Rist, "Student Social Class and Teacher Expectations."
10. Staiger, "Whiteness as Giftedness"; Tyson, *Integration Interrupted*.
11. SeeF erguson, *Bad Boys*.
12. Bourdieu& P aserone, *The Inheritors*.

4 How Parents Recreate and Reproduce the Boundaries

1. These are overall enrollment numbers because the district does not report the racial breakdown by G&T and Gen Ed programs by school.
2. This figure is based on what parents said, not what the NYCDOE or TCS provides because they do not break down enrollment numbers by G&T versus GenE d.
3. Raschka," RejectingG &T."
4. See Oakes & Wells, "Detracking for High Student Achievement"; Horvat & Lareau, "Moments of Social Inclusion and Exclusion"; Useem, "Middle Schools and Math Groups."
5. http://schools.nyc.gov/ChoicesEnrollment/GiftedandTalented/default.htm.
6. See examples from the peer effects literature: Hanushek et al., "Does Peer Ability Affect Student Achievement?"; Hoxby, "Peer Effects in the Classroom"; Summers & Wolfe, "Do Schools Make a Difference"; Zimmer & Toma, "Peer Effects in Private and Public Schools across Countries"; Boozer & Cacciola, "Inside the 'Black Box' of Project Star."
7. Tyson, *Integration Interrupted*,9 .
8. Gootman, "Children Face Rejection by Neighborhood Schools in Manhattan."

9. Mulkey et al., "Keeping Track or Getting Offtrack"; Oakes, *Keeping Track*; Darity et al., "Increasing Opportunity to Learn via Access to Rigorous Courses and Programs"; Hallinan, "Tracking."

5 "The Only Thing They Got out of This Is Segregation": TCS Revisited

1. Lareau, *Unequal Childhoods*.
2. Like Lareau in *Unequal Childhoods*, I classify parents of color as "working class" because neither parent was employed in a middle-class job. In the two African households, the father was employed in a professional career and both parents were college-educated. The two mothers had part-time positions. Therefore, I classified those two families as being lower–middle class.
3. Carter, *Stubborn Roots*,9 .
4. SeeP osey-Maddox, *When Middle-Class Parents Choose Urban Schools*.
5. Brooks et al., "Educational Leadership and Racism."

Conclusion   Putting Integration (Back?) on the Education Policy Agenda

1. Fessenden, "A Portrait of Segregation in New York City's Schools."
2. NewYorkAppleseed, "Segregation in NYC District Elementary Schools and What We Can Do about It."
3. Kucsera & Orfield, "New York State's Extreme Segregation."
4. Tyson, *Integration Interrupted*,6 .
5. Such as outreach to low-income families, free transportation, equitable means of selection (e.g., no standardized test scores), and so on.
6. Kucsera & Orfield, "New York State's Extreme Segregation."
7. Demerath, *Producing Success*.
8. MacLeod, *Ain't No Makin It*,2 68.
9. Tyson, *Integration Interrupted*.
10. Posey-Maddox, *When Middle-Class Parents Choose Urban Schools*.
11. Labaree, *How to Succeed in School without Really Learning*; Carter, *Stubborn Roots*.
12. Kucsera & Orfield, "New York State's Extreme Segregation."
13. And self-contained dual language programs that often admit disproportionate numbers of White students.
14. Ford, "Desegregating Gifted Education"; Borland & Wright, "Identifying Young, Potentially Gifted, Economically Disadvantaged Students."
15. NAGC," Identification."
16. Borland, "The Death of Giftedness"; Borland & Wright, "Identifying Young, Potentially Gifted, Economically Disadvantaged Students."
17. NewYorkAppleseed, "Segregation in NYC District Elementary Schools and What We Can Do about It."
18. Harris, "New York City Council to Look at School Segregation."
19. SeeB orland," TheD eatho fG iftedness."

20. Sapon-Shevin, *Playing Favorites*,1 29.
21. Borland, "The Death of Giftedness," 124.
22. See Hawley & Irvine, "Improving Teaching and Learning in Integrated Schools."
23. BELL Academy M.S. 294 in Queens uses the SEM approach. See Potter (July 14, 2014). http://ny.chalkbeat.org/2014/07/14/the-citys-gifted-education-system-needs-to-shift-one-school-at-a-time/#.VQxqXd7-WFI.
24. Raschka," RejectingG &T."
25. See the Stanford Center for Opportunity Policy in Education (SCOPE); https://edpolicy.stanford.edu/sites/default/files/publications/closing-opportunity-gap-what-america-must-do-give-every-child-even-chance.pdf.
26. Brooks et al., "Educational Leadership and Racism."
27. Burris & Welner, *Detracking for Excellence and Equity*.
28. Darity & Jolla, "Desegregated Schools with Segregated Education," 110.
29. Ibid.
30. Ibid,1 11.
31. Potter, "The City's Gifted Education System Needs to Shift, One School at a Time."
32. See Stillman, *Gentrification and Schools* and her recommendation to create White enclaves in "underutilized" zone schools in which "Gentry parents" are allowed to "congregate in the same classroom" to make them feel more comfortable (p. 144). This book does not recommend this approach because it leads to second generation segregation.
33. Hernandez, "Schools Chief Vows to Preserve Number of Gifted Programs and Their Exams."
34. Devor, "How We Devised a Pro-diversity Admissions Rule in a Changing Neighborhood."
35. Albrecht, "How a Park Slope School is Fighting to Stay."
36. *Parents Involved in Community Schools v. Seattle School District No. 1* (2007).
37. Scott," SchoolC hoicea sa C ivilR ight."
38. Frankenberg, "Integration after *Parents Involved*."
39. Eaton," TheP ullo fM agnets."
40. Robbins, "Integrating a School, One Child at a Time."
41. Baker, "Gifted, Talented and Separated."
42. Ibid.
43. Senior, "Myth of a Gifted Child."
44. Raschka," RejectingG &T."
45. See Campbell et al., "Early Childhood Education."
46. Reardon," Sourceso fE ducationalI nequality."
47. Brooks et al., "Educational Leadership and Racism."

References

Aja, A., Darity Jr., W., & Hamilton, D. (June 17, 2013). "Segregated Education in Desegregated Schools: Why We Should Eliminate 'Tracking' With 'Gifted and Talented' for All." *Huffington Post*. Available: http://www.huffingtonpost.com/alan-a-aja/segregated-education-in-d_b_3443865.html.

Albrecht, L. (December 10, 2014). "How a Park Slope School Is Fighting to Stay Diverse." *DNAinfo*. Available: http://www.dnainfo.com/new-york/20141210/park-slope/how-park-slope-school-is-fighting-stay-diverse.

Arum, R. & Beattie, I. R. (2000). *The Structure of Schooling: Readings in the Sociology of Education*. Mountain View, CA: Mayfield.

The Association of the Bar of the City of New York—ABCNY Report (2003). "Ending Discrimination in Gifted Education in New York City Public Schools." Available: http://www.abcny.org/pdf/report/giftedprogramreport.pdf.

Baker, A. (January 12, 2013). "Gifted, Talented and Separated." *The New York Times*, New York.

Barth, Fredrik (ed). (1969). *Ethnic Groups and Boundaries: The Social Organization of Culture Difference*. London: George Allen and Unwin.

Bifulco, R., Ladd, H. F., & Ross, S. (2009). "Public School Choice and Integration: Evidence from Durham, North Carolina." *Social Science Research: A Quarterly Journal of Social Science Methodology and Quantitative Research*, 38(1), 71–85.

Borland, J. H. (2003). "The Death of Giftedness: Gifted Education without Gifted Children." In *Rethinking Gifted Education*, edited by James H. Borland. New York: Teachers College Press.

Borland, J. H. (February 14, 2009). "Gifted Kids Deserve Better: Time to Fix the City's Failed G&T Plan", *The New York Times*, New York.

Borland, J. H. & Wright, L. (1994). "Identifying Young, Potentially Gifted, Economically Disadvantaged Students." *Gifted Child Quarterly*, 38, 164–171.

Bourdieu, P. (1984). *Distinction: A Social Critique of the Judgment of Taste*. Translated by Richard Nice. Cambridge, MA: Harvard University Press.

Bourdieu, P. (1986). "The Forms of Capital." In *Power and Ideology in Education*, edited by J. Karabel and A. H. Halsey. New York: Oxford University Press.

Bourdieu, P. & Paserone, J. (1977). *The Inheritors: French Students and Their Relation to Culture*. Translated by Richard Nice. Reprint, Beverly Hills: Sage.

Bourdieu, P. & Wacquant, L. D. (1992). *Outline of a Theory of Practice*, 8th edn. Cambridge: Cambridge University Press.

Brantlinger, E. M., Majd-Jabbari, M., & Guskin, S. L. (1996). "Self-Interest and Liberal Educational Discourse: How Ideology Works for Middle-Class Mothers." *American Educational Research Journal*, 33, 571–597.

Brooks, J. S., Arnold, N. W., & Brooks, M. C. (2013). "Educational Leadership and Racism: A Narrative Inquiry into Second-Generation Segregation." *Teachers College Record*, 115, 1–27.

Burris, C. C. & Garrity, D. T. (2008). *Detracking for Excellence and Equity*. Alexandria, VA: Association for Supervision and Curriculum Development.

Campbell, F. A., Ramey, C., Pungello, E., Sparling, J., & Shari Miller-Johnson (2002). "Early Childhood Education: Young Adult Outcomes from the Abecedarian Project," *Applied Developmental Science*, 6(1), 42–57.

Carter, P. L. (2012). *Stubborn Roots: Race, Culture and Inequality in U.S. and South African Schools*. New York: Oxford University Press.

Civil Rights Project. (2011). "Federal Education Policy Should Promote Diversity." Available: http://civilrightsproject.ucla.edu/.

Corcoran, S. P. & Baker-Smith, C. (2015). "Pathways to an Elite Education: Exploring Strategies to Diversify NYC's Specialized High Schools." *The Research Alliance for New York City Public Schools* Policy Brief. Available: http://steinhardt.nyu.edu/research_alliance/publications/pathways_to_an_elite_education.

Crozier, G., Reay, D., James, D., Jamieson, F., Beedell, P., Hollingworth, S., & Williams, K. (2008). "White Middle-Class Parents, Identities, Educational Choice and the Urban Comprehensive School: Dilemmas, Ambivalence and Moral Ambiguity." *British Journal of Sociology of Education*, 29(3), 261–272.

Cucchiara, M. (2013a). *Marketing Schools, Marketing Cities: Who Wins and Who Loses When Schools Become Urban Amenities*. Chicago: University of Chicago Press.

Cucchiara, M. (2013b). "'Are We Doing Damage?' Choosing an Urban Public School in an Era of Parental Anxiety." *Anthropology & Education Quarterly*, 44(1), 75–93.

Darity, W., Castellino, D, Tyson, K., Cobb, C., and McMillen, B. (2001) *Increasing Opportunity to Learn Via Access to Rigorous Courses and Programs: One Strategy for Closing the Achievement Gap for At-Risk and Ethnic Minority Students*. Raleigh: North Carolina State Department of Public Instruction.

Darity, W. & Jolla, A. (2010). "Desegregated Schools with Segregated Education." In *The Integration Debate: Competing Futures for American Cities*, edited by Chester W. Hartman and Gregory D. Squires. New York: Routledge.

Darling-Hammond, L. (2010). *The Flat World and Education: How America's Commitment to Equity Will Determine our Future*. New York: Teachers College Press.

Delale-O'Connor, L. (2009). *Drawing the Line: Race, Ethnicity and Class Boundaries in Education*. New York: American Sociological Association Annual Meeting.

Delgado-Gaitán, C. (2001). *The Power of Community: Mobilizing for Family and Schooling*. Lanham, MD: Rowan and Littlefield.

Demerath, P. (2009). *Producing Success: The Culture of Personal Advancement in an American High School*. Chicago: University of Chicago Press.

Devor, J. (2013). "How we Devised a Pro-Diversity Admissions Rule in a Changing Neighborhood." WNYC, Schoolbook. http://www.wnyc.org/story/303296-how-we-devised-a-pro-diversity-admissions-rule-in-a-changing-neighborhood/.

Eaton, S. (June 14, 2010). "The Pull of Magnets." *The Nation*. http://www.thenation.com/article/pull-magnets#.

Farkas, S. & Johnson, J. (with Immerwahr, S. & McHugh, J.) (1998). *Time to Move on: African-American and White Parents Set an Agenda for Public Schools*. New York: Public Agenda.

Ferguson, A. A. (2000). *Bad Boys: Public Schools in the Making of Black Masculinity*. Ann Arbor: University of Michigan Press.

Fessenden, F. (May 11, 2012). "A Portrait of Segregation in New York City's Schools." *New YorkTimes*. Available: http://www.nytimes.com/interactive/2012/05/11/nyregion/segregation-in-new-york-city-public-schools.html.

Ford, D.Y. (2003). "Desegregating Gifted Education: Seeking Equity for Culturally Diverse Students." In *Rethinking Gifted Education*, edited by James H. Borland. New York: Teachers College Press.

Ford, D.Y. & Grantham, T. (2008). "Gifted and Talented." *International Encyclopedia of the Social Sciences*. Retrieved on September 12, 2010: Encyclopedia.com: http://www.encyclopedia.com/doc/1G2-3045300925.html.

Frankenberg, E. (2011). "Integration after *Parents Involved:* What Does Research Suggest about Available Options?" In *Integrating Schools in a Changing Society: New Policies and Legal Options for a Multiracial Generation*, edited by Erica Frankenberg and Elizabeth DeBray. Chapel Hill: University of North Carolina Press.

Frankenberg, E. & DeBray, E. (2011). "Introduction: Looking to the Future." In *Integrating Schools in a Changing Society: New Policies and Legal Options for a Multiracial Generation*, edited by Erica Frankenberg and Elizabeth DeBray. Chapel Hill: University of North Carolina Press.

Gamoran, A. (1992). "The Variable Effects of High School Tracking." *American Sociological Review*, 57, 812–828.

Gootman, E. (March 24, 2009). "Children Face Rejection by Neighborhood Schools in Manhattan." *The New York Times*, New York.

Gootman, E. & Gebeloff, R. (June 18, 2008). "Gifted Programs in the City Are Less Diverse." *The New York Times*, New York.

Haimson, L. & Kjellberg, A. (Eds) (2009). *NYC Schools Under Bloomberg and Klein: What Parents, Teachers, and Policymakers Need to Know*. New York: Lulu. Retrieved April 20, 2010, from the World Wide Web: http://www.lulu.com/product/download/nyc-schools-under-bloombergklein-what-parents-teachers-andpolicymakers-need-to-know/4970769.

Hallinan, M. T. (1994). "Tracking: From Theory to Practice." *Sociology of Education*, 67, 69–83.

Hanushek, E. A., Kain, J. F., Markman, J. M., and Rivkin, S. G. (2003). "Does Peer Ability Affect Student Achievement?" *Journal of Applied Econometrics*, 18(5), 527–544.

Harris, E. A. (October 21, 2014). New York City Council to Look at School Segregation. *The New York Times*. http://www.nytimes.com/2014/10/22/nyregion/new-york-city-council-to-look-at-school-segregation.html.

Hawley, W. & Irvine, J. J. (2011). "Improving Teaching and Learning in Integrated Schools." In *Integrating Schools in a Changing Society: New Policies and Legal Options for a Multiracial Generation*, edited by Erica Frankenberg and Elizabeth DeBray. Chapel Hill: University of North Carolina Press.

Hernandez, J. C. (June 17, 2014). "Schools Chief Vows to Preserve Number of Gifted Programs and Their Exams." *The New York Times*. Available: http://

www.nytimes.com/2014/06/18/nyregion/schools-chief-vows-to-preserve-number-of-gifted-programs-and-their-exams.html?_r=1.

Hess, F. (June 3, 2014). "America's Future Depends on Gifted Students" in Room for Debate: New York City's Gifted Classrooms Useful or Harmful. *The New York Times*. Available: http://www.nytimes.com/roomfordebate/2014/06/03/are-new-york-citys-gifted-classrooms-useful-or-harmful/americas-future-depends-on-gifted-students.

Holme, J. J. (2002). "Buying Homes, Buying Schools: School Choice and the Social Construction of School Quality." *Harvard Educational Review*, 72(2), 177–205.

Holzman, M. (April 27, 2012). "Gifted and Talented: A Road to Segregation?" *Daily Kos*. Available: http://www.dailykos.com/story/2012/04/27/1086903/-Gifted-and-Talented-Road-to-Segregation#.

Hoxby, C. (2000). "Peer Effects in the Classroom: Learning from Gender and Race Variation." NBER Working Paper No. 7867. Cambridge, MA: National Bureau of Economic Research.

Insideschools.org (2009). "Is a Gifted Program Right for Your Child?" *Insideschools. org: Your Independent Guide to NYC Public Schools*. Available: http://insideschools.org/index12.php?s=1&a=74.

Johnson, H. B. & Shapiro, T. M. (2003). "Good Neighborhoods, Good Schools: Race and the 'Good Choices' of White Families." In *White Out: The Continuing Significance of Racism*, edited by Ashley Doane and Eduardo Bonila-Silva. New York: Routledge.

Katch, D. (March 24, 2013). "Gifted and Talented School are Segregation by Another Name." *Truthout*. http://truth-out.org/news/item/15293-gifted-and-talented-schools-are-segregation-by-another-name.

Kershaw, S. (December 29, 1996). "Agony on the Upper West Side over a Battle to Shift a Gifted Students' Program." *The New York Times*, New York.

Kimelberg, S. M. (2014). "Beyond Test Scores: Middle Class Mothers, Cultural Capital and the Evaluation of Public Schools." *Sociological Perspectives*, 57(2), 208–228.

Kimelberg, S. M. & Billingham, C. M. (2013). "Attitudes Toward Diversity and the School Choice Process: Middle- Class Parents in a Segregated Urban Public School District." *Urban Education* 28(1), 85–108.

Kohli, S. (November 18, 2014). "Modern Day Segregation in Public Schools." *The Atlantic*. Available: http://www.theatlantic.com/education/archive/2014/11/modern-day-segregation-in-public-schools/382846/.

Kucsera, J. & Orfield, G. (March, 2014). "New York State's Extreme Segregation: Inequality, Inaction and a Damaged Future." The Civil Rights Project/Proyecto Derechos Civiles. Available: http://civilrightsproject.ucla.edu/research/k-12-education/integration-and-diversity/ny-norflet-report-placeholder/Kucsera-New-York-Extreme-Segregation-2014.pdf.

Labaree, D. (1997). *How to Succeed in School Without Really Learning: The Credentials Race in American Education*. New Haven, CT: Yale University Press.

Lacireno-Paquet, N. & Brantley, C. (2012). "Who Chooses Schools, and Why? The Characteristics and Motivations of Families Who Actively Choose Schools." In *Exploring the School Choice Universe: Evidence and Recommendations*, edited by

Gary Miron, Kevin Welner, Patricia Hinchey, and William Mathis. Charlotte, NC: Information Age Publishing.
Lamont, M. (1992). *Money, Morals and Manners: The Culture of the French and American Upper-Middle Class*. Chicago: University of Chicago Press.
Lamont, M. (2000). *The Dignity of Working Men: Morality and the Boundaries of Race, Class, and Immigration*. Cambridge, MA: Harvard University Press.
Lamont, M. & Lareau, A. (1988). "Cultural Capital: Allusions, Gaps and Glissandos in Recent Theoretical Developments," *Sociological Theory* 6(2), 153–168.
Lamont, M. & Molnar, V. (2002). "The Study of Boundaries in the Social Sciences." *Annual Review of Sociology*, 28, 167–195.
Lareau, A. (2000). *Home Advantage: Social Class and Parental Intervention in Elementary Education*. Lanham, MD: Rowman and Littlefield.
Lareau, A. (2003). *Unequal Childhoods: Class, Race, and Family Life*. Oakland CA: University of California Press.
Lareau, A. & Horvat, E. M. (1999). "Moments of Social Inclusion and Exclusion: Race, Class and Cultural Capital in Family-School Relationships." *Sociology of Education*, 72(1), 37–53.
Legal Defense Fund (October 22, 2014). "New York City Councilmembers Introduce Measures to Expand Access to Specialized High Schools." http://www.naacpldf.org/update/new-york-city-councilmembers-introduce-measures-expand-access-specialized-high-schools.
Lewis, A. (2003). *Race in the Schoolyard: Negotiating the Color Line in Classrooms and Communities*. New Brunswick, NJ: Rutgers University Press.
Losen, D. (1999). "Silent Segregation in Our Nation's Schools." *Harvard Civil Rights Law Review*, 34, 1–27.
Loveless, T. (2013). "The Resurgence of Ability Grouping and Persistence of Tracking." Brookings Report Online: http://www.brookings.edu/research/reports/2013/03/18-tracking-ability-grouping-loveless.
Lucas, S. & Berends, M. (2002). "Sociodemographic Diversity, Correlated Achievement, and De Facto Tracking." *Sociology of Education*, 75, 328–348.
Macleod, J. (2009). *Ain't No Makin' It*. Philadelphia, PA: Westview Press.
Makris, M. V. (2015). *Public Housing and School Choice in a Gentrified City: Youth Experiences of Uneven Opportunity*. New York: Palgrave Macmillan.
Meier, K. J., Stewart, J., & England, R. E. (1989). *Race, Class and Education: The Politics of Second-Generation Segregation*. Madison: University of Wisconsin Press.
Merriam, S. B. (2009). *Qualitative Research: A Guide to Design and Implementation*. San Francisco, CA: John Wiley.
Mickelson, R. A. (2001). "Subverting Swann: First and Second-Generation Segregation in the Charlotte-Mecklenburg Schools." *American Educational Research Journal*, 38(2), 215–252.
Mickelson, R. A. (2003). "When Are Racial Disparities a Result of Racial Discrimination? A Social Science Perspective." *Teachers College Record*, 105(6), 1052–1086.
Mickelson, R. A., Bottia, M., & Southworth, S. (2008). "School Choice and Segregation by Race, Class, and Achievement." University of North Carolina at Charlotte: Education Policy Research Unit.

Mulkey, L. M., Catsambis, S., Steelman, L. C., & Hanes-Ramos, L. (2009) "Keeping Track or Getting Offtrack: Issues in the Tracking of Students." In *International Handbook of Research on Teachers and Teaching*, edited by L. J. Saha, A. G. Dworkin. Philadelphia: Springer Science + Business Media LLC, pp. 1059–1078.

NAGC, National Association for Gifted Children. "Identification." Available: http://www.nagc.org/resources-publications/gifted-education-practices/identification.

NewYorkAppleseed. (2014). "Segregation in NYC District Elementary Schools and What We Can Do About It: Addressing Internal Segregation and Harnessing the Educational Benefits of Diversity." Available: https://www.appleseednetwork.org/wp-content/uploads/2014/02/Within-Our-Reach-2nd-Brief-February-2014-FINAL.pdf.

New York City Department of Education. School Report Cards. Retrieved April 20, 2010 from the World Wide Web. http://schools.nyc.gov/default.aspx.

New York City Independent Budget Office (May 2013). "New York City Public School Indicators: Demographics, Resources, Outcomes." Available: http://www.ibo.nyc.ny.us/iboreports/2013educationindicatorsreport.pdf.

Oakes, J. (2005). *Keeping Track: How Schools Structure Inequality*. New Haven, CT: Yale University Press.

Oakes, J. & Wells, A. S. (1998). "Detracking for High Student Achievement." *Educational Leadership*, 55(38), 41–48.

Oakes, J., Wells, A. S., Jones, M., & Datnow, A. (1997). "Detracking: The Social Construction of Ability, Cultural Politics, Resistance to Reform." *Teachers College Record*, 98(3), 482–510.

O'Leary, A. (January 18, 2013). "What Is Middle Class in Manhattan?" *The New York Times*. Available: http://www.nytimes.com/2013/01/20/realestate/what-is-middle-class-in-manhattan.html?_r=0.

Orfield, G., Eaton, S. E., & Harvard Project on School Desegregation. (1996). *Dismantling Desegregation: The Quiet Reversal of Brown v. Board of Education*. New York: New Press.

Orfield, G., Kucsera, J., & Siegel-Hawley, G. (2012). *E Pluribus...Separation? Deepening Double Segregation for More Students*. Los Angeles, CA: UCLA Civil Rights Project.

Otterman, S. (June 21, 2011). "More Preschoolers Test as Gifted, Even as Diversity Imbalance Persists."*The New York Times*, New York.

Parents Involved in Community Schools v. Seattle School District No. 1 (2007).

Posey-Maddox, L. (2014). *When Middle-Class Parents Choose Urban Schools: Class, Race & the Challenge of Equity in Public Education*. Chicago: University of Chicago.

Potter, H. (July 14, 2014). "The City's Gifted Education System Needs to Shift, One School at a Time." *Chalkbeat NY*. Available: http://ny.chalkbeat.org/2014/07/14/the-citys-gifted-education-system-needs-to-shift-one-school-at-a-time/#.VQxqXd7-WFI.

Potter, H. & Tipson, D. (June 3, 2014). "Eliminate Gifted Tracks and Expand to a Schoolwide Approach" in Room for Debate: New York City's Gifted Classrooms Useful or Harmful. *The New York Times*. Available: http://www.nytimes.com

/roomfordebate/2014/06/03/are-new-york-citys-gifted-classrooms-useful-or-harmful/eliminate-gifted-tracks-and-expand-to-a-schoolwide-approach.
Raschka, L. (May 1, 2008). "Rejecting G&T: Despite the Drama Surrounding Admissions, Some Parents Opt Out of Gifted Programs Altogether." *West Side Spirit*. New York.
Ravitch, D. (2010). *The Death and Life of the Great American School System: How Testing and Choice are Undermining Education*. New York: Basic Books.
Reardon, S. F. (2003). *Sources of Educational Inequality: The Growth of Racial/Ethnic and Socioeconomic Test Score Gaps in Kindergarten and First Grade*. University Park: Population Research Institute, Pennsylvania State University.
Resmovits, J. (March 26, 2014). "The Nation's Most Segregated Schools Aren't Where You'd Think They'd Be." *The Huffington Post*. Available: http://www.huffingtonpost.com/2014/03/26/new-york-schoolsegregated_n_5034455.html.
Rist, R. C. (1970). "Student Social Class and Teacher Expectations: The Self-Fulfilling Prophecy in Ghetto Education." *Harvard Educational Review*, 40, 411–451.
Roberts, A. (2011, February). "Gentrification and School Choice: Where Goes the Neighborhood." Paper presented at 63rd annual conference of the Southeastern Philosophy of Education Society, Decatur, GA.
Robbins, L. (June 15, 2012). "Integrating a School, One Child at a Time." *The New York Times*. Available: http://www.nytimes.com/2012/06/17/education/brooklyn-magnet-schools-see-hurdles-to-integration-even-in-kindergarten.html.
Roda, A. & Amy Stuart Wells (2013). "School Choice Policies and Racial Segregation: Where White Parents' Good Intentions, Anxiety, and Privilege Collide." *American Journal of Education*, 119(2), 261–293.
Rubin, B. C. (2008). "Detracking in Context: How Local Constructions of Ability Complicate Equity-Geared Reform." *Teachers College Record*, 110(3), 646–699.
Sapon-Shevin, M. (1994). *Playing Favorites: Gifted Education and the Disruption of the Community*. Albany: State University of New York Press.
Sapon-Shevin, M. (2003). "Equity, Excellence, and School Reform: Why Is Finding Common Ground So Hard?" In *Rethinking Gifted Education*, edited by James H. Borland. New York: Teachers College Press.
Saporito, S. & Lareau, A. (1999). "School Selection as a Process: The Multiple Dimensions of Race in Framing Educational Choice." *Social Problems*, 46, 418–435.
Sattin-Bajaj, C. (2014). *Unaccompanied Minors: Immigrant Youth, School Choice, and the Pursuit of Equity*. Boston, MA: Harvard Education Press.
Saulny, S. (November 16, 2005). "Gifted Classes Will Soon Use Uniform Test, Klein Decides." *The New York Times*, New York.
Scott, J. (2011). "School Choice as a Civil Right: The Political Construction of a Claim and Its Implications for School Desegregation." In *Integrating Schools in a Changing Society: New Policies and Legal Options for a Multiracial Generation*, edited by Erica Frankenberg & Elizabeth H. Debray. Chapel Hill: University of North Carolina Press.

Senior, Jennifer. (February 8, 2010). "Myth of a Gifted Child." *New York Magazine*.
Staiger, A. (2004). "Whiteness as Giftedness: Racial Formation at an Urban High School." *Social Problems*, 51(2), 161–181.
Stillman, J. B. (2012). *Gentrification and Schools: The Process of Integration When Whites Reverse Flight*. New York: Palgrave Macmillan.
Summers, A. A. & Wolfe, B. L. (1977). "Do Schools Make a Difference." *American Economic Review*, 67(4), 639–652.
Swartz, D. (1998). *Culture and Power: The Sociology of Pierre Bourdieu*. Chicago: University of Chicago Press.
Tyson, K. (2011). *Integration Interrupted: Tracking, Black Students, & Acting White after Brown*. New York: Oxford University Press.
Useem, E. L. (1992). "Middle Schools and Math Groups: Parent's Involvement in Children's Placement." *Sociology of Education*, 65, 263–279.
Valenzuela, A. (1999). *Subtractive Schooling: U.S.-Mexican Youth and the Politics of Caring*. Albany: State University of New York Press.
Watanabe, M. (2008). "Tracking in the Era of High-Stakes Accountability Reform: Case Studies of Classroom Instruction in North Carolina." *Teachers College Record*, 110(3), 489–534.
Weiher, G. & Tedin, K. (2002). "Does Choice Lead to Racially Distinctive Schools? Charter Schools and Household Preferences." *Journal of Policy Analysis and Management*, 21, 79–92.
Wells, A. S. & Crain, R. (1997). *Stepping over the Color Line*. New Haven, CT: Yale University Press.
Wells, A. S. & Crain, R. (1994). "Perpetuation Theory and the Long-Term Effects of School Desegregation." *Review of Educational Research*, 64(4), 531–555.
Wells, A. S., Holme, J. J., Revilla, A. T., & Atanda, A. K. (2009). *Both Sides Now: The Story of School Desegregation's Graduates*. Berkeley: University of California Press.
Wells, A. S. & Serna, I. (1996). "The Politics of Culture: Understanding Local Political Resistance to Detracking in Racially Mixed Schools." *Harvard Educational Review*, 66(1), 93–118.
Winerip, M. (July 25, 2010). Equity of Test Is Debated after Children Compete for Gifted Kindergarten. *New York Times*, New York.
Wise, J. (June 30, 2013). "Too Many Geniuses: The Real Talent of the City's Gifted- and -Talented Program Is Getting in." *New York Magazine*. Available: http://nymag.com/news/intelligencer/gifted-and-talented-2013-7/.
Yin, R. K. (1994). *Case Study Research: Design and Methods*. Thousand Oaks, CA: Sage.
Zimmer, R. W. & Toma, E. F. (2000). "Peer Effects in Private and Public Schools Across Countries." *Journal of Policy Analysis and Management*, 19(1), 75–92.

Index

advantaged parents. *See also* boundaries, critical mass, and school choice
anxiety, pressure, and competition of, 3, 11, 39, 45, 60–1, 70, 79, 81, 85–6, 93–4, 152, 155–6, 161–2
concerned with segregation, xv, 2, 35, 57–8, 68, 52, 103, 109–10, 118–20, 123, 161, 165
and looking past it because there's more competition for a G&T seat, 128, 143–8
definition of, 9–10, 48–53, 57, 101, 167
getting the best teachers, 22, 66, 95, 116, 130–1, 150–3
and getting the kindergarten Gen Ed teacher who used to teach G&T, 100, 103–4, 117–18, 130, 144
role in changing demographics, 8, 29–30, 45–6, 105, 109, 150, 155
afterschool programs
segregation of, 33, 137, 145–6

behavior problems. *See also* standardized testing: reasons for retesting for G&T
in segregated schools, 31
and in Gen Ed programs, 69–70, 86–8, 90, 115, 118, 120–1, 132, 140
boundaries
recreating, 102–11, 150, 161

adapting, 10, 111–22
and reproducing/maintenance of, 3, 5, 20, 24, 29–30, 38, 53, 87, 102–4, 122–7, 134–5
setting up/"boundary work," 58–61, 64, 68–9, 129
use of race, SES and cultural signals to distinguish where they and others belong ("Us" and "them"), 13, 23, 53, 58–60, 70–3, 91–5, 101, 111, 125–7, 135–6
social and symbolic, 12–13, 58, 67, 92
when symbolic boundaries do not translate into social boundaries, 13–14, 71–3, 130, 135–6
Bourdieu, P., 169, 173–4
cultural capital, 11–12, 40, 49, 82, 89, 132, 141, 154, 156
and field, 59
Brown v Board of Education, 3, 17

Carter, P., 135, 167, 169, 175, 178
case study. *See* research methodology
City Limits Community School District. *See also* school choice
description of, 7, 33–4, 44, 163
G&T policy, 158
school options/school choice, 7–8, 31–2, 35–6, 46–7, 55–6, 61–2, 106, 144, 155, 163, 169
and opening new G&T programs, 27–8, 39, 42–3

Civil Rights Project, 31, 155, 170, 178, 180, 182. *See also* Orfield, G.
concerted cultivation. *See* Lareau, A.
Conflicted Followers, 10, 23, 49–50, 77–8
contradictions. *See* G&T program/label
controlled choice, 163
critical mass of advantaged parents
  desire/preference for, 21, 46–7, 60, 64–5, 80, 90, 109, 114, 118
  of lower-income families of color, 104, 111
  racial/SES dimensions of, 25, 27–8
Cucchiara, M. B., 167–8, 173–4

demographic change, 45–8, 96, 109. *See also* boundaries and *The Community School*
  reasons for, 21, 32, 76, 105–6, 163
  responding to, 8, 47, 103–4, 111–14
desegregation, 3, 17, 31, 145
  relationship to school integration, 4, 6, 14, 155, 157–8, 163
de-tracking, 19, 21–2, 24, 107, 125. *See also* G&T programs/label
  approaches to, 159–60
diversity. *See also* school choice
  benefits of, 18–24, 75, 107, 139, 166
  by choice, 20, 157, 162
  conceptions of, 14, 62, 150, 156, 170, 172
  school-level vs. classroom-level, 15–16, 33, 56, 67–9, 156
  by default, 10, 14, 59, 68, 73, 122, 149, 156
  desire for, xiii–xv, 11, 42, 57–60, 62, 67–70, 78, 99, 109, 149, 162

facilitation of natural growth. *See* Lareau, A.

G&T Defenders, 9–10, 49, 78, 81–2, 91–5, 114, 174

G&T policy
  context, 11, 70, 156
  de-tracking G&T/Schoolwide Enrichment Model, 159–60
  shift from decentralized to centralized admissions policy, 14–15, 29–30, 32–3, 37–41, 47, 85, 105
G&T programs/label
  academic self-concept and, 87–90, 142
  hidden curriculum of privilege and superiority, 138, 153, 166
  "smart kids" class, 132, 151–3
  admissions process, 37–8, 41
  competition for seat at TCS, 143
  factors beyond test scores that determine track placement, 141–2
  fairness of cutoff score, 15, 85
  reasons for not applying, 134, 140
  advantages of, 3, 56, 86–7, 110, 127, 140
  less supplementing at home, 151
  citywide programs, 4, 37–9, 42, 114, 168–9, 172
  curriculum and, 22, 33–4, 41–2, 83–4, 100, 114–17, 149
  debate over, 14–19, 35–6, 110–11, 164–5
  internalizing G&T label, 12, 73, 90–5, 102
  marginalized parent communities and, 29, 66, 136, 146
  reasons for keeping/implementing [to attract White parents, and their valuable resources, into the public system], 27–8, 43, 66, 100, 108, 144–5, 148
  to avoid their failing zoned school, 45, 55, 57, 60–1, 63, 93, 125–6, 143
  because of the 'diversity' within the school, 126–7, 140–1, 145, 148

to elevate a school, 110, 123–6
opening more G&T programs/
diversify G&T, 148–9, 157–8
and threat of White flight from
public schools, 160
reasons for phasing out, 10, 77,
90, 102–3, 107–8, 110, 113,
122, 137, 139, 142–3, 145–7,
158–9
support for phase out, 165
tool for segregation, 134–5, 146
G&T test. *See* standardized testing
G&T vs. Gen Ed parents, 60–1. *See
also* advantaged parents and
low-income and working-class
families
attracting the right type of G&T
parent, 24, 28, 100–2, 123–7
low-income Gen Ed parents, 44,
126–7, 130, 145
cultural deficit perspective of,
65–7, 86, 92–3, 101, 119, 127,
145, 173
out of zone parents, 45, 57, 93,
102–3, 122, 125, 127
G&T vs. Gen Ed programs
academic differences/curriculum is
the same, 107, 114–18,
144, 149
downplaying/ambivalence of
G&T, 10, 22, 103, 112
resource disparities, 146–7
and changing the name of the
programs, 147–8
silence about the two programs, 101,
103, 111–14
vs. talking about two programs
openly in front of children,
103, 120–1, 138, 147
and using code language,
113, 136
student/parent interaction with
'other' G&T/Gen Ed program,
33, 72, 96, 115–16, 130

students realizing which program
they are in, 77, 88–90, 113,
118–20
teacher matters more than program,
116–18
G&T vs. Gen Ed students
perceptions of 'other' G&T/Gen Ed
students, 118–21
Gen Ed program/label
becoming an acceptable option for
advantaged families, 8–9, 13,
28–9, 45–7, 106
and diversity of, 20–1, 109, 150
as a fallback, 45, 57, 60–1, 93
stigma and, 3, 10, 52, 56–8, 60–72,
134, 141, 147, 149, 151
and academic self-concept, 87–90,
113, 132, 138, 142, 145
sense of belonging in the school,
132
versus G&T, 1, 63
Gen Ed Reconcilers, 9–10, 52
gentrification
school choice and, 31, 105, 134,
162–3
giftedness
definition of, xiii, 78–9, 131,
136–7, 141
question the definition of,
128–31, 136–7
identification of, 19, 80–1, 85–6,
155, 157–60
social construction of, 3, 56, 79–81,
91–3, 131, 137, 157, 165
test taking skills and, 38–9, 83–4
good schools
indicators of, 36, 124, 162, 55–6,
61–7
versus bad or "failing" schools, 36, 108

Hobson v. Hansen, 17
Holme, J., 20, 70
hyper-segregated school, xiii,
34–5, 169

integration. *See* desegregation

Lareau, A., xiv, 70, 83–4, 131
low-income and working-class families, 129. *See also* G&T vs. Gen Ed parents
    definition of, 44, 49, 51, 93, 133
    marginalization of, 29, 66, 136
    relationship with advantaged families, 134
    school choice practices, 6, 62, 100, 132–3

magnet schools. *See* school choice
Makris, M. V., 6–7

NAACP Legal Defense Fund, 17–18

Oakes, J., 16
Office for Civil Rights, 17–18
opportunity gap, 18–19, 159
Orfield, G., 31, 155, 157
overview of chapters, 22–5

parenting/parent involvement, 52
    fundraising and parent donations, 29, 66, 71, 146–7
    parent involvement at home (e.g. homework assistance), 93, 131
    PTA, 52–3, 66, 71, 99, 113, 120, 124, 147–8
    race/SES, cultural G&T/Gen Ed differences, 56, 64–6, 69–71, 93, 100–1, 131, 136–7, 146
    school choice and, 57
        applying to G&T and, 44, 64–7
        being considered a "good parent," 94, 140
        test prep and, 1–2, 76, 141–2, 150–1
Pathways of Educational Advantage, 15–16, 20, 22, 68, 83, 110, 137, 140, 145, 150–1

peer effects
    peer environment/"good kids" and, 60–4, 115, 145, 149
People Who Care v Rockford Board of Education, 17
Posey-Maddox, L., 29–30
post-civil rights era, 19, 24, 30, 155
preschool, 38, 59, 64, 79, 93, 157–8
    and Universal pre-k, 165–6
principal. *See* school leadership
private schools
    choosing public schools instead of, 99, 105–6, 135
privilege, 5, 11–12, 21, 60, 95, 156–8. *See also* advantaged parents and status
public school
    as a value, 58, 75, 99
    zoned school, 1, 7–8, 32, 34–6, 55, 60, 63, 169, 171

race
    intersection of race and SES/social class, 1, 7–12, 30–1, 64
    perception of advantaged families being "better," 59, 64, 136
    perception of low-income parents/parents of color, 60, 64
    perceptions of low-income students/"dark-skinned kids" or "brown-skinned kids," 77, 118–21, 132, 138–9
    racial composition of *The Community School*, 8, 42–3, 45–8
    of *City Limits*, 33–7
    of New York City public schools, 31–3
    TCS neighborhood, 43–5
research methodology
    interviews, 48
    observations, 52–3

Sapon-Shevin, M., 6, 86, 159
Savvy Negotiators, 9–10, 23, 49, 52, 77–8, 157
school choice, 4–6, 125–6
   advantaged families and, xiii–xv, 1, 7, 11, 19–22, 31, 34–6, 40, 46–8, 93, 95–6, 121
   influenced by social networks, 11, 47, 70, 75, 99, 131
   "parents who have options," 2, 35, 100, 131, 153–4
   deregulated/color-blind, 6, 19, 31–2, 155, 166
   low-income parents and, 131
   barriers to the school choice process, 24, 131–2, 154
   options in New York City, 30–3
   in *City Limits*, 33–7, 169
   magnet schools, 163–4
   private vs. public school choice, 75, 91, 99
   unzoned schools, xiii–xiv, 7, 32, 42, 162–3, 169
   preferences, 61–3
      to be with other similarly advantaged families (*see* critical mass of advantaged parents)
      not wanting to be in the minority, xiii, 59, 119, 144
      wanting the best for your child, 36, 107, 110
   pro-diversity admissions policy, 162–3
   professional school choice consultant, 1, 52–3, 114, 124
   tool for diversity, 31, 157
   tool for segregation, 11, 31, 125, 155
school leadership
   focus on testing, 144
   responding to Gen Ed demographic change, 103–4, 117–18, 144
   school climate and, 11–12, 143–4, 147
   enabling second-generation segregation, 159–60
segregation. *See also* hyper-segregated schools
   dual, 29, 31
   first-generation, 3
   second-generation, 3, 125, 157–8, 166
   effects on students, 132, 138–9, 146
social class, 4, 12, 108, 173, 175. *See also* race
social reproduction, 4, 6, 12, 30, 86, 156, 162
Specialized High Schools, 17–18, 158
standardized testing/G&T test
   anxiety and pressure on students, 161–2
   critique of G&T test, 80–1
   cultural bias and, 5–6, 12, 15, 17, 37, 85
   fairness of using a single test score, 2, 76–7, 158
   G&T test prep, 38, 56–7, 81–2, 84–5, 99, 136–7, 141, 152–3
      compromising parental values, 152
   test prep for middle school and high school placements, 18, 136–7, 150–2
   G&T testing process, 32, 39
   sibling priority, 8, 32, 39–40, 81–2, 92, 94, 100, 141–3, 148, 153
   G&T tests (OLSAT and BSRA), 38–9
   reasons for retesting, 10, 21, 44, 61, 69–70, 72, 83, 115–19, 140–3, 149–54
status and entitlement
   distinctions between schools/programs, 68, 123
   of G&T label, 19, 58, 68–70, 72, 95–6, 130, 136, 147–8, 151

structures of inequality, 5–6, 11, 14, 22, 73, 111
work/"game" the system, 11, 40, 56, 78–82, 152, 156

The Community School
description of, 7, 41–2, 75–6
becoming more White and higher income over time, 8–9, 21, 45–7, 82, 105–6, 109, 122–4, 142, 155
and demographic changes, 101–4 (*see also* boundaries)
neighborhood/and reasons for moving there, 43–4, 49, 99, 134
diversity overall, 67–8
"feeling of segregation," 110, 132, 134, 138, 145
vs. segregation within, 28–9, 56, 59, 64, 69, 110, 129–30, 132–4, 161
school culture/community, 65, 111, 113, 157
divisive educational environment/"one school" instead of two, 29, 89, 96, 103, 122–3, 132, 134, 138, 144–5, 157
student achievement, 62, 145
tracking, 1–5, 21–2, 88
debate, 15–18
de-tracking and, 107, 125, 159–60, 168
racialized, 6, 17, 118
Tyson, K., 17, 118

"UrbanBaby" blog, 35–6

Watanabe, M., 88
Wells, A. S., 20, 159, 167

The manufacturer's authorised representative in the EU is Springer Nature Customer Service Centre GmbH, Europaplatz 3, 69115 Heidelberg, Germany. If you have any concerns regarding our products, please contact ProductSafety@springernature.com

Printed and bound by CPI Group (UK) Ltd, Croydon, CR0 4YY
23/03/2026
02076734-0009